THE SMILING POPE

THE LIFE AND TEACHING
OF JOHN PAUL I

RAYMOND AND LAURETTA
SEABECK

Our Sunday Visitor Publishing Division
Our Sunday Visitor, Inc.
Huntington, Indiana 46750

Dedicated to

Elizabeth and Steven	Monique and Douglas
Kailey	Allison
Stevie	Matthew
Emily	Joseph

Special thanks to Mother Teresa, O.C.D.,
and Nancy Beaton

Contents

Introduction   7

PART I — *A Biographical Sketch*
1. Albino Luciani, Pope John Paul I: An Early Vocation   11
2. Seminary Life   16
3. Papa Living His Priesthood   21
4. The New Bishop   28
5. Patriarch of Venice   39
6. *Habemus Papam*   50
7. The Smiling Pope   58
8. The World Mourns   70

Epilogue   74
Notes for Part I   79

PART II — *Words from the Heart*
1. Written on Dust   87
2. I Hope You Will Help Me with Your Prayers   92
3. "Why Do I Suffer?"   94
4. Faith   99
5. Hope   104

6. Love	109
7. The Lesson of the Christmas Donkey	117
8. Never Lose Heart: Liberation from Sin	122
9. Christ, the Physician of Souls	127
10. The Way of the Magi	132
11. Proper Veneration of the Real Presence	138
12. Education in the Family	143
13. You Too Must Do the Same	149
14. Crosses	153
15. We Bring Love	155
16. Our Lady of the People	159
17. The Gifts of the Spirit	163
18. Presiding in Charity	170
19. The Three Levels of the Pyramid	174
20. You Have Been Sent	189
21. The Bishop, the Keeper of the Faith, the Man of Charity	194
22. Sunday, the Lord's Day	199
23. We Are Running Dry: Letter to Charles Dickens	212
24. Joy, Exquisite Love: Letter to St. Thérèse of Lisieux	217
25. We Are the Astonishment of God: Letter to Charles Péguy	223
26. Confession Six Hundred Years Ago: Letter to Francesco Petrarch	227
27. In What Kind of World . . . : Letter to Gilbert Keith Chesterton	232
28. Restless People	236
29. Honoring the Human Person	240
30. Love Can Do Everything	245
Chronology	247
Mother Teresa of Calcutta	253

Introduction

*A*lbino Luciani, Pope John Paul I, is known in Italy as the Pope of the "smile." We listened closely to what he said in his thirty-three-day reign. During his funeral Mass, we received the inspiration to found our mission society, the Missionary Servants of Pope John Paul I. Our purpose is to provide missionaries with the supplies they need to accomplish their ministry.

We began as a family of four, Elizabeth, Monique, Lauretta, and Ray. We, in the words of Pope John Paul I, consider ourselves "worthless servants." We know we are the weakest of God's creatures, but we place ourselves in St. Joseph's hands. God our Father placed His own Son in St. Joseph's loving arms, so how can we do less? Over the last few years, thousands of people have joined us in seeing and loving Christ in His poor. Because so many little mission groups and individuals have joined us, we have been enabled to send millions of dollars in aid to the poor. We do not beg for anything; we depend on Divine Providence. God continues to smile upon our work, and as we make our visits to the poorest countries of the world, we smile for the poor. We try to continue Pope John Paul I's smile to the world. We try to radiate Christ's joy. We try to love Christ in His poor. We try to be a little instrument in the hands of God. We try to be Missionary Servants.

In addition to packing and shipping ten-ton sea containers of goods for the poor from our home, we also publish *Humilitas*, a magazine devoted to the writings of Pope John Paul I and our mission work. We publish a prayer book yearly that has been given to thousands in our extended family. We host daylong women's retreats in our home three or four times a year. We host "Work Days for the Poor" throughout the winter months where groups of adults or students will come to spend a few hours learning about the poor and help us with special projects for the poor. And, we have published a limited edition of *The Good Samaritan*, Pope John Paul I's retreat for his priests.

Now that the process for the beatification of our little Pope has officially been started by the bishops of the Vittorio Veneto region of northern Italy, we feel that it is important to publish more of his collected works in English. His writings in Italian fill nine volumes and they are called *Opera Omnia*. Our little smiling Pope, Albino Luciani, is affectionately called "Papa" by his fellow Italians. We hope as we publish this series of books by or about Pope John Paul I, to convey Papa's spirit, and his message, to a world hungry for holiness. Papa states over and over in his writings that we are all called to be saints. With his compelling stories, his simple style, and his humble example, we can all, in Papa's own words, try "to be what God wants us to be and do what God wants us to do."

— RAY AND LAURETTA SEABECK

PART I

A Biographical Sketch

1

Albino Luciani, Pope John Paul I

An Early Vocation

It is difficult to imagine the kindly and gentle Pope John Paul I ever having been a "holy terror." But he was. His brother, Edoardo, describes him as a high-spirited, mischievous child, full of pranks and given to pulling the girls' hair at school and fighting with his schoolmates. In fact, at an audience during his tragically brief pontificate, he said, laughingly, that he hoped no one would look up his conduct marks during his elementary schooling because they were so bad.

Albino Luciani, the future Pope John Paul I, was born on October 17, 1912, in Canale d'Agordo, a small village nestled in the Dolomite mountains in northern Italy and whose inhabitants were rugged, hardworking, mountain people who had to struggle to make a bare living from the rocky soil. Their houses were mostly small, wooden buildings clustered around the central piazza, now called Piazza di Papa Albino Luciani, where stood the parish church of St. John the Baptist.

Albino's father, Giovanni Luciani, was a bricklayer who, like so many others of that poverty-stricken area, had to seek work in Switzerland and Germany. This was his second marriage. His first wife had died and left him with two small girls, both deaf-mutes. When he met his second wife, Bartolomea Tancon, or Bortola as she was called, who was also from Canale, they were both working in Venice. She had had three years of schooling, more than most of the other women of Canale, and had worked for eleven years for a religious community in Venice. Many of her friends thought she would become a religious. She was thirty-two when she married Giovanni Luciani who was thirty-nine. He was a lax

Catholic and she accepted him only on the condition that he would not in any way hinder their children being brought up as good Catholics. Such was her example and goodness that, little by little, she brought her husband back to the practice of his faith.

Albino was their first child. When he was born, the midwife who attended Bartolomea baptized him immediately because he was so frail, she feared he would die. All his life he would suffer from poor health and, at times, intense pain.

Three more children followed Albino: Frederico, (who died in infancy), Edoardo, and Antonina (Nina). To them, as to her two little deaf-mute stepdaughters, Bartolomea was a warm and loving mother, and frequently had to be both father and mother to all of them, as Giovanni had to seek work elsewhere so often that the children saw little of their cheerful, hardworking father.

Bartolomea was a strong-willed woman of deep faith and whenever she could, she rose early in the morning to attend Mass at the village church of St. John the Baptist. Years later, then Cardinal Luciani wrote of his experience as a youngster when he used to enter the church, while the organ was playing with full voice: "I forgot my usual poverty and had the impression that the organ was welcoming especially me and my little companions as if we were princes. From this first vague intuition came the strong conviction that the Catholic Church is not only something great, but also makes great the little and the poor, honoring and ennobling them."[1] More than once his mother took little Albino by the hand and, on foot, fasting and praying, went on pilgrimage to the Shrine of Our Lady of Grace. She imbued her family with a rich spirituality nourished by frequent Communion and the family recitation of the rosary. Albino never forgot the lessons she taught him both by word and by example, and all his life he retained the most tender affection for her. As Pope he expressed his gratitude and admiration for all mothers.

The family was very poor, especially right after World War I when everyone in that area suffered a great deal from hunger because of the devastation left by the German occupation. Sometimes Albino would go out with his mother to gather roots and herbs in the countryside. Edoardo said, "Our family had very little money, very little, but there was a certain dignity in our poverty and [Mama] always found a way to buy books for school. Everyone had a smile on their lips and we knew a joyous childhood."[2] One day when Albino was about eight years old, he went to do some work for a woman who lived at a distance, and was rewarded with a piece of white bread, a delicacy almost unknown in that poverty-stricken area. Although he was hungry, he did not eat it, but walked home and gave it to his little brother, Edoardo, who says he has never forgotten the taste and smell of that piece of bread.

Giulio Bramezza, a carpenter in Canale, spoke of their childhood together. At school, they were desk mates. Albino far surpassed his little friend in composition and used to help him by giving him ideas and suggestions. Sometimes, when the teacher caught Giulio looking at Albino's notebook, he would fly into a rage and scold them both.

The winters were long and bitterly cold. Twice a day the boys had to trudge to school through ice and snow, wearing galoshes and old military jackets to try to keep warm. In the spring and summer, they went barefoot, wearing shoes only to church.

"We made our First Holy Communion together when we were seven or eight," Giulio said. "I remember it so well because usually he was very vivacious and playful, but on that day he was different, less carefree, more pensive. That day and for some time after, we spoke less, nor did we confide in each other. Albino seemed to be thinking of things he could not explain. But in a few days he was the same as before, full of fun and pranks.

"Sometimes we played hooky in order to catch birds. Albino loved birds, and we would climb up into the mountains with birdlime to catch them, in order to raise them and hear them sing. Then we let them go. If we caught goldfinches, then our day was a great success."[3] One summer Albino had the idea of building a kind of pool up in the mountains, and he and Giulio used to play in it. Actually they did not have much time to play because the children in the village had to pasture the cows during the summer, and there was work at home looking after the younger ones and helping their mothers.

Giulio continued: "We always remained friends. Anyway, it was impossible to quarrel with him; he always managed to convince me to do what he wanted to do, even if I didn't want to. He had a way of saying things that made one quickly give in to him. He even succeeded in teaching me doctrine and was always there when I needed help. He never changed.

"In 1945, I was a prisoner of war in a German concentration camp. My wife had not heard from me for over a year, and in desperation, she went to Don Albino who was then teaching in the seminary. Shortly afterwards, two German soldiers brought me to a radio and said, 'You may speak. Your wife is listening.' Somehow, Albino had succeeded in finding me.

"I was a little in awe of him when he became bishop and patriarch, but that was nonsense on my part. The last time he came to Canale we met in front of the church and he called to me, 'Giulio, do you remember the goldfinches? And when we went up on the 'Pici' mountain which seemed so close to the skies?"[4]

When he was ten, Albino attended a mission given by a holy Capuchin priest, and knew then that he wanted to become a priest. He would gladly have gone off with the Capuchin, but his mother and the parish priest told him he had to wait until he was eleven before he could go to the minor seminary. A year later, Albino was still firm in his decision to become a priest and wrote to his father asking his permission, for unless his father consented, the minor seminary would not accept him. It was an anxious time for Albino. Not only did his father belong to a political party that was frequently anticlerical, but being the eldest son, he would normally be expected to help support the family as soon as he was old enough to do so.

Every day Albino trudged over to the little post office hoping for an answer. At last it came in an envelope that was posted with a stamp of Our Lady. Despite his socialist ideas, his father was enthusiastic. "And I hope," he wrote, "that when you are a priest you will take the part of the poor and the workers, because Christ took their part." Albino cherished that letter and kept it by him until his death.

That summer in the mornings he took extra lessons from a teacher who was staying in the rectory, and in the afternoons took his books to the field where he had to keep an eye on the cow. There he would study a while and then play with the other boys. One day he left his notebook under a tree while he played. When he returned he found, to his horror, that he had left it near the salt lick and that the cow had chewed it. He was in despair. He would have no homework to show the teacher. He was so apprehensive as to what the teacher would say, that his mother went with him to the rectory. The teacher put on a long face and said jokingly, "Since the cow has eaten his lessons, Albino won't be able to go to the seminary."

Albino took him seriously and burst into tears. The pastor, who was present, patted him on the head and reassured him, "Now, now, there are other notebooks, and you will still be able to go to the seminary."[5]

At last on October 1, 1923, Albino, smiling and happy, climbed into the carriage that was to take him to the minor seminary in Feltre, and gaily waved farewell. But as the carriage disappeared around the corner, poor little Edoardo began to cry.

2

∞∞∞

Seminary Life

*A*t first, seminary life was very difficult for the exuberant eleven-year-old. He was used to running freely through the fields and woods, and climbing up the mountains. How he loved those mountains, the white snow and the trees, the sunset behind "his" mountain, which he could see from his window, and the fresh, invigorating air. He missed his devoted mother and brother and sisters, and his poor, but beloved home. Now his freedom was gone. He was confined to a dark barrack-like building, and his days were filled with a rigid discipline. His health, never very good, suffered from the austere life of the seminary. But with the tenacity of hard-working mountain people, he was determined that nothing would stop him on the road to the priesthood.

A young priest, Don Giulio Gaio, now in his nineties, took a special interest in Albino and helped him greatly in those first years. What struck Don Gaio most about his little charge was his penetrating intelligence and his total unawareness of his abilities. Among his companions he was vivacious and talkative, with a Venetian wit and delightful sense of humor.

Each summer he and a few other boys returned to Canale for their vacation. The saintly pastor, Don Filippo Carli, continued the work of the seminary professors by introducing the boys to the practical field of their future work as priests. They accompanied him on his visits to the sick, and watched how he comforted those who were ill, and had just the right word for each member of the family; they saw him at prayer; they noted his zeal for souls and his love for all that was good and beautiful. All this made a tremendous impression on Albino. Don Filippo endeavored to keep the boys busy and invented all kinds of work for them: teaching catechism, taking care of the church, directing the singing, typing, even beekeeping. "Once I tried to teach myself bookbinding and he encouraged me," said Luciani years later. "Another time I collected stamps and took up typewriting." One day when Don Filippo saw that Albino had nothing to do, he gave him an alarm clock to repair. "The clock never worked again once it got into my hands!" said Albino ruefully.

When he was cardinal he once spoke about that period of his life and said that he was far from being a model student. "One day, at the end of vacation, Don Filippo called me into his room where he was seated, writing something. I stood there, waiting. Every now and then he stopped writing, looked up at me, perplexed, and shook his head. I felt guilty and miserable. Finally he finished writing, signed the letter, sealed it, and gave it to me. 'This letter is for you to give to the rector. I have been very unhappy about you this year, and I am asking him to reprimand you.'" Albino was spared neither rebukes nor punishments for being too vivacious, too full of pranks, sometimes disobedient and thoughtless. The seminary professors said of him, "Albino Luciani [is] too exuberant. He has such an original personality, only God knows how he will turn out."

He had a passion for reading, and devoured any book he could get his hands on. Don Filippo was not happy about this. Gently and wisely, he guided Albino's reading. "I am glad that you read," he said to Albino, "but I want you to read only the books in the rectory." "That was easy," said Luciani, "the library had a collection of very good novels, *Twenty-Thousand Leagues Under the Sea,* etc...." After a while Don Filippo was worried again: "You read too many novels. Be more moderate and read some lives of the saints." Years later, as professor in the seminary, Luciani warned a young seminarian who also had a passion for reading: "Do you know that I risked losing my vocation when I was your age, by reading unsuitable books?" Luciani then asked his brother, Edoardo, to get ten good books for the youngster to read during his vacation.

Don Filippo urged Albino to write for the parish bulletin. The first article he wrote was a tirade, full of flowery phrases. Don Filippo read it calmly, put it on the table, and said thoughtfully, "It is well written but reeks of a sermon and it is too long and difficult to understand. Think of some poor old peasant woman trying to read your article, full of long words and complicated sentences. Poor old lady! Imagine her looking at those words full of "isms" and trying to understand those long sentences! Do it again, stick to the point, write short sentences with simple ideas. Illustrate your ideas with word pictures," and again, "think of that old peasant woman!"

"How much I owe to my parish priest," commented Cardinal Luciani as he recalled the episode.[1] Surely it was because he had followed the advice of the village pastor that Pope John Paul I excelled in expressing himself so simply, so directly that children as well as adults could easily understand. This was beautifully illustrated by the child who came with his mother to pray before the body of Pope John Paul I. The little boy brought flowers with him and said, "I want to give these flowers to the Pope who spoke like Jesus."

When he was about fifteen or sixteen, Albino changed. Pope John Paul II, in speaking to the faithful of Vittorio Veneto on August 28,1979, said, "We can say that what was deeply striking right from the years of his adolescence was his certainty of God's love and the greatness of his call to the priesthood."[2]

From that time on, Albino was determined to become a saint, but in a quiet, hidden way, so that no one would notice. His goal was to become just like Jesus, gentle and humble of heart. This meant a constant, daily struggle, for he was not gentle by nature and had a fiery temperament, which occasionally burst into sudden flames. But with God's help, a will of iron, and a deep interior life, little by little, he became the gentle, smiling man who brought such joy to the Church during his thirty-three-day pontificate.

As patriarch, he revealed something of his own interior life in a talk he gave on April 30, 1972, the fiftieth anniversary of the death of St. Bertilla Boscardin. A Sister of St. Dorothy, she died at the age of thirty-four, and had spent most of her religious life as a nurse in a hospital in Treviso, Italy. Luciani, who had been a patient at that hospital several times, asked some of the Sisters who had known Sister Bertilla if they had recognized her sanctity. They replied that they had realized she was a very good religious, a hard worker, very obliging and always tranquil, pious, and faithful to the Rule, but that was all. In his talk, the patriarch said, "She had a hunger and thirst for holiness . . . she was straight as a steel arrow in her tenacity and constancy in loving God. St. Bertilla was a person who for years said every morning, 'I want to love the Lord so much, and I will, I will, at any cost. I am *resolved* with His help to become a saint.' And, for me, the most beautiful aspect of St. Bertilla was that she became a saint doing everything so as not to attract attention to herself. She wrote, 'To suffer and mortify myself, but without letting it be noticed, all for the love of Jesus alone.' "[3]

When Luciani was a boy, his mother gave him a child's edition of *Introduction to a Devout Life* by St. Francis de Sales. As he grew older, he read and reread all this saint's works and tried to follow his example of gentleness and amiability. When he was seventeen, and in the Diocesan Major Seminary of St. Gregory in Belluno, he read the autobiography of St. Thérèse for the first time and it made a great impression on him. "It was like a bolt from the blue," he said. St. Thérèse's spirituality also had been greatly influenced by St. Francis de Sales; she was a living example of his spiritual doctrine. In his writings and sermons Luciani would often refer to both saints, and although his references to St. Francis de Sales are far more frequent than those to St. Thérèse, one feels that he lived totally her "Little Way." However, he preferred to call his way "the way of the carts," which is not that of a comfortable car on a smooth highway, but that of an ox-drawn cart on a rough dirt road, requiring much sacrifice, patience, and fatigue. Like St. Thérèse, he would say, "Let us trust above all in the mercy of God, Who, knowing that we are poor and little, is happy with our sincere desires and daily efforts to grow in holiness."[4] And like St. Francis de Sales, "God carries us, He holds us by the hand, He carries us in His arms. It is enough to entrust ourselves to Him. He leads us on the right path even if we do not see where it ends."

In the major seminary, history, biblical exegesis, and Latin were his best subjects, and to the solace of many, mathematics his worst. He was always ready to help his fellow students who frequently came to him with their problems in Greek or Latin or any other subject except mathematics. He loved to sing in the choir. "I can still see him, happy and content, singing with 'gusto' with that characteristic twist of his mouth, which we used to tease him about," said one of his fellow seminarians.

One evening as he and another seminarian were returning to the seminary, his friend suddenly yelled, "Fire, fire!" and began to run. Albino rushed after him, and they came to a barn, flames leaping from its roof. Both dashed in to rescue the animals, and they managed to save them all, to the great gratitude of the farmer who had been away.

During the summer vacations he went back to Canale and divided his time between church, study, and work. It was during one of these vacations that he indexed and catalogued all the books of the parish library. There were hundreds of them, and he read them all. Father Giuseppe Strim, S.J., an old friend, said, "One day I went to visit him at Canale, and I found him reading as usual, his cassock stained with grass as he had been haymaking all day. He looked up, smiling. 'What a workhorse you are,' I said to him, 'do you want to go crazy with your books?' 'Don't worry,' he answered, 'this is the last book in the library, and since I have no money to buy books, I'll start reading them all over again!'"[5]

One Sunday afternoon in Canale, when the people had left the church after Vespers and were milling about the square, a distinguished-looking gentleman got on a box and began to harangue the crowd, trying especially to attract the youngsters. He was a Fascist, and, therefore, violently anti-Catholic. All of a sudden, Albino was there, talking and gesticulating to the man, and telling him in no uncertain terms to leave immediately. The man fled. Later on, after World War II, this same man became a Franciscan friar.

Finally, the longed-for day of his ordination arrived, July 7, 1935. Albino was twenty-two years old. The next day he celebrated his first Mass at Canale, a bittersweet occasion because only a few months earlier, his beloved Don Filippo Carli had died. A saintly man, loved by all who knew him, he was greatly mourned by everyone, but especially by Albino who owed so much to his fatherly watchfulness and encouragement during the long road to the priesthood.

3

Papa Living His Priesthood

*D*on Albino's first assignment from July to December, 1935, was to his own parish at Canale where Don Augustin Bramezza was pastor. Then from December 1935 to 1937 he was chaplain and teacher at the Technical Mining Institute at Agordo.

"I gave him the job of entertaining the children and he did it splendidly," said Don Augustin. "He was a genius in telling stories, and he always knew how to draw a significant moral from them in a very humorous way. The children gathered around him listening with mouths open, hanging on his every word."[1]

Many years later, whenever Bishop Luciani introduced Don Augustin to anyone, he would say, "Here is the priest who used to make me get up at 4 a.m. every day," and then went on to tell how much he owed to Don Augustin for making sure that he, as a newly ordained priest, formed strict habits, making plenty of time for prayer before the day's work began because prayer is of the utmost importance in a priest's life.

One of his first decisions as a young priest was to join the Apostolic Union of the Clergy, an international association of secular priests endeavoring to live a life of intense Eucharistic piety and prayer. In 1936, after six months of probation, he made the Promise required of the members of that Union, saying in a letter to the rector of the seminary, Monsignor Angelo Santin, "I want very much to make the Promise because the Apostolic Union does me so much good. I consider it a grace from Our Lord to belong to it." His act of consecration, in his own handwriting, is still extant, and part of it reads as follows, "I, Don Albino Luciani . . . for the greater glory of God and in order to bind myself with greater efficacy to my sanctification and to the salvation of souls . . . freely adhere to this Union, and with all my heart I consecrate and offer myself, confiding in the Heart of

Jesus and through the intercession of Mary, and promise to observe the Rules of the Union with constancy and fidelity. Amen. The Epiphany of the Lord, 1936."[2]

Within a year of his ordination, his health, never good, broke down and he was taken to the sanatorium, a very ill young man. The antibiotics, which could have helped him, had not yet been discovered, and Albino expected to die soon. He was ashamed at feeling a bit afraid. He said to himself, "I'm a priest, wake up, don't be stupid." So well did he succeed in hiding his feelings, that the doctor said of him, "He accepted it all with serenity and even with cheerfulness." Later, Luciani wrote, "I was ill in the sanatorium. I can tell you it is completely different to be ill having the faith, and not having it. If one has faith, one beats it willingly; if one has no faith, one gets discouraged."[3] He recovered, but several years later he again spent many months in the sanatorium.

Two years after his ordination, Monsignor Santin, rector of the Gregorian Seminary, appointed Don Albino as vice rector of the seminarians. His day began at 4 a.m. He woke the boys up in the morning, he recreated with them, kept his office door always open for them to come to him with their problems, to share their joys and sorrows, and he adamantly refused any job that would take him too far away from his seminarians. Every day he went to visit the sick ones and spent time consoling and comforting them.

One of his former students said that Don Albino, although he was strict and took his job of disciplinarian seriously, was the most patient and understanding of all the professors and never lost his temper. "When I did not understand him in class I went afterwards to his study to ask for explanations. He always listened to me very willingly, and since he never showed the least sign of impatience with me, I kept going back to him, never dreaming that I might be asking too much or wasting his time."

Albino loved to take his students for long hikes through the countryside and the forests, up to the foothills of the Dolomites. Once by mistake, he wore a pair of hiking shoes that were too small for him. After a while the students noticed him walking with difficulty and guessed what had happened. Each step must have been painful, but he uttered no word of complaint, nor did he slow his pace, and the students were in admiration of his extraordinary self-control.

One day a student found him in his room numb with cold, huddled over a book. "Why don't you light the fire and get warm?" he asked. Don Albino replied, "Because your rooms are not heated, and it is not right that I should be warm while you are cold."[4]

Another student was most anxious to discover something about Don Albino's interior life, but with little success. However, he once caught a glimpse of it. Don Albino was trying to persuade his students to read certain books on the perfections of God, but they were only half-listening, as they expected the bell for recreation at any moment. He urged them to read it, and said, "At your age, when I got these volumes, I read them right through, and I was so struck by them that for some days I was incapable of thinking about anything except God." When the student told this story, he added, "Recently I read some words which reminded me of that incident: 'The face of Pope John Paul I is like that of someone who has seen more than we, and is still enraptured by it.'"[5]

Around this time, he was afflicted with an extremely painful ailment that could have quickly been cured by an operation. He refused so that he could offer this pain to the Lord. But as time went on he found it impossible to continue his duties with such excruciating pain, and common sense prevailed whereby he submitted to the surgery, which cured him.

As professor he taught at various times, from 1937-1947, dogmatics, philosophy, canon law, sacred art, history of art, history, patristics, sacred eloquence, and catechetics. He was in the habit of taking copious notes from his readings and had indexed them all, a practice he urged on his students. After he was elected Pope, the first thing he sent for from Venice were his boxes of notes, a fund of documentation which was the result of many years of hard work. Recently, one of Luciani's old students recalled the lessons given by the future Pope on the history of art. Belluno and Feltre are filled with works of art, dating from Roman times, and Feltre has been called an "open air museum" because of its many houses whose walls are decorated with frescoes from the 16th-18th centuries. He used to bring his students on field trips to study the paintings, sculptures, and architecture, and he taught them to interpret all these works of art, including the modern ones. He explained that the artist is trying to create beauty and said, "Beauty is not truth, but the radiant expression of truth. One cannot judge the artist only by his technical ability because the artist must have above all, spiritual and moral qualities.... Art must be neither pure realism, nor exaggerated idealism which devalues truth and sacrifices reality.... Nature must be seen with the eyes of a poet.... The artist retouches nature in such a way as to bring it back to that purity and holiness which it had at the beginning of the kingdom of goodness and innocence in which we would all like to live ... entering into the kingdom of art, each one should become better."[6]

Don Albino well realized the growing importance of the communications media. For this reason he initiated his seminarians into the techniques of printing, radio, and movies to help them understand the tremendous influence of the mass media, so that they could use them efficaciously, combating error and spreading the gospel.

He told his seminarians that good manners are essential to charity. In the many retreats that he gave to priests as a bishop, Luciani spoke at great length about courtesy and of its great importance. "People greatly appreciate our courtesy and kindness. This is a little thing, but sometimes the success of our work depends on just these little things: pay attention; be kind and polite with everyone, but subservient to no one."[7]

He spent the long hard years of World War II at the seminary and suffered all the hardships and privations that it brought on Italy and, indeed, on most of Europe. Nor did the ending of the war bring an immediate cessation to either the hardships or the violence. After the German army had been driven from the country by the Allies, the Resistance party came down from their hiding places in the mountains. Some of them were determined to take justice into their own hands and punish those accused of collaboration with the Germans. One night a group set up a gallows and planned to hang twelve collaborators. Someone quickly told Don Albino what was happening. No one knows how he did it, but the next day the gallows had gone and no one was hanged. Twelve men owe their lives to Don Albino.

It was at this time that one of the students, whose home and everything in it had been burned by the Germans, arrived at the seminary with only the clothes on his back. Don Albino immediately gave him one of his cassocks and some money. Then seeing how the youth suffered from the cold, he went to a great deal of trouble to have his old overcoat repaired and gave it also to the destitute student.

In 1947, he received his doctorate from the Gregorian University in Rome. He passed his exams brilliantly, and his thesis was on "The Origin of the Human Soul according to Antonio Rosmini," prepared under the direction of Father Charles Boyer, S.J., which won for the author the special congratulations of the theology faculty at the Gregorian as well as that of the Congregation for Seminaries and Universities (now the Congregation for Education).

Pope Pius XII named him monsignor, and one day a new seminarian called him "Don Luciani" instead of "Monsignor Luciani." His companions reproached him for this, but Luciani took his side, saying, "You see, these titles are a farce . . . men are like footballs, and if the football is deflated, people ignore it and leave it in a corner; if it is pumped up, everyone thinks they can use it as they please and kick it around."[8]

The Diocesan Eucharistic Congress was organized by Monsignor Luciani in 1949, and as director of the Catechetics Center, he drew up a very clear and simple book, *Catechetics in Crumbs,* for the formation of catechists. When he became Pope, he was asked permission to re-publish it, but he refused because by 1978 parts of it were out of date due to the renewal of catechetical methods since Vatican II. After his death, however, several Italian publishers printed it again. A section was translated into English and given to a young American catechist in 1983. Her reaction was, "Here I find some things I have wanted to do with the children, but was hesitant . . . now I am encouraged to do them."

The book begins with "The Mission of the Catechist." "There is a painting by Murillo called 'The Children of the Seashell.' In a tranquil and serene background, while angels from on high are looking on and smiling, the boy Jesus is giving little John the Baptist some water in a shell drawn from a limpid brook which is flowing at their feet. This is the mission of the catechist: to take the place of Jesus and give, with the catechism, the water of eternal life to children."

Among many other subjects, he emphasized teaching children how to pray. "Praying means talking with the Lord, and not only about heaven, the soul, but about anything, really to "chat" as one does with a friend. We can speak to Him of Papa and [Mama], of homework, of play. He is not far away but very close. He hears us and He is very happy that we talk to Him. We should not pray only in church, but everywhere and often, in the street, at school, at home, during games. We can recollect ourselves for a moment greeting Jesus, giving thanks, asking His pardon without anyone noticing it."[9] Luciani continues at length on this subject, giving ideas on methods to be used in teaching prayer to children. And of course, the catechist must be a person of prayer in order to be effective and teach others how to pray.

Catechesis was his love and great passion all his life, from the time of his first priestly assignment to the very day of his death as Pope.

John Paul II said of him in his apostolic exhortation *Catechesi Tradendae* (On catechesis in our time), "Pope John Paul I's zeal and gifts as a catechist amazed us all. To all of us he gave an example of catechesis at once popular and concentrated on the essential, one made up of simple words and actions that were able to touch the heart." And he was a catechist in the total sense of the word, having had direct experience for years as well as years of study. Another witness, Cardinal Marco Ce of Venice, said, "Luciani was a great catechist of humble people, and the Church will always hold him up as a model. It is impossible now to speak of a pastoral style in fulfilling the duties of bishop and Pope without referring to Albino Luciani."[10]

Cardinal Angelo Roncalli of Venice, who became Pope John XXIII, went to Belluno for a few days, and on one of these days Don Albino offered to take the cardinal out driving. In this way they got to know each other, and afterwards Roncalli said to the vicar general of Belluno, "I have never met such a lovable man." When Luciani heard this, he smiled and said, "I don't know how he could know me; he did all the talking!"

When Cardinal Roncalli was elected Pope in 1958, the Episcopal See of Vittorio Veneto was vacant. After consultation with other bishops, he decided to name Albino Luciani as its new bishop.

At first, Monsignor Luciani was reluctant to accept the appointment. Rome insisted, and finally the Pope called Luciani to Rome and after a long talk, asked him to acquiesce.

He objected, "Holy Father, I don't have good health; I have respiratory problems."

"Excellent!" replied Pope John. "If that's all it is, I'll send you to Vittorio Veneto. The bishop's palace there is high on a hill; the air is wonderful and will do you good!"[11]

It was because of Pope John's appreciation of Luciani that he personally consecrated him bishop on December 27, 1958. The evening before, the Pope had a talk with the bishop-elect, and twenty years afterwards, Luciani spoke about that visit: "Pope John told me, with a confidence that dumbfounded me, a simple priest, even if I was a candidate for the bishopric, several things I must not say here. He even affectionately gave me some practical advice. Sitting close to me he said, 'I know that you have taught theology and other beautiful things. But school is one thing, being a pastor is another. Be careful to talk simply and clearly.' Then striking his knee with his fist he added, 'Humility! Humility!' With his usual simplicity, he took from his pocket the *Imitation of Christ,* and he read to me the four rules to acquire peace: 1. endeavor to do the will of another rather than your own; 2. always choose rather to have less than more; 3. always seek the lowest place and to be inferior to everyone; 4. always wish and pray that the Will of God may be entirely fulfilled in you" (Book 111, 23).[12]

Luciani considered Pope John XXIII a saint, and the *Imitation of Christ* was always one of his favorite books.

After the Ceremony of the Episcopal Consecration, Pope John turned to a monsignor and, pointing to Luciani, said, "Watch that little bishop, you will see . . . you will see. . . ."

4

The New Bishop

*I*t was a cold, dreary day in January 1959 when the train from Belluno pulled into the station in Vittorio Veneto. A delegation of ecclesiastics and city officials was waiting on the platform to welcome Albino Luciani, their new bishop. He got off the train and went forward to greet them, looking a little shy, and with the train of his long robes rolled up in a ball under his arm. Behind him came his trainbearer with nothing to carry. (Those days before the Second Vatican Council, bishops used to wear robes at ceremonies that trailed on the ground, necessitating the help of a trainbearer.) Surprise was the delegation's first reaction, but Luciani immediately won their hearts with his captivating smile.

He kissed the ground and went directly to the Cathedral of San Tiziano for the ceremony of taking possession of his diocese (a phrase he never liked: "A bishop is given to his diocese," he used to say). When he saw the crowds of people he felt very nervous, but no one ever forgot that first sermon, during which he said:

> *There are certain things that the Lord wants to write neither on bronze, nor on marble, but actually on dust, so that if the writing remains, not broken up, not scattered by the wind, let it be very clear that everything is due solely to the work and the merits of the Lord. I am the little one of once upon a time, I am the one who comes from the fields, I am pure and simple dust, on this dust the Lord has written the episcopal dignity of the illustrious Diocese of Vittorio Veneto. If anything good ever comes out of all this, let it be very clear from now on, it is only the fruit of the goodness, the grace, and the mercy of the Lord.*[1]

What God wrote on that "sand" has remained to this day in the hearts of the people of Vittorio Veneto, so greatly did they love and esteem their dear Bishop Luciani. In fact, at the audience he gave them shortly after his election as Pope, they told him that they had been sure he would become Pope after the death of Paul VI. He smiled and said teasingly, "I always knew that you had many beautiful qualities, but I never realized that you also had the spirit of prophecy."

The new bishop chose as his motto, "*Humilitas,*" as had St. Charles Borromeo, whom he looked upon as a model bishop. Luciani explained the virtue of humility as primarily an attitude of the heart, not merely something exterior such as looking for the last place, accepting blame or opposition, or being hidden. It is a deep awareness and lived experience of our nothingness before the greatness of God, and so it becomes the source of exterior humility. He said, "It does not bring approbation, admiration, or earthly satisfaction; but it is in fact the foundation which no one sees, no one except God."

His coat of arms represented the Dolomite mountains, where he was born, and the three theological virtues of faith, hope, and charity were symbolized by three stars. "I will always try to keep faith, hope, and charity before me in my episcopate. You too must try to do the same," he told the people of Canale d'Agordo in his first talk when he visited them as a new bishop. "If we put these three things into practice we are on the right road. Let us try to keep united with Our Lord Jesus Christ; let us try to be good at whatever cost in work or in sacrifice. The Lord will recompense and reward us."[2] Humility, faith, hope, and charity, these were the great themes of the four general audiences he gave during the thirty-three days of his pontificate.

Vittorio Veneto is a small diocese situated at the foot of the Italian Alps. The bishop's residence was an old and austere medieval castle high on the hill, built for the prince-bishops of those days. Luciani lived there in great simplicity, dressed as an ordinary priest. His meals were frugal, and his car was so old that his secretary finally persuaded him to accept the gift of a new one. He then sold the old one and gave the proceeds to the poor.

During his years in Vittorio Veneto he modernized the House of Retreats, completed the seminary, opened new churches and inaugurated various parochial works, organized the Diocesan Archives, and renovated the printing equipment at the seminary. But his first and most important concern was for his priests and his people. He gave many retreats to his priests, one of which was taped by a participant, who painstakingly typed the whole of it for his own use. This retreat was printed after the Pope's death under the title of *The Good Samaritan*. It was not edited, and therefore, reads exactly as he spoke, with the consequence that it has all the liveliness and disconnectedness of a familiar conversation. The "Retreat" has become famous in Italy today, and at the Synod of Bishops in 1980 Pope John Paul II said, "A short time ago I had occasion to read the text of these marvelous conferences, full of life, with figurative language which was adapted in every step to the reality of priestly life and centered around the figure of the Good Samaritan. We can see how dear this figure was to him, how much he identified with it."[3]

Luciani was particularly close and grateful to priests who were willing to work in small and unimportant parishes. "The people there have souls," he said. "If one truly loves the Lord, I don't understand how anyone can refuse this work, humble and yet great."

Bishop Luciani was especially interested in the missions. In 1962, then Bishop Makarakiza begged for priests to come to help his diocese in Burundi, Africa. Luciani not only sent some of his own priests as missionaries but also "adopted" the African diocese. When one of his priests returned to Vittorio Veneto to ask permission to collect funds, Bishop Luciani said to him, "Not only do I give you permission, but since you are a missionary, I ask your blessing." With that, the future Pope knelt down to receive his blessing.

He visited Burundi in 1966, and during that time, Bishop Makarakiza wanted Luciani to inaugurate the new church in Kitega, built mainly through the generosity of the people of Vittorio Veneto. He asked Bishop Luciani to preside, but he declined, saying, "Not for the world! You are the bishop here; we are only here to give you a helping hand."

One of the missionaries took Luciani all over the diocese in a jeep, and confided to Makarakiza that he had given him such a wonderfully bumpy ride that Bishop Luciani would never be able to forget Burundi. The African bishop exclaimed in horror, "Oh! You must not do that to a saint like him!"

After his visit Bishop Luciani wrote, "The missionaries brought home to me most forcibly the love of God, Who loves all men and wants all to reach salvation. He who encounters the missions encounters the Father, and also the Son, the First Missionary. A true Christian cannot but feel the problem of the missions."[4]

In urging the people to help the missions, he said, "It is beautiful to see people showing true gratitude to Our Lady for graces they have received. But it is sad to see necklaces and gold rings of great value, and even objects of superstition, placed on the statue of the Virgin, while so many people are dying of hunger. Is not Our Lady also the Mother of the Chinese, of the Africans, of the Vietnamese? Indeed she is. The most beautiful diadem on the Virgin's head is a row of clean beds in a hospital, a series of schoolrooms, a group of the poor being fed."[5]

The people of his diocese were very dear to his heart, and he frequently visited families, the sick, and the poor all over his diocese. Sometimes, because of bad roads or no roads, he had to walk through mud or snow in order to reach their homes or huts, where he comforted and encouraged them, and left gifts from his own pocket for the poor. Often he slipped money under the pillow of the sick. He made two pastoral visitations to all of the one hundred and eighty parishes, meeting one by one the youngsters in the catechetical classes of the elementary and middle schools, the teachers, catechists, associations, parish priests, and the many sick people. It was a joy to be present when he was with the children. His skill as a catechist fascinated everyone and often brought forth bursts of laughter.

"Is it easy or difficult to obey?" he asked the children.

Some said, "Easy," and some said, "Difficult."

"If your mother gives you some money and tells you to go and buy some candy, is it easy or hard?"

"Easy."

"And if she tells you to stay at home, do your homework, and help with the dishes, is it easy or hard?"

"Hard."

"And should we obey only when it is easy or also when it is hard?"

"Also when it is hard."

"Yes, that's it. We must always be obedient to our mother because inside we know that we truly love her. So we must also have the courage to love God at all times and obey Him when it is easy and when it is hard."

His burning desire was to make God known and loved by both children and adults. He said, "If here inside our hearts there is only a small flame of love, then a little wind of selfishness, of pride, of laziness, will extinguish that small flame. But if there is a bonfire of love for God inside us, difficulties will make this love burn higher and more splendidly. The bishop must be the first to try to get to know the Lord and make Him known and loved. And it is not enough to be content with a 'little,' or a 'somewhat' love, but only with a great and burning love, constantly fed."

At a parish mission one winter, seeing the church filled with men, Bishop Luciani was thrilled: "Oh, how wonderful, how wonderful, how happy I am, and how I thank the Lord!"[6]

Always smiling, he truly kept his promise made at his installation as bishop of Vittorio Veneto, "My dear brothers, my dear faithful, I would be a very unfortunate bishop if I did not love you. I can assure you that I do love you, that I desire only to enter into your service and to put at your disposal all my poor strength, the little I have and the little I am."[7]

He used to visit his beloved sick alone, and had an almost maternal tenderness with them. Having had so much illness himself, he could feel their sufferings, and knew how to console and comfort each one. When Luciani's doctor was asked, "What struck you most about Pope John Paul I?" he answered, "His compassion. He spoke so kindly that people listened and never forgot his words. His sensitiveness and human warmth were not only natural gifts, but were the privilege of a man who has suffered greatly and who has known suffering in all its aspects."[8]

One morning, one of his priests came to see him, unannounced. Luciani was sitting down, weary, and his face was strained. At a certain point in the conversation he confided to the priest, "Last night I did not sleep."

The priest asked him, "Excellency, don't you feel well?"

"No," he answered. "I couldn't sleep because I had to reprove a confrere and I carried in my soul all the bitterness which I must have caused him by my correction."[9]

On his way to Rome one day, he had a painful attack of illness. He refused to go to a doctor, so his secretary tried to make him as comfortable as possible in the car, propping him up with pillows, while they continued their journey to Rome. That evening, in spite of his pain, Bishop Luciani gave the final sermon at a novena being held in one of the churches. His secretary praised him, but the bishop merely replied, "We are useless servants. We only did our duty." Bishop Gioacchino Muccin, who knew him intimately, said of him, "In spite of his fragile physical constitution, he always showed great endurance in his work and an incredible strength of will which is rarely met with in healthy, robust persons."[10]

The Second Vatican Council took place while Bishop Luciani was bishop of Vittorio Veneto, from 1962-1965. He went in order "to learn rather than to teach," as he put it. Although he did not speak at the council, he made some written interventions.

During the council, he met Cardinal Stefan Wyszynski, Primate of Poland, and they became close friends. From then on whenever the cardinal came to Rome, he always stayed with Luciani before he went back to Poland. Through Wyszynski, Luciani came to have a great admiration and love for Poland, and was greatly impressed by the enthusiastic and deeply lived faith of the Polish people.

He said, almost prophetically, "I am convinced that only the Polish Church can save us. I do not know how, but I am certain that Poland has a great mission to fulfill. In the coming years, they will speak much about this nation, which is so devoted to Our Lady."[11]

Just before going to Rome for the conclave that would elect him Pope, he gave to his niece, Pia, a small statue of the Black Madonna, which had been given to him by Cardinal Wyszynski.

And it was on Poland's greatest feast, the Feast of Our Lady of Czestochowa, that he was elected Pope, to the great delight of Cardinal Wyszynski.

After the council, many problems arose even in the small Diocese of Vittorio Veneto. The bishop had to cope with various crises: crises of defections from the priesthood, of vocations, of catechetics, with wrong interpretations of the council, and with the advance of Marxist and materialistic ideologies.

Pope John Paul II, in speaking to the pilgrims from Vittorio Veneto on August 28, 1979, said to them, "How lucky you are, you who for so many years were able to enjoy the presence of such a good Father. His first concern as a bishop in that period, so difficult for the Church, was on the plane of doctrine. He strenuously defended orthodoxy and discipline. It was his concern and preoccupation, and also his glory."[12] Luciani spoke out strongly, but always with charity. His vicar general said of him, "When he was confronted with wrong interpretations of the council, he suffered but did not yield, always faithful to Christ and His Church. He united strength with gentleness and paid no heed to the criticisms leveled at him; the saints look to God and not to themselves. 'It is enough that God is content with me,' he would say. 'What I imagine myself to be must be cut down to size. What others think of me is of no importance. What God thinks of me is important.'"[13]

During the Year of Faith in 1968 he gave many talks to his priests concerning the faith. They were so impressed that they asked him to write down these talks for them, and the result was a small book entitled *The Little Syllabus*.

In his introduction, Bishop Luciani writes:

> *Dear Priests . . . Try to live this Year of Faith, speak enthusiastically to your people of the Word of God, of Jesus, of the Church, and speak of those things more than of errors. And do not be content that your listeners grasp it intellectually; see that they also live their faith. Show by your own actions and by your ardent words, with a chaste and compassionate life, that "you continue to run after Christ, to seize Him because*

*you in your turn have been seized by Him"(cf. Phil 3:12).
Faith is saying yes to God, clinging to Him with our whole spiritual being and making our own the truths which He has
revealed to us and proposes to us by means of the Magisterium
of the Church. We do not believe because such truths please us,
or agree with scientific data, or are the fashion of the day, but
because He has revealed them, He Who loves us and cannot
and will not deceive us.*[14]

As one French author said, "One can see that Albino Luciani
was not an inert and powerless spectator in his palace while 'the
assassins of the faith' came and threatened the doctrinal and moral
integrity of the priests and faithful entrusted to his care. He did
not belong to the category of pastors who became 'dumb dogs' for
fear of losing popularity. Nor did he belong to those who defend
truth but without charity."[15] No, he was a true shepherd of Christ
Who defended his flock.

He had made a thorough study of responsible parenthood and
consulted with many doctors and theologians. Like John XXIII
and Paul VI, he had studied the possibility of the "pill" being used
as a "natural" method of regulating births. But like them, when
further scientific investigation showed it to be contrary to the
Church's teaching, he discarded the idea. As soon as the encyclical *Humanae Vitae* was issued, he supported it vigorously, and, in
fact, was one of the first bishops to circulate it. He not only wrote
to his priests telling them to propagate the encyclical, but also
defended Pope Paul's considerable delay in settling the questions.
In his letter he says, "He (Pope Paul) knows that he will cause bitterness to many; he knows that different solutions would probably have brought him more human applause; but he places his trust
in God, and in order to be faithful to His Word, reproposes the
constant teaching of the Magisterium in this most delicate matter
in all its purity." Then he quoted from the encyclical: ". . . if sin
should still keep its hold over them, let them not be discouraged,
but rather have recourse with humble perseverance to the mercy
of God which is poured forth in the Sacrament of Penance . . . may
married couples always find in the words and heart of a priest the

echo of the voice and the love of the Redeemer." He ended his letter, "I am sure that all will have with me a sincere adhesion to the pontifical teaching, and in this faith I bless and greet you."[16]

Luciani was intransigent in upholding the teaching of the Church, and severe with those, who through intellectual pride and disobedience, paid no attention to the Church's prohibition of artificial contraception. To those who sincerely tried to live up to the Church's teaching but who fell through weakness, and then had recourse to the Sacrament of Penance, he was very compassionate, following Pope Paul's guidelines, and while not condoning the sin, he lifted them up and encouraged them. "How much mercy it is necessary to have," he would say. If some people think that his compassion and gentleness in this respect implies that he was against *Humanae Vitae,* one can only infer that it is merely wishful thinking on their part and an attempt to find an ally in favor of artificial contraception.

One of the rather widespread misinterpretations of the council documents was the downgrading of devotion to Our Lady. Luciani worried about his people who no longer prayed the rosary and he kept urging devotion to Our Lady and to the rosary. But he wanted more than mere superficial devotion. Sometimes he was approached by simple women who asked him out of pious curiosity which title of Our Lady he liked best. Without satisfying their curiosity, he would reply with a twinkle in his eye, "If you will let me give you some advice, may I suggest that you should have devotion to Our Lady of the Pots and Pans, or Our Lady of the Broom." He then went on, "You see, Our Lady became a saint without visions, without ecstasies. She became a saint as a simple housewife, washing the dishes, preparing the soup, peeling the potatoes, or things like that."

"What I was trying to tell them," he said to his priests in a retreat, "was that, yes, they should have great devotion to Our Lady, they must pray to Our Lady and have great confidence in her, but above all, they must imitate her virtues."[17]

Luciani loved the rosary and was frequently seen with it in his hands. In 1972, he wrote, "The rosary becomes a look at Mary, which grows in intensity little by little as one proceeds. It ends by being a refrain which springs from the heart and, which repeated, sweetens the soul like a song." Then he continued, "When they speak of 'adult Christians' in prayer, sometimes they exaggerate. Personally, when I speak alone with God and Our Lady, I prefer to feel myself a child, rather than a grown-up. The mitre, the zucchetto, the ring disappear. I send the grown-up on vacation, and the bishop along with him, and abandon myself to the spontaneous tenderness that a child has for its papa and mama. To be for a while before God as I am in reality, with the worst of myself and with the best of myself; to let rise to the surface from the depths of my being the child I once was, who wants to laugh, to chatter, to love the Lord, and who sometimes feels the need to cry so that he may be shown mercy, helps me to pray. The rosary, a simple and easy prayer, helps me to be a child, and I am not ashamed at all."[18]

In 1969, the cardinal patriarch of Venice, Cardinal Urbani, died suddenly, and no one was surprised when Pope Paul VI named Albino Luciani to the See of Venice. No one, that is, except Luciani himself. He was reluctant to accept because of his health, and because of his limitations, which he clearly recognized and admitted, but Pope Paul insisted. Perhaps the Pope felt that just such a man as Luciani — simple, humble, prayerful, and fearless in defending Church doctrine — was needed for the tormented and complex situation that prevailed in Venice.

Soon after his nomination, before he left Vittorio Veneto, Luciani and his secretary picked up two young hitchhikers who did not recognize him as a bishop because he was dressed as an ordinary priest. His friendliness and interest put them at ease, and they began to speak about the new nominee.

"Who is this Luciani! No one has ever heard of him. They should put someone else in Venice."

The bishop did not tell them his name, but explained to the young men that God's ways and man's ways are often very different. He must have impressed them, because as they left, thanking him for the ride, they said warmly, "We wish a priest like you would be made patriarch!"[19]

Luciani left a great void in the hearts of his people at Vittorio Veneto, where he is remembered with great love and affection as a bishop totally committed to the care of souls. When he was about to leave for Venice, he gave to his vicar general the money he had saved, as well as the collection taken up by his priests to cover the expenses of his installation at Venice. "Give it to the poor," he said. "I came without a penny in my pocket, and that's the way I want to leave." In his farewell discourse in the cathedral, February 11, 1970, he said, "I have always tried in these eleven years I have been with you to be 'God's Postman' for you. I have always exhorted you to be in love with God, to read His Word, and to put it into practice as He asks you to do."[20]

As close as he was to God, Luciani was not without his human weaknesses, and he made mistakes, even, it is said, to depriving a priest of parish work for nine years. It was a decision he made on the basis of insufficient evidence, just as St. Alphonsus Liguori penalized St. Gerard Majella on the same basis of insufficient information. But such was the love and admiration of the people and priests of Vittorio Veneto for their bishop, that when he became Pope, that same priest said, "I am very happy that they elected Albino Luciani. He learned and grew from his mistakes, and he will be a very good Pope."[21]

5

Patriarch of Venice

Pope Paul VI called Bishop Luciani to succeed Cardinal Urbani as pariarch of Venice on December 15, 1969, and he took possession of the diocese on February 3, 1970. In the consistory of March 5, 1973, the Pope appointed thirty-nine new cardinals, with Albino Luciani in their number. Venice was a difficult and sometimes explosive assignment, but the new patriarch was able to do his work with humility and simplicity. On the one hand there was the ancient, aristocratic city with its pomp and splendor, its artiness, and its centuries-old social system. On the other hand, there was the new city, its industry developing at a tremendous rate, with the consequent problems of overpopulation, materialism, housing, schooling, and pollution. Marxism and religious indifference thrived, and the churches were becoming mere museums of antiquity.

Here in this ancient, splendid city, Luciani kept to his hidden and simple lifestyle, much to the displeasure of some of the society-minded and even some of the priests. Instead of the cortege of gondolas to welcome him to Venice, he kept the ceremony a strictly religious one. He accepted few invitations to secular functions, unless their purpose was to raise money for the poor. Then he always appeared, hoping the presence and the urging of the patriarch would inspire people to be generous. But as for the rest, he said he did not like to put his prestige as patriarch at the service of secular and worldly vanities, nor did he have time for them. Naturally, this attitude did not please the Venetians.

Luciani loved to talk with the people as a friend and father to all, and made sure that everyone was welcomed at the patriarchate.

"My door is always open," he said. "Tell my secretary what you need, and I will gladly do anything I can for you."

As a result, every day there was a long line of people who came for help of some kind.

"Eminence," said his secretary, "you will ruin me! They won't leave me in peace."

Smiling, the cardinal replied, "Someone will help us."

And so they kept coming — the poor, the abandoned, the jobless, ex-convicts, ex-prostitutes, drunkards. They were all his friends.[1]

If anyone wanted to speak personally with him, he was always available if his work permitted. One Easter Sunday while he was dining with his brother, the Sister announced that two boys, aged twelve and thirteen, wanted to speak to him because they had a big problem. The patriarch immediately left the table and went to them. Their problem was that they were both "in love" with a girl their own age. Their parents said they were too young. What were they to do? Luciani spoke with them for over fifteen minutes. A few days later two grateful mothers told the patriarch that their boys were happy and at peace.[2]

In 1977, Cardinal Hyacinthe Thiandoum, archbishop of Dakar, spent a few days in Venice with the patriarch. On All Saints' Day, at the request of Cardinal Luciani, the African cardinal presided at the ceremony, seated on the patriarchal throne, and he was deeply moved by this gesture of love and friendship for the African Church. He was greatly impressed by the popularity the patriarch enjoyed. "When we walked in the streets or went in the gondolas or vaporetti, each time there were handshakes, smiles, manifestations of sympathy, which spoke much to me about the affection which the Venetian people felt for their pastor."[3]

People called Luciani a progressive because he loved the little ones, the sick, the castoffs, and defended the rights of the workers. To the latter he said, "If you should meet up with big problems, knock at my door. I am the son of workers and I can understand you."[4] He tried to be the mediator between the feuds of the employers and the workers, but did not always succeed.

He constantly preached charity to all. "A truly Christian life cannot be confined to church and Sunday Mass. Mass and prayers yes, but, 'I go to Mass, I approach Holy Communion, and then outside of church I do not approach my brothers.' Is not the Eucharist then incomplete? The Lord has said we would find Him in the poor and the needy. When we speak of the needy, we think of the Third World, the oppressed, outcasts, persecuted. That is right, but it is also necessary to include the old and the sick in your own homes, your mother-in-law and father-in-law, your children, your husband or wife, your companions at work. The occasions for heroism and great actions are very rare. On the other hand, every day within easy reach are the occasions of doing little favors, interpreting kindly the actions of others, of being patient with those who displease us."[5]

And he practiced what he preached. When someone was unkind to him, he would smile and say, "It's not important. We'll both go to Paradise." He had a marvelous and surprising capacity to recover himself quickly after painful misunderstandings or failures of his plans due to people's negligence or other reasons, simply saying, "It will be as the Lord wills" or "The Will of God is my Paradise." His joy and his peace were contagious, and as his secretary said, "To everyone who lived with him or came to speak to him, he constantly radiated an indescribable feeling of serenity and peace."[6]

A monsignor said of him, "If you want to understand the gospel and love the Lord more, get to know Cardinal Luciani."[7]

Luciani had a special predilection for retarded children and treated them with kindness and understanding. Once, after a ceremony, a retarded boy asked the patriarch to pose with him for a photograph.

"Certainly, my son."

The boy added, "I would like you to put on your red robes and fancy surplice again."

"Certainly," and he immediately went back to the sacristy, donned his cardinal's robes again, and had his picture taken in different poses with the boy. When they were developed, he sent them to the boy's mother who wept with gratitude."[8]

He frequently went to the home for retarded children run by the Don Orione Fathers, where he loved to gather the little ones around him to their great delight. He celebrated Mass there often, and although he was criticized by some priests, he gave the children their First Holy Communion. Because of a lack of funds, the home was about to close, and so the patriarch sent out an appeal to his priests, asking them to sell the valuable rings and other jewelry, *ex-voto* gifts offered to the churches by the faithful, but he insisted that nothing be sold that had any artistic value. He himself said, "I want to set an example myself by offering the golden chain which used to belong to Pope Pius XII and which was given to me by Pope John XXIII when he ordained me bishop."[9] Contrary to what has been said, it was not a question of selling the art treasures of Venice — even the Pope cannot sell the Vatican art treasures — but of selling religious objects and things of no artistic worth. Through his efforts he was able to collect enough money so that the home for his beloved children was saved.

His sermons and homilies were simple but profound, and often he called a child over to himself and questioned him in order to get a point over to the adults, just as he did with Daniele[10] at one of the papal audiences. Most of his listeners not only loved this, but also learned a great deal themselves, though not all. Some of the clergy felt his style was "puerile" and "unworthy of a bishop," and this criticism followed him even to the Chair of Peter.

Cardinal Marco Ce, the former patriarch of Venice, said of Luciani, "A preference for the poor, the little ones, was his personal way of imitating Christ, Who made Himself the lowest and servant of the lowest. It was an evangelical choice, a pledge to follow Christ, an act of obedience to the gospel; he made himself small to break bread with those who were small. This way brought him much pain and humiliation."[11]

The greatest cross for this man of God was having to confront religious indifference. He once confided to a friend, "Often I have thought of asking Cardinal Wyszynski to take me to Poland when I retire. A little diocese would be enough, or simply a parish.... I would like to end my life working among Christians who truly believe, in order to taste in full the joy of being a pastor of souls."[12]

His motives were sometimes misunderstood and his efforts opposed, even by his own priests, which caused much suffering for him. This was brought out in a very telling remark made by the vicar general of St. Mark's at the audience given to the Venetians by John Paul I: "Holy Father, we do not tell you to remember us, because we feel you cannot forget us, if only, and we say it with a request for forgiveness, for what we have cost you in concern, in sacrifice, in grief and sorrow, in love, in such great love. Forgive us."[13]

If some called the patriarch a progressive, others called him a conservative because of his attachment to traditional doctrine and fidelity to the Holy Father. As at Vittorio Veneto, he constantly spoke out against abuses, urged not only by St. Paul's words, "If you wish to please men, you are not a servant of Jesus Christ," but also because, as he said, "The faith of the people is being compromised, not only by those who write and spread errors, but also by those who keep silent and do not write, whereas they should speak out."[14]

When the youth organization FUCI (*Federazoni Universitaria Cattolica Italiana*) decided to support the referendum on divorce, he spent the night in prayer, and the next morning made his decision, which caused a sensation in Italy. He disbanded the FUCI in Venice, and suspended the faculties of any priest who supported it.

One of the patriarch's last talks before his election as Pope was in Belluno at a Mariopolis meeting of the *Focolare*, a lay movement founded by Chiara Lubich in 1943, whose spiritual aim is unity. Among other things Luciani said, "I particularly admire Chiara's passion for the Church, it is truly a *passion....* "He went on to say, "Remember that the focal point of Christianity is God Who loves us; he who has not understood this has not understood Christianity. And I add that this love is not only alive, it is unceasing. It is a love that never gives up. Even if I sin and go away from Him, He runs after me. This must be understood at any cost, otherwise we do not understand Christianity. Jesus is someone Who loves us. The Church is the continuation of Christ."[15]

Often he spoke of the extraordinary happiness of being a member of the Church, and he felt urged to communicate this happiness to others. "It is not enough that I save my own soul; I must help others as much as I can. I will draw close to them with courtesy, with humility, full of respect for them, with the one desire to serve them."[16]

He constantly spoke of Jesus' love for each individual soul and for the Church, and he said, "Those who speak ill of the Church end up like one who cuts off the branch of the tree on which he is sitting."[17] Love for the Church absorbed him, and he served her with all his energy, up to his last breath.

Luciani loved the Pope, no matter who he was. "What I as a bishop say is a little bell ringing a summons, a gentle invitation. What the Pope says is a real tower bell which keeps one awake and puts each one's conscience face-to-face with his own duty."[18] He often spoke of Pope Paul VI with admiration and affection: "He was a great Pope and suffered much. He was not understood. . . ."[19]

There is a picture of him being greeted by Pope Paul, and the intense love and compassion on Luciani's face is very moving.

Everyone knows the story of Pope Paul's visit to Venice in 1972, where he showed his great esteem for the patriarch by the prophetic gesture of placing his own stole on Luciani's shoulders. The following year, the Holy Father elevated Albino Luciani to cardinal. Yet another "incident" occurred between the two at the audience of Pope Paul with the bishops of the Veneto region in 1977. At the end of the visit, Pope Paul inexplicably could not find the little buzzer on his chair with which to call the papal attendants. Noticing his embarrassment, Luciani delicately put his hand on Pope Paul's and guided it to the buzzer. The Pope looked attentively at him and, smiling, said, "So you have already learned where the buzzer is!"[20] He once said of Luciani, "Looking at him pray makes one want to pray too."[21]

Pope Paul was even more grateful to him in the following incident: in 1977, an Italian bishop wrote an open letter to Enrico Berlinguer, head of the Communists in Italy. This bishop wanted some sort of dialogue between the Church and the Communist party, and Berlinguer publicly agreed. The bishop's action caused a furor in Italy, and Catholics were waiting for the episcopal conference to make a public reply. No reply came. As more and more comments were being made about the Church's unwillingness to reply, Luciani took up his pen. He told what had just been said to him at the bishops' synod, which was taking place at that time. "In the Synod Hall, a bishop met me and referring to this 'dialogue,' said, 'Be careful. The maneuver is classic. In Poland we know it well. They do everything in order to divide the bishops. If just one of you withdraws a little from the others and hints at even a reserved esteem for the Communist party, leftists everywhere will converge upon him through the press to take advantage of the situation. The Polish bishops have opposed this tactic with absolute unity.'" This bishop was the archbishop of Krakow, Karol Wojtyla, the future John Paul II. Shortly after Luciani's answer was published, he was received by Pope Paul who said to him gratefully, "We thank you, Eminence, for what you did for us on that occasion."[22]

The seminary was the apple of his eye, and he sometimes invited two or three seminarians to dinner so that he could get to know them personally and follow them in their spiritual life. It has been said that no priest of Venice has defected who had been formed under his guidance. He had an extremely exalted idea of the priesthood, stemming from his experience as an adolescent, and he deeply loved his priests, especially those who were ill. He gave recklessly of his own money to priests in financial difficulties, causing some to criticize him for being imprudent and improvident.

With those who were thinking of leaving the priesthood, he spent many hours, patiently and lovingly trying to persuade them to remain, and praying for them constantly. When a priest finally decided to leave, the patriarch suffered physically as well as emotionally, to the point of not being able to eat or sleep. He wrote a great deal on the priesthood: "Let us priests not waste too much time wondering who we are, because it is not so much a question of defining our priesthood, as of living it. We have the example of Christ before us, He was meek, humble, poor, chaste, obedient. He prayed intensely, keeping in continuous touch with the Father, and He taught people to pray. He gave Himself entirely and generously, for the spiritual and material needs of men. There we have all we want: to imitate Him; to aim at a holiness perfected day by day, by the generous exercise of the ministry and of charity, and to live with Him a life of intimacy, bound to Him by trusting love and intense prayer."[23]

During Lent, before his election as Pope, the patriarch wrote an amusing yet hard-hitting letter to his priests, which he titled, "A Bit of Purgatory." He described the seven cliffs in Dante's Purgatory, where, on each cliff, souls were being purified by enduring punishment and by meditating on an episode from the life of Our Lady. From this structure Luciani gave some lively exhortations and lessons. In his retreat, "The Good Samaritan," he says, "Dear Priests, unless you love the Lord greatly, it is impossible to preserve chastity for very long. Let us remember that the foundation of the priestly life, lived in its totality, is the spirit of sacrifice, the readiness to sacrifice oneself for the Lord at every moment. A chastity which is almost second nature presupposes great love for God, great mortification, great faith. When one is truly chaste, one flings oneself yet more into the love of God."[24] Above all he prayed to Our Lady for his priests and urged them to "pray to her to protect their priesthood, and to help them always be true and holy priests."[25]

The patriarch also spoke to many groups of religious. In talking of authority as service, he says, "What service does the superior render, if he does not exercise his duty of commanding? And to command is the most difficult service in the community."[26] He noted that the superior must certainly imitate Jesus, Who came to serve; but also the brother or sister must imitate Jesus, Who humbled Himself and became obedient even to death on the cross. He felt there should be fewer meetings, assemblies, and workshops, "in order to pray more, to create more silence, and then to roll up our sleeves and get to work."[27]

Perhaps one of the most delightful and simple talks to Sisters given August 5, 1978, was on "Mary, Model of the Religious Soul." After commenting on Our Lady as our Mother he then spoke of her as our sister, and counseled imitation of Our Lady in the ordinary things of daily life. He went on to say, "The other day I met one of your Sisters, and I asked her, 'What did you do today, sister?'

"'I prepared the clothes,' she said, 'and every stitch was for Him, for the Lord.'"

"How beautiful," he exclaimed, "to work for Him!"

He next spoke of silence, "Not in order to sleep," he said smilingly, "but in order to talk with my Lord."

He urged intimacy with God. "I read the life of St. Catherine of Siena by Blessed Raymond. He says that Jesus appeared to her and invited her to read the Office with Him, each one saying a verse. You do not have to believe this, but I like the idea, to chat with the Lord!" He then spoke of the importance of putting into practice the examples and teachings of Jesus and said, "Lord, if You were here now, in the midst of this mess, how would You get out of it? I want to imitate You, I want to try and do what I think You would do. . . ."

He advised peace of soul, optimism, cheerfulness, and above all charity, and ended his talk, "So remember, Our Lady is 'Mother.' I invoke her, venerate her, and have complete confidence in her. She is 'Sister,' in order to imitate her! Imitate her in her virtues, especially in recollection, without which there are no profound or lasting virtues."[28]

Luciani loved to speak about joy. He himself radiated joy to all who met him. He insisted that joy is a Christian obligation, and that "whoever wishes to reproduce in himself the sentiments of the Heart of Jesus must give a large place for joy. Besides the ordinary human joy lived in a Christian way, there are others, the spiritual joys, ordinary as well as extraordinary ones. To know that one is loved by God and that one can love Him is ordinary Christian joy. Unbelievers laugh at this; you invent God, they say, and then love this imaginary Being. No, God is not an invention nor is He far off; He dwells within each one of us, a true Person Who loves, and works. In certain moments, the joy of possessing Him is such as to make all other joys grow dim; in times of spiritual dryness, some healthy human joys can be an encouragement to us."[29] His advice to Sisters was that they "should become merchants and distributors of joy, adorning their charity with a smile, showing by means of their own patient and joyful life that the yoke of the Lord is easy and His burden is light."[30]

It was when he was patriarch of Venice that he wrote *Illustrissimi*, now translated into twelve languages. To someone who asked him what made him decide to write these letters for the Italian *St.*

Anthony's Messenger, he replied, "When I preach in St. Mark's, 100, 150, or at most 200 faithful listen to me; half of these are tourists who do not understand Italian, and the other half are darling old ladies, already strong in their faith. The director of the Italian *St. Anthony's Messenger* said to me, 'If you write for us, you will multiply your listeners by a thousand.' He convinced me." Luciani's wisdom, his wit, and his love for God and the Church all shine forth in these refreshing letters, each of which has a special lesson for the modern world.

But above all, Albino Luciani was a man of prayer. He deeply felt both the need and the power of prayer. In the morning when all was quiet, there he was in his private chapel praying in front of the tabernacle. Here too was his favorite corner, where he had a little table and shelves for his religious books. If his secretary or the Sisters had to pass by, they almost walked on tiptoe in order not to disturb him. But if he noticed them, he would interrupt his prayer, greet them, and then return to his dialogue with God.[31]

A monsignor recalls that when he was a young altar boy, Luciani, then vicar general of Belluno, used to visit Canale, and what amazed him most were the long hours Monsignor Luciani spent in church. Another witness said of him, "His day was immersed in prayer. When he had a quiet moment he would take refuge in prayer. When everything seemed to be questioned, it was in prayer that he found the strength of his choices and solutions to problems. When he had to write something important, perhaps a letter to a priest, or a homily, or an article for a magazine, you would find him in church."[32] The retired bishop of Belluno, Maffeo Ducoli, remembers that on the day after Luciani's election, August 27, 1978, at about 4:20 p.m., "I spoke on the phone with Don Diego, his secretary, who informed me that the Pope was in the chapel in prayer at that moment."[33] He never failed to ask prayers for himself, often asking people to pray an "Hail Mary" for him.

As bishop and patriarch, Luciani frequented Our Lady's shrines, either as a simple pilgrim or by leading pilgrimages or presiding at Marian anniversaries in the various sanctuaries in Italy, and also in Yugoslavia and Brazil. An incident at Lourdes is typical of his modesty. During one of the diocesan pilgrimages he could not be found. Finally someone spotted him, dressed in a simple black cassock with no insignia, just one priest among others in a group of French pilgrims. In 1977, he had a two-hour talk with Lucy, the only surviving seer of Fátima, whom he described as very vivacious and talkative.

Every year for his vacation he went to the beautiful Shrine of Pietralba, surrounded by snow-capped mountains, near the border of Austria. He liked to share the cloistered life with the Servite Fathers who took care of the shrine and to offer Mass at the privileged Altar of Our Lady of Sorrows, where he often spoke during his homilies of the love and the mercy of the Mother of God at the foot of the cross.

His love for nature and for his mountains found expression in this magnificent spot. He liked to put on his climbing boots and, wearing his cassock, make the hour's climb up to the top of Corno Bianca where the view was awe-inspiring. Once he began to climb, he never stopped to rest, even for a minute, moving slowly but steadily until he reached the summit. He also loved to walk in the woods near the shrine. "In these woods," he wrote, "hearing the songs of the birds, and watching the leapings of the squirrels, I sometimes feel like Sturm, the monk who opened the way for St. Boniface in the German forest. Like me, Sturm was also a friend of squirrels and had discovered the fact that they could keep jumping and leaping from one tree to another for about eight miles without touching the ground."[34]

Luciani's last visit to Pietralba was in July 1978. In one month he would be catapulted from the small but important Diocese of Venice to the See of Peter, where he would be shepherd of 850 million Catholics belonging to the Universal Church.

6

Habemus Papam

The sun rose gloriously over the lagoon of Venice on the morning of August 10, as the cardinal patriarch and Don Lorenzo, his secretary, left St. Mark's Basilica. They were on their way to Rome for the conclave that would elect a new Pope to succeed Paul VI, who had died four days previously on the Feast of the Transfiguration of Our Lord. Only a few priests had known the time of his departure and were waiting in the square to say goodbye. He wanted to slip away with as little fuss as possible. His housekeeper, Sister Vincenza, was also there.

"Eminence," she said in a worried tone of voice, "I hope you return."

"My dear Sister, of course I will. Don't worry."[1]

In Rome he stayed with his old friends, the Augustinian Fathers, at St. Monica's International College near the colonnade of St. Peter's Square. The cardinal took his place in the community as if he were a simple religious.

The superior wrote about his stay with them: "His life was a prayer. His interior life, his union with God, his holiness radiated from his smiling face. His fatherly love encouraged everyone to feel he was his closest friend. He once said to us, quoting St. Augustine, 'To be preachers, you must first be pray-ers,' which he translated into, 'In order to talk about God, you must first talk *with* God.'"[2]

While with the Augustinians, the cardinal often met with the ninety-year-old lay brother, Brother Franceschino.

"How are you, Franceschino?"

"Thank God, Eminence, I am well. And I am old."

"Blessed are those who reach such a venerable age as you," replied Luciani.

He did not want to be treated any differently than the rest of the Fathers, but this did not please Franceschino. He felt the cardinal should be given some distinction. And so one day Franceschino, without telling anyone, went shopping. That evening at dinner, the Fathers noticed with amusement that Cardinal Luciani had a red placemat instead of the white ones used by the Fathers.

Each day he participated in the General Congregation of the Cardinals, and the rest of the time he spent reading and praying, and in preparing notes for a retreat which he was to give to the priests of Veneto. In the afternoons, Luciani liked to walk in the Augustinians' garden, meditating and reading his breviary. Afterwards he used to sit on an old bench, take out his beads, and pray the rosary. Franceschino, seeing him there, would go over and sit on a bench opposite him and also say the rosary.

One day Franceschino accompanied the cardinal to the great bronze doors of St. Peter's. A Swiss Guard who knew Franceschino, seeing his friend in a simple black cassock, asked who he was.

"The cardinal patriarch of Venice," Franceschino said proudly. Whereupon the Swiss Guard immediately gave him the great salute, much to Franceschino's delight.

Two days after his election, Pope John Paul I sent a handwritten letter to the rector of the Augustinians, thanking him for his hospitality: ". . . I bless you with all my heart, together with all the brethren (including Franceschino!) and the good Sisters."[3]

Friday, August 25, the Mass of the Holy Spirit was concelebrated in St. Peter's by all the elector cardinals with Cardinal Jean Villot presiding. After the Mass, the cardinals returned in procession to the Chapel of the Pieta, and had to cross through the central nave of St. Peter's. Some of the cardinals smiled at the people watching them; others, including Luciani, seemed thoughtful and recollected. All present knew that in a few days one of these cardinals would exchange his red robes for the white robes of the Pope. No one dreamed that within two months a second cardinal would also don the papal white.

Before the conclave that evening, Luciani met an old friend, Camillo Cibin, a papal guard. They had been talking together for a few minutes when another friend, Giusto Antoniazzi, also a papal guard, joined them.

"Let me wish you every success, your Eminence!" said Antoniazzi.

Quickly Luciani responded, "What are you saying! You are wishing me misfortune!"

Cibin interrupted, "Yes! I did not wish you success because the papacy is too heavy a cross."

"I know, I know, but there is nothing to be worried about; it's not for me."

Antoniazzi replied, "They say John XXIII once said that someone has to accept that cross."

"Yes, that's true," answered the cardinal. "Well, if I were sure it would carry me to heaven, I'd have no difficulty in accepting it!"[4]

Before the conclave opened, reporters, journalists, and newsmen along with television cameras, were to be seen interviewing a cardinal or group of cardinals talking together. Some noticed that at these times Luciani would slip away quietly, true to his desire to remain hidden. When at last they found him, he was walking in a quiet corridor praying his rosary. They pestered him with questions about the "politics" of electing a Pope, but he kept silent. Finally he said, "Journalists should learn to write less, talk less, and pray more. I am thinking only of praying that the Lord will enlighten me in such a way that I may vote for the right person."

The evening of August 25 at 5 p.m. the cardinals sang the *"Veni Creator Spiritu"* as they proceeded into the Sistine Chapel for the opening of the conclave. The doors were then shut and locked. The cardinals from every continent and almost every country in the world were now completely cut off from the world. Nothing more would be heard from them until the white smoke from the chimney announced that a new Pope had been elected.

In a letter to his niece, Pia, Luciani wrote:

Dear Pia,   Rome, August 24, 1978
I write to you so that you can have the new stamps "sede vacante" and also to congratulate you on the success of your first exam. We hope that the Lord will also help you with the rest. Today we have finished the pre-conclave with the last "Congregatio Generalis." Afterwards, the cells were chosen by

lot and we went to see them. I have #60, a parlor made into a bedroom. It is like the seminary in Feltre in 1923, iron bed, mattress, a basin for washing. Cardinal Tomasek of Prague is in #61. Farther on, Cardinals Tarancon (Madrid), Medeiros (Boston), Sin (Manila), Malula (Kinshasa). Except for Australia there is a "concentration" of the whole world.

I do not know how long the conclave will last. It is difficult to find the person able to face so many problems, which are very heavy crosses. Luckily, I am out of danger. Even so, it is a very grave responsibility to vote in these circumstances.

I am sure, that being a good Christian, you will pray for the Church at this time. Greet Francesco, papa and [mama]. I did not write to them as I have a bit to do at this time.

Yours affectionately ,
Luciani[5]

Cardinal Joseph-Albert Malula had room #65, and he and Cardinal Luciani met for the first time in the corridor when both were on their way to fill their old-fashioned pitchers with water. "The next time I met him," said Cardinal Malula, "was when we were going to the chapel for the afternoon voting. He grasped my hands and said, '*Tempestas magnas super me*' ('A great storm is upon me.'). I said, 'Courage, courage. You must have confidence. If the good God calls you to the task, He gives the necessary grace to fulfill it well.' I noted that he quoted my words during the first Angelus Message."[6] This shows that by the end of the second voting, Luciani must have received a great many votes.

Meanwhile, the world was waiting to see who the new Pope would be. But since Saturday, August 26, was only the first day of voting, no results were expected. There had been lists and pictures of the various "papabile," but only in Northern Italy was the name of Albino Luciani mentioned, and not only mentioned but foretold as the next Pope. After all, he was their favorite son! A long and difficult conclave was expected. It was the most diverse, cosmopolitan, and largest group of cardinals in history, and surely it would be difficult to agree in choosing one man among them to be the Vicar of Jesus Christ. Afterwards, most of the cardinals said that at the beginning of the voting, no one stood out as an obvious choice, as had been the case in the election of Pope Pius XII and Pope Paul VI.

As the voting continued, Luciani's name was repeated over and over, and his face became more and more strained.

"I saw him put his head in his hands several times," said Cardinal John Patrick Cody, and Cardinal John Deardon added, "Then the tension gave place to a kind of resignation or better, to a great serenity."

Toward the end of the voting, Cardinal Pericle Felici, feeling deeply for Cardinal Luciani, who was obviously profoundly upset, went to him and said lovingly, "A message for the new Pope." Luciani replied, "Thank you, but it's not yet definite," and then opened the envelope to find a small Way of the Cross. He said, "The path of the Popes is marked by the cross. Help this poor Christ to carry the cross; help the Pope to climb Calvary for the good of the Church, of souls, and of humanity."[7]

The day after the election he told Cardinal Felici that he had the Way of the Cross on his table and added, "It is beginning already."

Felici pointed out to him that above the little *Via Crucis* was pictured the triumphant, resurrected Christ.

"Yes," he answered, "but the Resurrection comes only after death."[8]

Finally the fourth voting was over. Albino Luciani had been elected on the first day. He sat deep in prayer. A cardinal was heard to murmur, "*Et exaltavit humiles*" ("He has exalted the humble").

Cardinal Villot approached Luciani to ask, "Do you accept?" He was silent. Then he stood up, smiled, and said gently, "I accept."

A cardinal heard him say to himself, "How unsearchable the designs of God and how inscrutable His ways." He was asked what name he chose. He paused. All waited in silence. *"Joannes Paulus Primus"* ("John Paul the First") he said quietly.[9]

John Paul II said a year later, "I remember that moment when in the Sistine Chapel he said, 'I wish to take the name of John and Paul.' This decision had its own convincing eloquence. To me personally it seemed to be charismatic."[10] It was the first double name in the history of the papacy, except for Simon Peter. Later, some cardinals expressed their feelings concerning the election. Cardinal Corrado Ursi of Naples said, "An interior inspiration indicated a choice, a name." Cardinal Vicente Enrique y Tarancon of Spain said, "There was no one in particular whom we felt would get a two-thirds vote. Suddenly, however, I don't know how or why, the name of Cardinal Luciani came to our minds." Cardinal Wojtyla, later to become Pope John Paul II, said, "God chose Cardinal Luciani. At first He kept him, so to speak, in the shade, and he himself, the predestined one, sought to be hidden. Then all of a sudden the Lord revealed the face and the name of him whom He had chosen."[11]

The new Pope went to the so-called Room of Tears, and from there to the room where the tailor was waiting for him. Large, medium, and small white cassocks were ready. He put on the smallest, but it was too big for him and had to be adjusted so he would not trip. When he returned to the Sistine Chapel in the white and red papal robes, he seemed totally transfigured. His face was radiant with a deep spiritual joy, joy in his *fiat*, in his total abandonment to the Will of God. The cardinals, also exultant with joy, began the "*Te Deum*." One by one they knelt before him to kiss his hand as a pledge of obedience to the new Vicar of Christ, and he had a kind word for each as he asked their prayers. To Cardinal Jaime Sin of Manila, who earlier that day told Luciani, "I am sure you will be the new Pope," he said, "You were a prophet, your Eminence! But my pontificate will be short." Cardinal Sin himself recounted this.[12] To Cardinal Eduardo Francisco Pironio, prefect of the Congregation for Religious, he said, "Tell the religious to pray for me." And to Cardinal Leo Jozef Suenens who thanked him for saying yes, he replied with a twinkle in his eyes, "Maybe I should have said no."

In the meantime, people began to fill the square. They did not think the election would be over that day, but they wanted to see the smoke even if it was black, as it had been after the morning voting.

When the afternoon voting ended, smoke billowed out of the chimney, first black, then white, and then gray. The crowd grew excited, and there was much arguing and questioning: was it black or was it white? No one was sure. Just as people were beginning to leave the square, someone noticed that there was movement behind the central balcony of St. Peter's. Now there was no doubt, a new Pope had been elected. Word spread like lightning, and radio announcers leapt to their microphones. More and more people poured into the square waiting to hear the name of the new Pope and to receive his blessing. After a few minutes of excited waiting, the large door of the loggia opened, and Cardinal Felici in his magnificent voice announced, *"Annuntio vobis gaudium magnum, Habemus Papam!"* ("I announce to you a great joy, we have a Pope.") The crowd thundered its applause, then grew silent. Cardinal Felici continued, relishing each word, "He is the Most Eminent and Most Reverend Lord, Albino Cardinal Luciani, who has taken the name John Paul the First!"

The crowd went wild with joy although few people had expected Luciani to be elected, and most foreigners had never heard of him. When the new Pope appeared on the balcony at 7:31 p.m. with his transparent goodness, his disarming humility and the warmth of his smile, the storm of enthusiasm reached indescribable proportions. Monsignor Virgilio Noe, Master of Ceremonies, held up a large scroll for the Pope to read, and John Paul I gave his first blessing, *"Urbi et Orbi,"* ("To the City and the World") in his frail voice with the lilting Venetian accent. He was deeply moved, in spite of his broad smile, and at times seemed a little bewildered. In this short time, by his presence alone, he conquered the hearts of not only the people in the square, but also millions of men and women who saw him on television. Still smiling, the Pope turned and went inside to the waiting cardinals. It was at this moment, and not at the election, that the Pope joked to the cardinals, "May God forgive you for what you have done."

As the crowd kept applauding and chanting "Gianpaolo, Gianpaolo," (diminutive for John Paul) the cardinals persuaded the Pope to go out to the balcony again to bless them. "Unending applause filled with enthusiasm and affection thundered from the square. It was unforgettable. I was convinced that I was witnessing an amazing historical event," said Monsignor Giulio Nicolini, a priest-journalist.[13]

The conclave was now officially over and the cardinals were free to leave, but the new Pope asked them to remain so that he could be with them one last time for supper.

A Spanish cardinal, who desperately wanted to smoke (all smoking was forbidden at the conclave), went to the Pope to ask permission. Pope John Paul's eyes twinkled as he said, "I willingly permit you to do so, as long as the smoke is white,"[14] referring of course to the white smoke announcing the election.

That night, after meeting with several cardinals, he returned to his little room, #60, to prepare his long talk for the cardinals at Mass the next day. Not until the next afternoon would he go to the papal apartments, where according to custom he would untie the cords that since the death of Paul VI had roped off the Pope's rooms.

7

The Smiling Pope

The next day, Sunday, August 27, people began filling the square hoping to see the new Pope and to hear his first Angelus Message. By noon there were at least 100,000 people present. The shutters on the loggia opened, and Pope John Paul I appeared, smiling broadly.

"Yesterday morning," he said, and the crowd interrupted with cheers and applause, "I went to the Sistine Chapel to vote tranquilly. Never could I have imagined what was about to happen," and he laughed and so did the crowd, delighted by the simplicity of the new Pope. He spoke of the encouragement given by fellow cardinals, his acceptance of the election, and then he told why he had taken the names of John and Paul. John XXIII had himself consecrated him bishop,and Paul VI named him a cardinal. He also told how Pope Paul "made me blush to the roots of my hair in the presence of 20,000 people because he removed his stole and placed it on my shoulders. Never have I blushed so much! Furthermore, during his fifteen years of pontificate, this Pope has shown, not only to me, but to the whole world, how to love, how to serve, how to labor, and how to suffer for the Church of Christ."

The crowd was enchanted. Never before had a Pope spoken so informally; they felt he was one of them. He concluded his brief talk by saying, "I have neither the wisdom of heart of Pope John, nor the preparation and culture of Pope Paul. But I am in their place. I must seek to serve the Church. I hope that you will help me with your prayers."

An American lady who had lived in Rome for years described the reaction of the people: "We were on the edge of a crowd of about 100,000 in the piazza. It was like an electric charge, a spiritual electric current from the loggia to the square. It was a current of love, Godly love, and he, the Pope, so simple, so gentle, almost boyish, but with a firmness and a trueness in him that said, 'I represent God.' We [she and her two sisters] who have seen five Popes *never* felt anything like it. God's touch on the world, on our poor humanity."[1]

Earlier in the day the new Pope had offered Mass in the Sistine Chapel. He wanted all the cardinals over eighty, who could not vote because of age, to be with the elector cardinals at this Mass, and had the doors of the conclave opened to bring in the "ultra-octogenarians," a loving gesture which touched them deeply. It was during the Mass that the Pope outlined his program for his pontifical service.

That evening, Pope John Paul I made his first telephone call, and it was to an old friend, Maffeo Ducoli, bishop of Belluno.

"Excellency," he said, "you see the wolf has changed his clothes but not his nature!" (He was referring to his habit of making frequent telephone calls.)

The bishop, delighted and touched to be the first to receive a call from the new Pope, replied, "Holy Father, the joy of Canale, the joy of Belluno is indescribable! . . . Holy Father, how are you?"

"Well, I didn't sleep last night. I was filled with scruples. It was so unexpected and so sudden . . . give my greetings to everyone, my brother, my nephews and nieces, relatives and all my friends at Canale. Give my blessing to everyone."[2]

The next few days were taken up with various audiences, including one with the cardinals. He did not use the prepared text but spoke with them in a brotherly way. He recalled that the journalists had wrongly interpreted his remark to the cardinals the day before, "What have you done, may God forgive you!" He said, "I was not scolding you. I was repeating St. Bernard's remark when one of his monks was elected Pope. . . . I must thank you for the faith you have placed in me, by giving me your vote, which was absolutely unexpected and also unmerited. I hope the Lord will not find me unworthy of such faith. Help me with your prayers."

He told them of his work in his small Diocese of Venice (430,000 Catholics) and urged the cardinals to think not only of their own dioceses, but of the Universal Church. "Today there is a great need that the world see us united. We must work together.... Let us give the world a show of unity, even by sacrificing things now and then. We have everything to lose if the world does not see us united."[3]

On September 1, he spoke to the journalists, charming them by using the familiar "I" and departing from the text to tell them some stories. As he was walking down the aisle, a reporter from Argentina held up the microphone to the Pope and asked him to say a word to the Argentinians. The Pope smiled sweetly, put his finger to his lips, and said "shh" very audibly, much to the amusement of the other reporters.

The Italian emigrants were so dear to his heart that just a few days after his election, he wrote a letter to a group of them in his own hand:

> *Dear Emigrants,*   *Rome, September 2, 1978*
>   *I wanted so much to be with you at Einsiedeln on September 10 in order to honor Our Lady . . . and also to be with you who remind me of my father, my mother and my sister, who like you, were emigrants in Switzerland. My heart will be with you, as well as my Apostolic Blessing which I impart to all of you, your families and your work.*
>
>   *John Paul I*[4]

On September 3, before the Inauguration Ceremony, he had audiences with pilgrims from Venice, Belluno, and Vittorio Veneto. He was still their beloved "Don Albino," speaking simply, greeting them by name, telling little stories, giving encouragement to all, and asking prayers for himself. "Don't believe all the praise about me, it is exaggerated; what I really need are prayers. Prayers are truly a strength, a help." He told the priests they should have common sense and high principles, and once again urged them to be prayerful. "We need to pray. If the people see that the priest truly prays, is really united to the Lord, he is a witness that attracts many others."[5]

On their way out of the audience some Bellunese said to one another, "Don Albino always makes one want to be better and to do more."[6] A few who knew him well felt uneasy. They noticed that the strain of his heavy burden as Pope was already beginning to show, no matter how much he tried to hide it with his smile.

The inauguration took place that same evening. The new Pope had decided to simplify the centuries-old ceremony that had been formed when popes still wielded temporal power. He wished it to be a deeply spiritual experience for himself, for all who were participating in the ceremony, and for the millions who were watching it from the square or on television. He began by praying at the Tomb of St. Peter. Then, with all the bells of St. Peter's pealing, the Sistine Choir singing the Litany of the Saints, and the crowd applauding joyously, he walked in procession to the papal chair prepared for him between the massive pillars of the loggia. As the litany ended, the people grew silent, and Cardinal Felici, the senior cardinal deacon, came forward, not with the triple tiara worn by previous popes, but with only the special papal pallium, which he placed over John Paul's shoulders as a sign of his spiritual authority as Vicar of Christ. The choir then began the "*Tu es Petrus*" ("Thou art Peter") as each cardinal went up to the Pope, knelt before him, and kissed his ring as a sign of obedience. They were joyfully embraced by the Pope, who conversed warmly with each one.

The Mass proceeded and the Pope gave the sermon, ending it by calling on Our Lady, invoking her as the resplendent star "who guided with delicate tenderness our life as a boy, as a seminarian, as a priest and as a bishop. May she continue to enlighten and direct our steps in order that with Peter's voice and with our eyes and mind fixed on her Son, Jesus, we may proclaim to the world with joyous firmness our Profession of Faith, 'You are the Christ, the Son of the Living God.'"

Twilight was falling as the Mass ended. After blessing the crowd, the Pope then proceeded with the cardinals back into the basilica, and the people once again erupted into applause and shouts of joy. This happened every time he appeared, and once, when Sister Vincenza commented on these tremendous ovations, the Pope smiled and said, "Remember how quick the crowds were to shout 'Hosanna' and equally quick to shout 'Crucify Him.' We must rely only on God and work for Him."[7]

The four Wednesday audiences drew so many people that at the last one on the day before he died, the crowd had to be divided and the Pope gave an audience to each group, first in St. Peter's and then in the Nervi Hall, in order to satisfy everyone. He had an extraordinary gift of communication, and the people were enraptured by everything he said, with smiles on their faces and sometimes tears of emotion in their eyes.

Father Angelo Beghetto, O.F.M., described it well in his introduction to *Illustrissimi*, October 4, 1978: "Papa Luciani is a marvelous, moving figure in the history of humanity. Like Jesus he attracted the crowds with his simple, captivating words which were enlivened by examples, stories, 'parables,' and references to persons and happenings of today. He made the life and Word of Christ real to all, not an abstract philosophy or theology, but livable and comprehensible to persons of all ages and extraction."[8] These four audiences, as mentioned before, were on humility, faith, hope, and charity. He had intended to continue with the four cardinal virtues of prudence, justice, fortitude, and temperance. Instead, it was his successor who continued the talks, using the notes left by his predecessor.

His Sunday Angelus messages were short, but, like his audiences, they were models of catechesis, the fruit of years of experience.

On September 10, he asked prayers for the success of the meeting at Camp David, where President Carter, President Sadat of Egypt, and Prime Minister Begin of Israel were trying to draw up peace plans for the Middle East. After quoting from Jesus, the Koran, and Isaiah, the Pope went on to say, "We are the objects of undying love on the part of God. We know He always has His eyes on us, even when it seems to be dark. He is our Papa, even more, He is our Mother. He does not want to hurt us; He wants only to do good to us, to all of us. If children are ill, they have additional claim to be loved by their mothers. And we too, if by chance we are sick with badness, if we are on the wrong track, have yet another claim to be loved by the Lord."

In his audience on faith, he urged each one to try to help the Church by becoming better themselves and to say the prayer he was accustomed to pray: "Lord, take me as I am, with my limitations, my failings and my sins, and make me become what You want me to be." After his death, Sister Vincenza found a holy card, dating from his years in Venice, on which he had written this same prayer, prefacing it with, "Lord, I want so much to please You. . . ."[9]

On September 23, he spoke of violence, and of seven-year-old Luca Locci, who had been kidnapped three months earlier. Then he went on to say, "People sometimes say that we are in a society that is all rotten, all dishonest. That is not true. There are still so many good people, so many honest people. Rather, what can be done to improve society? I would say, let each of us try to be good, and to infect others with a goodness imbued with the meekness and love taught by Christ. Christ's golden rule was, 'Do not do to others what you do not want done to yourself.' And He always gave. Put on the cross, not only did He forgive those who crucified Him, but He excused them. He said, 'Father, forgive them for they know not what they do.' This is Christianity; these are sentiments which, if put into practice, would help society so much."

Luca's kidnappers must have been deeply touched by the Pope's talk, for at midnight that very same day, they left the little boy at the door of his home. One can imagine the child's joy, the joy of his parents, and the joy of the Pope. Luca and his family planned to visit the Pope, but there was not time. Four days later the Pope was dead. Instead, they attended the funeral.

Three times during his pontificate, Pope John Paul I spoke about the dramatic situation in Lebanon. In fact, he wished to go there himself to see if he could in some way help bring peace to that tortured country, and had already fixed the date of the meeting with the Maronite bishop of Lebanon in order to arrange the details of the visit.

When he met with the clergy of Rome he spoke of discipline and recollection: "Today it is the desire of many good faithful to feel that their priest is habitually united with God." And quoting St. Gregory the Great he said, "Let the pastor avoid the temptation of wishing to be loved by the faithful instead of by God and of being too weak for fear of losing men's affection. The pastor must indeed try to make himself loved but in order to win a hearing, not to seek this affection for his own profit." Pope John Paul I himself put these words into action throughout his priestly life.

At the end of the talk he spoke of the Orthodox Metropolitan Nikodem, who had died two days previously in the Pope's arms as the Pope was replying to his address. Pope John Paul I was deeply impressed by Nikodem's beautiful talk, by his extraordinary love for the Church, and by his great desire for unity, and later said of him to a friend, "*un vero santo!*" ("a real saint").

On September 26, his brother, Edoardo, paid the Pope a surprise visit. They had supper together, and the Pope told him he would say Mass at 7 a.m. the next day. Edoardo stayed the night in the so-called attic of the Vatican, where a guest room was prepared for him. But as he could not sleep he went down to the chapel at 6 a.m. The Pope was already there, praying, and Edoardo joined him. At Mass the Pope gave his brother Holy Communion, and after talking together for a while "like good brothers," Edoardo left, worried because his brother seemed very tired but never dreaming he would not ever again see him alive.

Was John Paul I overwhelmed by the task required of him? Was he confused and uncertain? Cardinal Giuseppe Caprio, substitute secretary of state, who worked with the Pope every day, has written a very interesting account, all the more so because he was utterly devoted to Pope Paul, and could not imagine how it would be working with another Pope.

> *I asked myself what reaction I would have, faced with another Pope who would be seated at the same table and ask me the same questions....*
>
> *Our first meeting, however, was most natural. Without giving me time to kneel down or express my sentiments, the Pope embraced me as if he had known me for a long time, and with a broad, fatherly smile he said, "I am at your service, Excellency." Such was his welcome that at the end of our talk I spontaneously encouraged him and gave him some practical advice. Going home, I went into the chapel to thank the Lord for having given a good and holy Pope to His Church.*

The following days were full of work, much of it burdensome, but the Pope accepted it and did it calmly, with self-assurance and with so much naturalness as to make one think that he had had years of preparation. The very words which he used when he called me on the telephone gave me the impression that he had been Pope for a long time: "It's the Pope. Would you come here a minute?"

It was his faith and filial abandonment to God's will which gave him this assurance. I was convinced of this a few days later when he confided to me, "Last night I really slept. It was the first time. Only now do I begin to realize what it means to be Pope."

For a moment I was afraid that this realization would crush him beneath its tremendous burden, would paralyze his smile and his natural way of acting. Fortunately, I was immediately convinced to the contrary. The Pope did not hide from himself either the gravity of the task which the Lord had entrusted to him, nor the importance of the problems submitted to his judgment. He examined everything calmly, and his decisions were clear, firm, and precise.

I confess that at the beginning his spontaneity disconcerted me; but, little by little as the days went by, I noticed that his understanding of men and his ability to face situations were far more superior than his humility would admit. The faith and confidence which he placed in divine assistance were unlimited.

We must not be deceived by his smile. He listened, he asked for information, he studied. But once he made a decision, he did not go back on it, unless new facts came to light. The brief hints he made about discipline in the audience to the Roman clergy, and about obedience at the ceremony of taking possession of St. John Lateran, are enough to testify to this firmness.

The bond of secrecy prevents me from citing particular and more explicit facts. But the short time I spent at his side persuaded me that, with absolute respect to persons, the Pope had no intentions of deviating from what had been his rule of life and the direction of his pastoral action; fatherly, yes, but absolutely firm in the guidance of the souls entrusted by God to his care.[10]

At the same time, he was deeply distressed by the enormity of the problems facing the Church. Bishop Van Lierde, vicar-general of Vatican City, recounts an incident during a talk he had with Pope John Paul I: "At one point the Pope looked me steadily in the eye and said to me lovingly, 'I wish to tell my vicar-general something in confidence. Look, Monsignor, I smile, and I always smile, but believe me, inside I suffer.'"

Cardinal Villot, secretary of state, who also had been utterly devoted to Pope Paul, was likewise captivated by the new Pope, who always accompanied him to the door at the end of their daily meeting. Finally Villot, a little embarrassed, told him that it was not the usual custom for the Pope to go to the door with anyone.

"I know it," he replied smiling, "but this Pope does!"

"Being at his side," recalled the cardinal, "was a very rich spiritual experience for me."[11]

Again, unlike former Popes, each morning he shook hands with all his collaborators, greeted them warmly, and made little jokes to cheer them up. He felt uneasy with crowds and did not care for formal official meetings. He liked meetings on a personal basis, and "knew how to look into the depths of a person's soul and to speak to his heart."[12]

On September 21, he gave an audience to some American bishops in which he spoke of the family. "The indissolubility of Christian marriage is important, although it is a difficult part of our message. We must proclaim it faithfully as part of God's Word, part of the mystery of faith. At the same time we are close to our people in their problems and difficulties. They must always know we love them."

At the end of the talk, he asked if any of the American bishops spoke Italian. When he was assured that some did, he told the Vatican personnel always present at an audience, including the official translator, to leave. Somewhat disconcerted, they went out. The Pope then smilingly told the bishops to ask him questions, which they did, after they got over the shock of such a request.

As bishop of Rome, he "took possession" of his cathedral on September 23. This cathedral is the Archbasilica of St. John Lateran. During the Mass he gave a striking homily, applying the readings of the Mass to concrete situations of the Church in Rome. He insisted on obedience, correct liturgy, love for the poor; he touched on authority and freedom, and on the service of guiding and governing. He ended with the words, ". . . It is God's law that one cannot do good to anyone if one does not first wish him well. I can assure you that I love you, that I desire only to enter into your service and to place the poor powers that I have, however little they are, at the disposal of all."

At this ceremony, some bishops, seeing the Pope's exhaustion, were deeply concerned about his health. He had noticeably lost weight, and there were dark circles under his eyes. Those who knew him had wondered why he did not stand up in the car to greet the crowds on the way to the Lateran. Later it was discovered that his legs had become swollen and painful.

Wednesday, September 27, was his last general audience. What he said that day could be considered as his "last will and testament." It was a hymn to charity: "My God, with all my heart and above all things I love You, Infinite Good and our eternal happiness, and for Your sake I love my neighbor as myself and forgive offenses received. O Lord, may I love You more and more." He went on to explain this prayer word for word.

Toward the end of the audience he called a little boy in the fifth grade to come up in order "to help the Pope."

The Pope asked him, "Do you want to stay in the fifth grade always, or do you want to graduate to the next class?"

Contrary to expectation, the boy, named Daniele, answered, "Well, I want to stay in the fifth grade, because if I go to the next grade, I'll have to leave my teacher."

The Pope was surprised. "Then do you always want to stay in the fifth grade?"

"Yes, always."

Greatly amused, the Pope turned to the people and said, "Oh! This boy is different from the Pope! Because when I was in the fourth grade I would say, 'if only I could be in the fifth grade,' and when I was in the fifth, 'if only I could go on to the next grade.'"

As a skilled and experienced catechist, the Pope used these remarks to describe man's insatiable yearning for progress in every aspect of life, and said that we must also desire to make progress in the love of God.

"Look, Daniele, the Lord has put within us a strong desire to progress, to go forward. I first said that the love of God has an aspect of travel, of going forward, then it is always necessary to go ahead and to progress. Lord, that I may love You always more, that I may never stop loving You. Do you understand?"

"Yes," said Daniele.

"Then I'll let you go. Do you see how much you've helped me?" the Pope said as he laughed and patted Daniele's cheek. Later Daniele was asked if he had learned the lesson. "The Pope said one must go forward. So I will go forward even if I'd rather stay where I am," he replied.

The Jesuits were having a general congregation at this time, and the Pope expected to meet the members on September 30, and had prepared a talk for them. John Paul I loved the Jesuits and in his youth had wanted to enter the Society, but could not do so because he was being educated for the Diocese of Belluno through the charity of a benefactor. He was closely bound to the Society through a distant relative, Father Felice Cappello, S.J., who was from Agordo. The Pope's prepared talk, published and sent to the Jesuits after his death, was affectionate and yet very frank concerning the problems of the Society in 1978. It is a talk which every religious would do well to ponder. Pope John Paul II, in his address to Father Pedro Arrupe, S.J., on September 21, 1979, urged the Jesuits to put into practice the recommendations made by his predecessor.

On Thursday, September 28, all was as usual. The Filipino bishops had an audience with the Pope; Cardinal Bernardin Gantin spoke with him; and the Pope joked with Monsignor Bosa, vicar-general of Venice who came to see him, "They have machines for writing — why don't they invent one for reading?" referring to the enormous amount of material a Pope has to read. In the evening, he spoke with Cardinal Colombo on the phone, and ended by begging his prayers for the Pope. He went to the chapel for Compline, the Church's night prayer, which contained the following verses:

> *You will show me the path of life*
> *the fullness of joy in your presence,*
> *at your right hand happiness forever.*
> *(Ps 16, Thursday Compline)*
> *May the God of peace make you perfect in*
> *holiness. May He preserve you whole and*
> *entire, spirit, soul and body, irreproachable*
> *at the coming of the Lord Jesus Christ.*
> *(I Thess 5:23, Thursday Compline)*

A few hours later, suddenly and unexpectedly, the Lord Jesus Christ did indeed come for him.

8

The World Mourns

*I*t was Sister Vincenza who found him. At 4:30 a.m., she left, as she always did, a cup of coffee outside the Pope's room and knocked on the door. There was no answer. Thinking he was up she went off to her other duties and came back around 5 a.m. to pick up the empty cup. The cup was still full. She knocked again, and again there was no answer. Now she was seriously concerned. She opened the door and looked inside. The Pope was in bed, with his glasses on, and papers in his hand. He was smiling and seemed asleep, but she knew he was dead. Frantically, she called Father Magee, his secretary, who rushed to his bedside, and seeing that the Pope was indeed dead, gave him absolution. He quickly called Dr. Buzzonetti, the Pope's doctor; his other secretary, Don Diego Lorenzi; Cardinal Confalonieri; and Cardinal Villot. In the meantime, Sister Vincenza ran to tell the other Sisters and they knelt in tears praying for the soul of their beloved friend and father. Dr. Buzzonetti, after examining the body, stated that the Pope had died of a myocardial infarction — that is, a massive heart attack — around 11 p.m., Thursday, September 28. Usually victims of this kind of heart attack suffer pain and distress, but John Paul belonged to the fortunate few who felt nothing.

The bells of St. Peter's began to toll, and soon all the bells of Rome joined in the slow, mournful tolling. People on the streets looked up in surprise. What could it mean?

Those at home, listening to the radio, were startled by the interruption announcing the death of Pope Luciani.

Shocked disbelief was the reaction of most. As the realization grew that the Pope was indeed dead, people began to crowd into the churches of Rome, and soon all over the world as well, to pray for the soul of their beloved shepherd who had roused such hopes and had filled them with an indescribable joy.

His body was laid in the Vatican Clementine Chapel. It was an extraordinary tribute to John Paul I to see for two days the endless lines of people who waited in pouring rain or scorching sun for two hours or more in order to see once again the Pope to whom they had felt so close and who had loved them so much. In mute sorrow, they passed his body, gazing on his face stilled in death. Many wept openly. Until darkness fell and the doors of the chapel were shut, the long lines of people continued.

A worker from Brescia traveled eight hours on the train in order to view the Pope's body, but the chapel was locked. He was desperate; he had to see him. Finally a priest saw him, listened to his story, and then went to get permission for him to go into the chapel. The man was in tears. "We went in," said the priest, "and knelt down by the Pope's body. The man gazed at him, bowed his head, closed his eyes, and murmured a prayer. After two or three minutes we left. The man was suddenly happy, deeply moved, and was crying for joy. He grasped my hands."

"And now what are your plans?" I asked him.

"Now I will take the train so that I can be at my job tomorrow at 7 a.m."

"Won't you be tired tomorrow?"

"No! I am so full of joy, I could go for a week without rest. I have seen him!"[1]

On September 30, the Pope's body was removed to St. Peter's. Here 50,000 people were waiting, and when his body was carried in, sustained applause greeted it. For three days thousands more streamed by, many of them young people, and by the end of the viewing it was estimated that about 750,000 had passed by the body. "He was too good," "He was a saint," "We did not deserve such a Pope," they said.[2]

The funeral was on October 4 in the late afternoon. The weather was overcast and it was drizzling. Because of the expected crowds, the cardinals decided to have the Mass in St. Peter's Square. The casket, a plain wooden one like Pope Paul's but with a gold cross on top, was placed in front of the altar. During Mass, rain fell in torrents and only let up a little when it was time to distribute Holy Communion to the people. The large paschal candle beside the casket flickered, but in spite of the rain, it did not go out.

During the homily, Cardinal Confalonieri asked the question that was on the lips of countless people: "We ask ourselves, why so quickly? The apostle tells us why: '. . . How deep His wisdom and knowledge and how impossible to penetrate His motives or understand His methods! Who could ever know the mind of the Lord?' We have scarcely had the time to see the new Pope. Yet one month was enough for him to have conquered hearts, and for us, it was a month to love him intensely. He passed as a meteor which unexpectedly lights up the heavens and then disappears, leaving us amazed and astounded. In the brief contact we had with him we were quickly struck and fascinated by his instinctive goodness, by his innate modesty, by his sincere simplicity in deed and word. The pontificate of John Paul was a dialogue of love between father and children."[3]

After the Mass the coffin was carried back into St. Peter's, and as the procession disappeared, the crowd clapped smartly four times, a Roman tribute of gratitude to their deceased Popes. Then the people, quiet and solemn, dispersed as night fell.

Nine days of official mourning followed, called the *Novemdiales*. A Solemn Requiem Mass was offered each day for the deceased Pope by some of the Church's highest officials. One of these was Cardinal Felici, who spoke of his smile: "The smile of suffering love.... He was a holocaust offered with joy and consuming itself in an autumn night, in complete solitude, when Jesus 'meek and festive' came to meet this blessed soul of His good and faithful servant, who, even in his lifeless body, left a trace of his smile, the smile of perfect abandonment to the Will of God."[4]

All over the world not only Catholics, but Protestants, Jews, Moslems, and even atheists were deeply saddened and felt as though they had lost a member of their own family. Thousands of people wrote or spoke about him. Mother Teresa of Calcutta said of him, "He was the most beautiful gift of God, a ray of the sun of God's love that shone in the darkness of the world, like the hope of eternal happiness. He was an ardent flame of the love of God . . . even our people in India when they saw the figure of John Paul I said,

'This is a Pope who is close to the heart of Mother Teresa because he is full of love for the poor.'"[5]

"We all felt the loss of Pope John Paul I," said a French Jesuit priest, "who had just time to unchain a tidal wave of loveliness and love. I felt very much he had done his task, which was to turn the world once more to Christ and His Church."[6]

"His pontificate brought me back to the Church," declared another person.[7]

Perhaps the greatest testimony of all is that given by Pope John Paul II on the occasion of his pilgrimage to Canale d'Agordo, on the first anniversary of the election of his predecessor.

He went there in order "to fulfill a need of my heart," he said, to render testimony to his predecessor, and to give joy to the people of that region who had been so deeply saddened by the death of "their" Don Albino. The people were greatly moved by this touching gesture of the Pope, and they prepared for his coming with much prayer and tremendous enthusiasm. Here are the words of Pope John Paul II at Canale d'Agordo and Belluno:

> *My pilgrimage in this blessed land, my presence here today, is meant to testify before the world that the mission and the apostolate of my predecessor continues to shine as a brilliant light in the Church, with a presence that could not be cut off. Rather it has given to it a new impulse, and a continuity that will never fade. With the teaching about charity, the theological virtue which has God as its source and principle, as model and reward, and which will never fade, the earthly page of John Paul I was closed. Or better still, it opened forever, in eternity, face-to-face with God, Whom he had loved so much, and Whom he taught us to love. . . . Be strong in the faith, strong in your hardworking activity, strong in the spirit of sacrifice. This will be the most adequate and the most worthy manner to honor in deeds the lovable figure of your, and our, John Paul I. He remained faithful, making real before the world the good and encouraging image of the Divine Shepherd. "Learn of me, for I am meek and humble of heart." This is how he remains forever, in our hearts.[8]*

Epilogue

I t is now over twenty-five years since the death of John Paul I. His pontificate was so brief that it would seem by this time his memory should have faded away. But such is not the case.

Soon after his death, people of all ages and from all over the world began to pray to "the Smiling Pope," and letters began to come into the chancery at Belluno and to the little church at Canale, telling of graces received, of small and big "miracles," of prodigious cures, all obtained through the intercession of John Paul I. People began asking for his beatification. At first, the Diocese of Belluno did nothing except to allow the people at Canale d'Agordo to have a register in their church in which people visiting Canale could write their signatures petitioning the Holy Father to raise Pope Luciani to the altars. However, by 1980 there were so many signatures that Bishop Maffeo Ducoli gave his imprimatur to the following prayer:

> *Lord Jesus, You Who gave us the great joy of venerating Pope John Paul I as Your Vicar on earth, and then in Your inscrutable designs gave us the immense sorrow of his unexpected departure. Grant us the graces we ask of You, so that, sure of his intercession with You, we may one day venerate him on the altars; then his goodness and humility, presented as an example to the faithful, will be a perpetual invitation to translate his teaching into life and to spread serenity and love. Amen.*

By June of 2003, 300,000 signatures had been collected not only at Canale, but from all over Italy and in many other countries, and presented to the Holy Father.

There are many of the faithful who feel they have obtained special graces through the intercession of Pope John Paul I.

In Italy, Emilia Aresca had suffered for years from a pain in her back that was so severe she could not do her housework, and none of the doctors she consulted had been able to provide a remedy. She attended the funeral of John Paul I and in tears prayed, "Papa Luciani, you who are close to Jesus, pray for me and obtain my cure or at least let me be well enough to do my housework. If you speak to Jesus, He will listen to you. . . ." The next morning when she got up, all the pain had disappeared and has never returned.[1]

Here in the United States, a young mother, pregnant with her third child, had such serious complications that the doctors told her that not only was there no hope for the baby, but she too would die unless she had an abortion. She refused. A small piece of the white cassock worn by Pope Luciani was sent to her, along with the prayer for his beatification. To the doctors' complete amazement, a beautiful boy was born. Never had they seen a successful outcome to this type of complication and they planned to write up the case as medical history. David Matthew John Paul is now a healthy, happy young man with an irresistible smile.

Every day people come to visit the tomb of John Paul I. A touching example is that of a blind woman who went down to the Vatican Grottoes, where someone led her to Pope Luciani's tomb. "All I want is to be here, near him. I want to talk to him," she said.[2] And people come, not only from Italy, but from every part of the world, "to talk to him." They know he understands and loves them, and they are sure he will help them.

At the Papa Luciani Center for the Poor in the United States, beautiful letters are received like the following one from Belgium:

I'm 32 years old and I'm a priest for 5 years now. In 1988 I entered the order of Norbertines in Grimbergen (Brussels). Now I'm the parish vicar of Grimbergen. I like the work in the parish quite well. It brings me in contact with many people and I try to be a good priest to them. I'm convinced that if he (John Paul I) wouldn't have been Pope I wouldn't have become a priest! When I was a young boy, at the age of 10, I was touched by the appearance of Pope Luciani. He was kind, smiled at everyone, and he was simple and human. When he became Pope, I became interested in the Eucharist and I wanted to be an acolyte. I have to thank Pope Luciani for the fact that I wanted to become a priest and every day I pray to him that I may persevere with my daily tasks. I hope you understand that he's very important to me, even though I didn't know him personally.

Fr. Johan

Canale d'Agordo is the scene of countless pilgrimages, especially in the summer when people come by busloads every day. They go to pray in the church where he was baptized and received his First Holy Communion. They go to look at the house where he was born, although little remains of the original house, as it has been enlarged and remodeled through the years. His brother, Edoardo, once said, half in amusement and half complaining, "My wife cannot even go out into the garden to hang up the wash in peace."[3] These pilgrims like to talk with the villagers to discover more about the Pope who impressed them so profoundly, and they pray to him for their spiritual and temporal needs.

One of the most frequent visitors to Canale is a woman from Germany. She went to great trouble to learn not only Italian but also the Veneto dialect so that she could talk with the people, and she has been most generous in donating money for the restoration of the centuries-old church in Canale.

In Vittorio Veneto, a beautiful statue of "their" Pope has been erected outside the cathedral, close to the street. People bring fresh flowers every day to place at his feet, and every day people can be seen kneeling in prayer before him.

At Lourdes in 1983, a bishop, ill and in a wheelchair, saw the sign "Belluno-Feltre" carried by some pilgrims. He called them over to himself and said in halting Italian, "You are from the homeland of John Paul I, a saint! If you go to his tomb, pray for me too!"[4]

———

Memorials began to appear in various parts of the world. One of the most beautiful is the Papa Luciani Center of Spirituality in his home diocese of Belluno. For years, the bishops have felt a pressing need for a center of spiritual renewal, where instructions in Christian doctrine and morals could be provided for youth, as well as offering a place of prayer and continuing religious formation for people of all ages. Because of the poverty of the people there, it seemed an impossible dream. The now retired bishop of Belluno, Maffeo Ducoli, decided to entrust the project to the intercession of Pope John Paul I, and using the modest savings which his own mother had left to him at her death in 1980, he began to renovate some old farmhouses on a beautiful property which had been donated for the purpose. Begun in 1981, a lovely chapel and large conference room, a kitchen, a few simple bedrooms, and study halls have been completed and are already in use. First Communion and Confirmation classes are held there, and also programs to prepare the youngsters to resist the attractions of drug and alcohol abuse, as well as the errors of Marxism. Meetings of married couples and activities for the elderly are also well attended.

Connected with the center is the Papa Luciani Association. Its aim is to make Papa Luciani and his writings known. It also voices the requests and desires from people all over the world who pattern their lives on Christ after the Pope's example. The members of the association are entitled to receive the delightful and informative quarterly journal *Papa Luciani Humilitas* (at present, published only in English and Italian); to take part in all the spiritual, charitable, and cultural works performed in his name and in his memory; and to be informed of whatever happens in the world in relation to John Paul I. The Papa Luciani Association has its headquarters at Centro Papa Luciani, 32035 S. Giustina Bellunese, (Belluno) Italy.

A second center has been constructed in the United States by the Missionary Servants of Pope John Paul I and is called The Papa Luciani Center for the Poor, 22 Boyd Hill Road, Gilford, NH 03249. This center is used for retreats, to promote vocations, to host work days for the poor, to store and ship goods to Mother Teresa's sisters in Haiti and throughout the Caribbean, and to publish the English edition of *Humilitas*. The English edition of *Humilitas* includes articles by and about Pope John Paul I and articles about the plight of the poorest of the poor. The Missionary Servants have sent millions of dollars of aid to the poor in Pope

John Paul's name without begging or soliciting, but only by depending on Divine Providence.

On August 26, 2002, the 24th anniversary of Pope John Paul I's election as Pope, Bishop Vicenzo Savio of Belluno-Feltre announced that the research to promote the Pope's beatification had begun on the local level.[5]

On June 10, 2003, the Vatican's Congregation for Sainthood Causes gave its consent to begin the canonical process on the holiness of the Servant of God Pope John Paul I. The first postulator of the cause was Salesian Father Pasquale Liberatore, who died in November 2003. In the meantime, the vice postulator, Monsignor Giorgio Lise, rector of the Papa Luciani Center in Santa Giustina Belluno, Italy, is carrying on this very important work.[6]

"The Smiling Pope" continues to fascinate people all over the world. His was a strong and rich personality that death did not extinguish, but revealed in all its splendor. It is not only his simplicity, his serenity, and his joy that attracts, but also his unique spirituality and his radiant holiness. Therefore, in the words of his great successor, Pope John Paul II, "Let us pray to good Pope John Paul I, particularly for the Church, so greatly loved by him, that he may obtain for us the grace of unity and sanctity."[7]

Notes for Part I

Chapter I

1. *Su questa polvere il Signore ha scritto.* Istituto Bellunese di ricerche sociali e culturali. Serie "Quaderni" No. 8, 1979.

2. *Giovanni Paolo I* by Georges Huber, Edizione Pro Sanctitate, Roma (No date given in Italian translation. Original French Edition, 1979).

3. *L'Osservatore Romano,* September 29, 1978.

4. Ibid.

5. *L'Amico del Popolo,* Belluno, September 2, 1978.

Chapter II

1. *Il Magistero di Albino Luciani,* Edizioni Messaggero, Padova, 1979.

2. *L'Osservatore Romano,* August 30, 1979.

3. *Testimonianza di Cristo,* Edizioni Messaggero, Padova, 1981.

4. Ibid.

5. *L'Osservalore Romano,* English Edition, November 2, 1981, Bishop Maffeo Ducoli.

Chapter III

1. *Il dono della chiarezza* by Antonio Ugenti, Edizioni Logos, 1979.

2. *L'Amico del Popolo,* Belluno, 1978.

3. *Su questa polvere il Signore ha scritto.*

4. *Giovanni Paolo I* by Georges Huber.

5. Ibid.

6. *L'Amico del Popolo,* Belluno, August, 1983.

7. Ibid.

8. *Giovanni Paolo I* by Georges Huber.

9. Quoted in *Il dono della chiarezza.*

10. *L'Osservatore Romano,* September 28, 1980.

11. *Giovanni Paolo I* by Georges Huber.

12. Ibid.

Chapter IV

1. *Papa Luciani* by Msgr. Giulio Nicolini, Edizioni Messaggero, Padova, 1979.

2. Article in *Il Celentone,* Bollettino della parrocchia di Canale d'Agordo. September-October, 1978.

3. *L'Osservatore Romano,* September 28, 1980.

4. *Il Nostro Papa Luciani.* Tipse, Vittorio Veneto. 1979.

5. *L'Osservatore Romano,* September 28, 1978.

6. *L'Osservatore Romano,* August 26, 1981, Francesco Taffarel.

7. *Giovanni Paolo I* by Georges Huber.

8. Ibid.

9. *Il dono della chiarezza* by Antonio Ugenti.

10. "Gli ultimi Papi." Talk by Bishop Gioacchino Muccin, Pontificia Universi tas Urbaniana, 1980.

11. Article in "Il cuore della madre," Rome, 1983.

12. *L'Osservatore Romano*, English Edition, September 17, 1979.

13. *L'Osservatore Romano*, September 28, 1979, articles by Mario Ghizzi and Francesco Taffarel.

14. *Il dono della chiarezza* by Antonio Ugenti.

15. *Giovanni Paolo I* by Georges Huber.

16. *Cosi parlò ... Papa Luciani*. Editrice "Il carroccio" Vigodarzere, 1978.

17. *Il Buon Samaritano*, Edizioni Messaggero, Padova, 1980.

18. Article in "Il cuore della madre," Rome, September 1979.

19. *L'Osservatore Romano*, August 26, 1982, Francesco Taffarel.

20. Cosi parlò... Papa Luciani.

21. As quoted in *The Popes of Vatican Council II*, F. Peter Wigginton, Franciscan Herald Press. 1983.

Chapter V

1. *Gente Veneta*, September, 1982, "Papa Luciani, un ricordo della sua umanità" by Mario Senigaglia.

2. Sister Vincenza Taffarel, as told to M. Irma Dametto.

3. *Giovanni Paolo I* by Georges Huber.

4. Ibid.

5. Ibid.

6. Article in "Prospettive nel mondo" by Diego Lorenzi, *43*, January 1980.

7. *Giovanni Paolo I* by Georges Huber.

8. Sister Vincenza Taffarel.

9. To the People of Venice, February 1976.

10. See Part I, Chapter 7: *The Smiling Pope*, p. 67 and Part II, Chapter 6: Love, p. 112.

11. *L'Osservatore Romano*, September 28, 1980, Cardinal Marco Cè.

12. Article in "Il cuore della madre," Rome, September 1980.

13. "Rivista diocesana del patriarcato di Venezia," September-October 1978.

14. *Giovanni Paolo I* by Georges Huber.

15. Article in "Living City," Jamaica, New York, November *1978*.

16. *L'Osservatore Romano*, September 29, 1982.

17. Ibid.

18. Ibid.

19. Sister Vincenza Taffarel.

20. Bishop Maffeo Ducoli. Personal communication. October 5, 1984.

21. *Giovanni Paolo I, Il Papa del sorriso,* Arturo d'Onofrio, LER, Napoli-Roma, October 1978.

22. Article in "Prospettive nel mondo," Alberto Michelini, 43, January 1980.

23. *L'Osservatore Romano,* November 22, 1973.

24. *Il Buon Samaritano,* Edizioni Messaggero, Padova, 1980.

25. Ibid.

26. *Testimonianza di Cristo.*

27. Ibid.

28. Ibid.

29. Talk by A. Luciani in *Coy ad Cor Loquitur.* La Catechesi del Cuore di Cristo, Atti del secondo Convegno Sacerdotale Internazionale della Lega Sacerdotale Mariana Pompei 22-27 September 1977. Edizioni Centro Volontari della Sofferenza, Rome, 1979.

30. Ibid.

31. *Gente Veneta,* September, 1981, "Ci ha insegnato a pregare" by Mario Senigaglia.

32. *L'Osservatore Romano,* English Edition, November 2, 1981, Bishop Maffeo Ducoli.

33. Ibid.

34. *Il Magistero di Albino Luciani.*

Chapter VI

1. *Giovanni Paolo I* by Georges Huber.

2. *L'Osservatore Romano,* October 1978.

3. *Trentatre giorni: un pontificato* by Msgr. Giulio Nicolini. 4th Edition, Editrice VELAR, Bergamo. 1984.

4. Ibid.

5. *Su questa polvere il Signore ha scritto.*

6. *L'Osservatore Romano,* August 1978.

7. *L'Osservatore Romano,* August 29, 1979.

8. *L'Osservatore Romano,* September 28, 1980.

9. *Giovanni Paolo I* by Georges Huber.

10. *L'Osservatore Romano,* August 27, 1979.

11. *Giovanni Paolo Il parla di Giovanni Paolo I,* Homily, September 17, 1978, Piergiorgio Beretta, Edizione Paoline, Roma. 1978.

12. Bishop Maffeo Ducoli. Personal communication. October 5, 1984.

13. *Papa Luciani* by Msgr. Giulio Nicolini.

14. *Giovanni Paolo I* by Georges Huber.

Chapter VII
All quotes in this chapter which are not noted here have been taken from the English Edition of *L'Osservatore Romano,* 1978 (August 31, September 7, September 14, September 21, September 28, October 5).
1. Francesca MacMurrough. Personal communication. March 1979.
2. Bishop Maffeo Ducoli. Personal communication. October 5, 1984.
3. From the tape recording, "Mi chiamerò Giovanni Paolo I," Papa Luciani, Radiovaticana.
4. *Bellunesi nel mondo,* September 1978, No. 9.
5. Article in *Il Celentone.*
6. Ibid.
7. Sister Vincenza Taffarel, as told to M. Irma Dametto.
8. Father Angelo Beghetto, Introduction to *Illustrissimi: Letters from Pope John Paul I.* Translated by William Weaver, Little, Brown & Company, 1978.
9. Sister Vincenza Taffarel.
10. *Trentatre giorni: un pontificato* by Msgr. Giulio Nicolini. 4th Edition.
11. *Giovanni Paolo I* by Georges Huber.
12. *L'Osservatore della domenica,* October 8, 1978, Msgr. del Gallo.
13. From the tape recording "Il piccolo catechismo di Giovanni Paolo I" Edizione Paoline.

Chapter VIII
1. *Trentatre giorni: un pontificato* by Msgr. Giulio Nicolini. 4th Edition
2. Ibid.
3. *L'Osservatore Romano,* English Edition, October 12, 1978.
4. *L'Osservatore Romano,* English Edition, October 19, 1978, Cardinal Pericle Felici.
5. *Trentatre giornz: un pontificato* by Msgr. Giulio Nicolini. 4th Edition
6. Rev. Joseph Ledit, S.J., Personal communication. November 1978.
7. Mary Dorsey, *Newsweek.* Letter to Editor, October 16, 1978.
8. *L'Osservatore Romano, August* 1979.

Epilogue
1. A. M. Cicuta, Chaplain at the Hospital in Nizza Monferrato, in a letter to *Humilitas,* October 8, 1984.
2. *Giovanni Paolo I* by Georges Huber.
3. *Domenica del Corriere,* October 1982.
4. *L'Amico del Popolo,* September 1983.
5. Zenit.org
6. Zenit.org

7. *L'Osservatore Romano,* August 27, 1981.

Other Sources

Papa Luciani-Supplement to *Gente Veneta*, September 1979.

PART II

Words from the Heart

1

Written on Dust

Sermon in Canale d'Agordo, January 6, 1959

Papa Luciani gave this sermon in his native village shortly after his episcopal consecration in Rome by Pope John XXIII, which he mentions in the text. It was transcribed from a tape recording.

My Dear Fellow Villagers:

Who would have ever said that in this church in Canale, where I was born, where I played as a child, where you have seen me work with a scythe and a rake during vacations, in this church where I made my First Communion, where I have been an altar boy and a choirboy, where I came to confess my mischievous pranks and my poor sins — who would have said that today I would be appearing with these insignia to celebrate the Pontifical Mass and to preach?

At this moment my soul is filled with different emotions, but above all, with a feeling of confusion. I don't know what the Lord thought about me, what the Pope thought about me, what Divine Providence thought about me. I have been thinking these past few days that the Lord has been using His old system with me: He takes the little ones from the mud of the streets and sets them on high; He takes people from the fields, the seashore, and the lake and makes apostles of them.

It is His old system. There are certain things that the Lord wants to write neither on bronze, nor on marble, but actually on dust, so that if the writing remains, not broken up, not scattered by the wind, let it be very clear that everything is due solely to the work and the merits of the Lord. I am the little one of once upon a time; I am the one who comes from the fields; I am pure and

87

simple dust. On this dust the Lord has written the episcopal dignity of the illustrious Diocese of Vittorio Veneto. If anything good ever comes out of all this, let it be very clear from now on, it is only the fruit of the goodness, the grace, and the mercy of the Lord.

I know that you have been kind enough to take an interest in this event; they've told me that you have rung the bells, and you have sent a large delegation to Rome. What's more, at considerable sacrifice, you decided to give me a gold pectoral cross. Thank you; you have done too much for me. When I wear this cross, I will feel that I am wearing something that will stimulate me to do good, to work for souls and not to dishonor my village, which has loved and honored me so much.

I see around me several priests who are particularly dear to me, the rector of the seminary [Monsignor Angelo Santin], who preached the sermon at my first Mass in this very church, our dear archpriest [Monsignor Augusto Bramezza], who guided my first steps in the pastoral ministry, and my schoolmates, some of whom have been my students. I thank them in a very special way.

And I would stop now, but I know — they told me — that I am expected to say a few words by way of a sermon. I don't know where to begin. They have made me preach so many times in the past few days. I will say this. When new bishops are about to enter their diocese, they have to prepare a coat of arms. I've had to do the same. At the top of this coat of arms, I have had them put three stars. They can mean the three theological virtues: faith, hope, and charity, which are the center of the whole Christian life. I have chosen these three stars for myself and I have chosen them for my future people. I will say a few words to you about these three virtues.

Faith, for me, is a meeting of three people. "My God, I firmly believe everything that You have revealed and that the Holy Church indicates that we should believe." Me, you, the Church. We no longer see the Lord speaking. He has left, He has gone to heaven; He is no longer visible in this world. In His place, the Lord has left the Pope, He has left the bishops, and it is these who we must hear and listen to. Even if they say difficult things, if they talk about mysteries, it is always God speaking. We must accept what they say like children, accept. Faith is a gift of God. God alone gives it to those He wishes. It is not a question of understanding; it is not a question of being intelligent. When I find someone who does not believe, I cannot say to him, "You are a blockhead, you are ignorant." No, I must say, "I am lucky and he is not as lucky. The Lord has not been as good to him."

What would we do in this world without faith? I have been ill in a sanatorium, and I can tell you that having faith and not having it are completely different things. If we have faith, we bear it willingly; if we have faith, we do it for God. When we do not have faith, we lose heart. Two people have the same amount of money, the same amount of cash, but if one has faith, he is not attached to that money. If someone does not have faith, he becomes attached to it, and is restless and always brooding on it. To have faith is a whole other thing, a great gift of the Lord.

Then there is hope. Hope means to expect, to await. We Christians are people who are expecting something beautiful, something extraordinary, from the Lord. And we must await it with great trust. When we priests read the Psalms, it is all one hope. We say, "Lord, you are my refuge; Lord, you are my light; I am not afraid; Lord, I am with you; Lord, you are my comfort as long as you are at my side, I will not fear in eternity." This is hope. Hope is the smile of the Christian life.

What would we do without hope? And poor unfortunate people, those who no longer have hope, those who are discouraged, those who are disheartened, those who are in despair. Never despair! Woe! Never despair, always await help from the Lord! Look at Judas, he made a serious mistake. Poor man, he betrayed the Lord! But his real mistake was not that; his real mistake was when he no longer had hope, when he said, "My sin is too great." No sin is too great, no sin is greater than the boundless mercy of the Lord. The same day that Judas hanged himself, a thief who had been an assassin for his whole life, in two minutes had stolen heaven — in two minutes! He had first been a thief on the roads of the world, and he became a thief of heaven on the cross: "Lord, remember me when you are in your kingdom." "This very evening, this very day you will be with me in Paradise." Let's try to have hope, whatever our situation might be.

St. Francis de Sales has written something that seems exaggerated, a paradox. He said, "At times we are almost lucky to have committed a sin, almost lucky because then we are humble, then we understand what wretched creatures we are, then we no longer dare to look down on others because they are sinners." Never despair, always have courage because the Lord is goodness, always, as long as there are the merits of our Lord Jesus Christ.

Then there is the third star, the third virtue, love, the great Christian virtue. It was in this very church that I learned the Act of Love. "Oh Lord, I love You with all my heart, above all else, and for Your love, I love my neighbor as myself." It takes very little time to say it, but it is rather difficult to put it into practice. Above all else, more than anything we must love the Lord. We can also love other things, but not like God and nothing contrary to Him.

St. Francis de Sales, speaking of the love of the Lord, used this analogy precisely to make us understand that we must first love Him and, once the Lord is in the right place, we can love so many other things. Afterwards he said, "There was a saint, he was still a young man, and being a young man, one day he met a young lady, a girl friend. He fell in love." St. Francis said, "Listen to what happens now. While the holy young man Jacob, who had the Lord as his guest, fell in love, what did the Lord do? He didn't turn to Jacob, He didn't say to him, 'Listen, dear friend, either she goes or I do.' He didn't say that. Instead, He said, 'You are young; I understand, you have fallen in love. I understand, it is your time. I will move aside a little and make a little room for this girl who will be your wife.' We can love so many other things along with the Lord, it is enough that they not be loved more than God, that they not be loved contrary to God, that they not be loved in the same way as God."

And then we must love our neighbors, for the love of the Lord. "Ah," says St. John, "it is an illusion if someone believes that he loves God and does not love his own brother." We must also love our neighbors; we must forgive, we must bear with annoying people, we must love them for love of God, as ourselves, it is said, like ourselves. Treat our neighbors like we would want to be treated. Try to have great sympathy, try to have great understanding, try to have great compassion.

My dear brothers and sisters, I don't want to go any further; I will stop here. A single thought, as I have said. For my episcopate, during my episcopate I will try to have this motto before me, faith, hope, love. If we put these three things in practice, we are in order; if we have faith, if we have hope, if we have love. Try to do the same yourselves. We are all poor sinners. Being a Christian costs everyone a great deal. You see, in this world there is not a single adult who is good, unless he has first made an effort. Do you see an upright man? Do you see someone who is truly a Christian? Don't worry about being mistaken, say without a doubt, "If that man there is good, it means that he has made a great effort." It takes an effort to be good. But afterwards there is the recompense, afterwards there is the Lord Who will reward us. In this world, let us remember, there is no happiness, there is a bit of happiness here and there, every now and then. But there is no real happiness. That is only in heaven.

So then, let's try to stay united to our Lord Jesus Christ. Let's try to be good at the cost of any effort, at the cost of any sacrifice. The Lord will give a recompense, and He will reward us.

2

I Hope You Will Help Me with Your Prayers

First Angelus Address, August 27, 1978

*Y*esterday ... Yesterday morning, I went to the Sistine Chapel to vote ... tranquilly. I never would have imagined what was about to happen.

As soon as the danger began for me, the two colleagues who were near me whispered words of encouragement to me. One said, "Courage! If the Lord gives you a burden, He also gives you the help to carry it." And the other colleague, "Don't be afraid! All over the world there are so many people praying for the new Pope." When the moment came, I accepted.

Afterwards, there was the question of the name because they also ask what name you want to take, and I had not thought about it very much.... Well, I reasoned like this: Pope John wanted to consecrate me himself, with his own hands, here in St. Peter's Basilica. Then, although unworthily, I succeeded him in the Chair of St. Mark in that Venice which is still completely full of Pope John. The gondoliers remember him, the sisters, everybody!

But Pope Paul not only made me a cardinal, but a few months earlier, on the runway in St. Mark's Square, he made me turn red all over in front of 20,000 people because, he took off his stole and placed it on my shoulders. I have never been so red! Besides, in the fifteen years of his pontificate, this Pope showed not only me but the whole world how we should love, how we should serve, and how we should work and suffer for the Church of Christ. For this reason, I said, "I will take the name John Paul."

Let me make this clear: I don't have either the wisdom of the heart of Pope John, or the preparation and culture of Pope Paul, but I am in their place, and I must try to serve the Church. I hope you will help me with your prayers.

3

"Why Do I Suffer?"

On May 24, 1978, just three months before he was elected Pope, Cardinal Luciani gave a talk at the Cini Foundation in Venice to an international symposium of doctors studying pain in patients with advanced cancer. His subject was the problem of suffering and pain and the Christian response to it. He was able to bring a special insight to the subject from his own experience as one who had experienced sickness many times during his life.[1]

Gentlemen, I have been asked to say a few words on human suffering. On this subject you are appealed to as doctors and as researchers. "Doctor," people say to you, "soothe my pain, cure me, with your talent for research, take a new step forward in medicine." The questions that are posed to me on the same subject are generally of another kind. "Why is there so much suffering, which seems to hit directly on the best in humanity? Why do the innocent and the children suffer? If it is true that there is a good God, a God Who is a Father, how do you reconcile His providence with such phenomena, which just don't seem to fit in with it?"

These questions wound the heart of the one who asks them, and mine as well, because I don't have a clear and convincing answer to give, but only elements of, attempts at, fragments of an answer. And I respond, "I understand you; it is human for you to pose this problem. On the cross, Christ let out the moan, 'My God, my God, why have you forsaken me?' (Mt 27:46). And yet the same Christ has said no to those who want to resolve the problem on the basis of a 'religious mathematics.'" He meets a man blind from birth, and right away His disciples ask Him: "Rabbi, who sinned, this man or his parents, that he was born blind?" And Jesus answers, "Neither he nor his parents sinned" (Jn 9:1-3).

Pilate has had some Galileans massacred, and a tower has come crashing down just a few days previously, killing eighteen people; the disciples find themselves tempted to apply the "religious mathematics" once again. But Jesus says, "Do you think that because the Galileans suffered this way they were greater sinners than all the other Galileans? By no means! Or those eighteen, do you think that they were more guilty than everyone else who lived in Jerusalem? By no means!" (Lk 13:1-5).

Jesus thus shares the reasoning of Job, who answers the friends who say to Him "Your misfortunes are a proof of your misdeeds" with "You are glossing over falsehoods and offering vain remedies, every one of you!" (Job 13:4).

The *Bible* admits, then, that the good are not always rewarded in this world, nor the bad always punished. What then? Then we must remember that human life is an *Adventure in Two Worlds* by A. J. Cronin.[2] The story begins here, but it is concluded in another world. "The souls of the just are in the hands of God.... They seemed, in the view of the foolish, to be dead, and their passing away was thought an affliction and their going forth from us, utter destruction. But they are in peace ... their hope is full of immortality" (Wis 3:1-4). Faith and hope in a future life, certainly, are the first elements of the answer.

Francis de Sales wrote, "As a child, I built a sand castle near the brook. Along came a big boy, and with one kick, he completely destroyed it. How I wept! It seemed to me the greatest of misfortunes. Now, however, I smile about those long ago tears. And so too, in heaven we will smile about sufferings which here seem to us tremendous misfortunes."[3] Those who suffer with heaven in view understand something of suffering. These pains are not directly willed, but only permitted by God, Who wants to do only good to His children, even if He does not intend to intervene through miracles to obstruct the forces of nature and the course on which He has set it in motion with its own laws. Nor is God a lover of pain; He does not wish suffering for its own sake. Christ Himself, in the garden, prayed at first to the Father to take the chalice of suffering from Him; only after He had prayed and received courage did He add, "Not my will, but yours be done"

(Mt 26:42). It is not Christ's suffering, as such, which redeemed us, but rather the patience, the love, and the obedience with which Christ accepted His suffering.

And here emerges another partial answer to the why of suffering. If accepted it can actually become a teacher and a means which instructs us and helps us become better people. John Henry Newman wrote, "To be safe is to be unsafe." This might be translated,[4] "To be too safe is equivalent to being in danger," in danger of not doing anything noble, of standing still, and of loving only our own happiness. Instead, God has mysteriously arranged it so that the greatness of man is born of effort, responsibility, sacrifice, and mutual aid. We can tell a man's worth by the way he reacts to misfortune. Is he crushed by sorrow? It means he is mediocre. Does he remain on his feet? He shows himself to be greater than if he were raised on a pedestal. Napoleon wrote at Saint Helena, "Strike bronze with a glove, and it will give off no sound; strike it with a hammer, and you will hear it ring!"

A third partial answer to the why of suffering rests in the fact that it is a common condition; often it helps us to compare ourselves to others. A Chinese man said, "I had only one pair of old, ragged shoes, and I moaned about it. One day I met someone who had no feet. I never dared complain again."

I repeat, these are fragments of an explanation, and I emphasize that Christ did not teach us so much why we suffer as how to face suffering in ourselves and in others.

He showed that He loved the suffering. St. Mark tells us that after He cured Peter's mother-in-law in her home, "they brought to him all who were ill," until "the whole town was gathered at the door. He cured many who were sick with various diseases" (Mk 1:32-34). One day, on the shore of the lake, Jesus ordered that a boat be ready. Why? "Because of the crowd, so they would not crush him. He had cured a man, as a result, those who had diseases were pressing upon him to touch him" (Mk 3:9-10). Jesus had a passionate love for the suffering. He told the parable of the Good Samaritan, who had compassion on the man who was robbed and beaten by thieves and concluded it by saying, "Go and do likewise" (Lk 10:29-37). He made of Himself one person with the sick, saying, "I was ill and you cared for me. You did it for me" (Mt 25:34). Many have taken this invitation and these words seriously. Camillo de Lellis, when taking care of the sick, used to say to them, "Do not ask me, command me; you are my masters." When Pedro Claver, who had gone from Spain to Latin America to evangelize the Indians, went down, almost by chance, into the hold of a slave ship, and saw the horrors of the place and the unspeakable condition of the poor blacks, he changed his mind, took a vow and signed it this way, "Pedro, slave of the blacks forever." He spent the remaining forty years of his life in washing, nursing, giving medicine, and bringing the gospel to the slaves who were arriving in Cartegena in Colombia by the thousands from the Congo and Angola.

But the sufferings of Christ themselves contain precious indications of how the sick should bear their illness. In the garden He wanted to experience the fear of suffering, as if to say to us, "I myself have shown you the way, don't be surprised if you are also afraid of pain; only try to imitate Me." "Your Father," He once said, "knows what you need before you ask him" (Mt 6:8). And look at Him, in His fear, going straight to the Father, to ask for and obtain strength and confidence. Many Christian sick people, after the example of Christ, pray to have the strength to accept and bear their suffering with resignation and courage. Not only that; sometimes they move from resigned acceptance to offering their own suffering to God. One famous sick person, Blaise Pascal, wrote in his *Priere pour demander a Dieu le bon usage des maladies,* "I ask you neither for health, nor for sickness, nor for life, nor for death, but that you arrange my health and my sickness, my life and my death, for your glory, for my salvation, and for the good of the Church."

But Christ did not pass up more humble remedies. In the garden, He tried several times to find comfort in His favorite disciples, and it saddened Him to find them sleeping from exhaustion. It is an indication that those who suffer often feel the need to have the people they love near them. To feel that they are not alone, that they are not cut off, that they are understood, loved, and able to communicate with others instills in the sick hope and courage.

For this reason too, visits and associations among the sick should be encouraged. Hospitals themselves, in addition to being well-equipped in the clinical and technical areas, should promote the training of medical and paramedical personnel in giving sensitive and attentive treatment and in showing the proper openness to visits from relatives. "The way in which men are assisted when they are suffering and dying," wrote Charles Flory, "is one of the clearest signs of the level of civilization of an epoch and a regime."[5]

I will stop here. The few things I have said are only fragments of the Christian philosophy of suffering . . . it would be possible to extract from the writings of Seneca, St. Augustine, Boethius, and the already cited Pascal, as well as those of Dostoyevsky, Péguy, Bernanos, Cappee, and others. Our Manzoni, though, summed up very briefly this philosophy in the well-known "essence" of his novel.[6] Sufferings, he wrote, "come so often because there is a reason for them . . . the most prudent and innocent conduct will not keep them away; and when they come, whether our fault or not, faith in God will soften them and make them useful for a better life."

Notes

1. "Simposio internazionale sul dolore nel cancro avanzato," Prolusione tenuta alla Fondazione Cini il 24 maggio 1978, RD, vol. 63, nos. 4-5, (April-May 1978), pp. 161-63.

2. *Adventures in Two Worlds* was the title of the Scottish novelist's autobiography, published by McGraw Hill in 1952 (Trans).

3. Cf. St. Frances de Sales, *Oevres*, (Trans).

4. The quotation from Newman was in English in the original text (Trans).

5. *Settimana Sociale di Francia*, 1951.

6. *The Betrothed.*

4

Faith

General Audience Talk, September 13, 1978

*M*y first greeting goes to my brother bishops, many of whom I see here.

Pope John, in a note of his that was also published later, said, "This time I made my retreat on the seven lamps of sanctification. Seven virtues, he meant, faith, hope, charity, prudence, justice, fortitude, and temperance. Who knows if the Holy Spirit will help the poor Pope today (laughs) illustrate at least one of these lamps, the first one, faith (long applause).

Here in Rome, there was a poet, Trilussa, who also tried to talk about faith in one of his poems. He said, "The little old blind women whom I met the evening I became lost deep in the woods said to me, 'If you don't know the way, I will show it to you, for I know it. If you have the strength to stay close to me, from time to time I will give you a call; down to the bottom where there is a cypress tree, and up to the top, where there is a cross.' I answered, 'Maybe . . . but I find it strange that someone who cannot see can guide me. The blind woman then took me by the hand and sighed, 'Walk.' She was faith." (applause, cheers)

As poetry, charming; as theology, defective. Defective, because when it comes to faith, the great stage manager is God, because Jesus has said, "No one can come to me unless my Father draws him" (Jn 6:44). St. Paul did not have faith; in fact, he persecuted believers. God is waiting for him on the road to Damascus. "Paul!" He says to him. "Don't even dream of rearing up, of kicking like a frisky horse. I am that Jesus whom you are persecuting. I have plans for you. You must change!" Paul surrendered; he changed, he turned his own life upside down. Some years later, he would write to the Philippians, "That time, on the road to Damascus,

God seized me; from that time on, I have done nothing but run after him, to see if I too can seize him, by imitating him and loving him ever more" (Phil 3:12). This is what faith is, surrendering to God, by transforming our own lives. Something that is not always easy.

Augustine has told of his journey of faith, especially in the last weeks, it was terrible. He feels as though his soul is shuddering and writhing in inner conflicts. Over here, God calling him and insisting, and over there, his old habits, "old friends," he writes, "who pulled me gently by my garment of flesh and said to me, "What, Augustine? You are abandoning us! Just think, I wouldn't be able to do this, I wouldn't be able to do that other thing, ever again!" Difficult! "I found myself," he says, "in the situation of someone who is in bed in the morning. They say to him, 'Get up, Augustine, get out of bed!' And I said 'Yes, but later, just a little bit longer!' Ah, finally, the Lord gave me a violent pull, and I got up." So then, don't say, "yes, but . . ." Don't say "Yes, but later." You must say, "Yes, Lord! Right away!" This is faith, to respond generously to the Lord. But who is it that says this "yes"? We must be humble and have complete trust in God.

My mother said to me when I was growing up, "Oh, when you were little you were very sick once. I had to go from one doctor to another. I had to stay up whole nights, do you believe me?" How could I have said, "Mama, I don't believe you?" "But of course I believe you, I believe in what you tell me, but most of all, I believe in you." It is like that with faith. It doesn't mean only believing in the things that God has revealed, but in Him, Who deserves our faith, Who has loved us so much and has done so much for our love.

Of course, it is difficult to accept some truths because the truths of faith are of two types, some pleasant, others distasteful to our minds. For example, it is pleasing to hear that God has such tender love for us, even more tender than that which a mama has for her children, Isaiah says. This is pleasant; it is congenial. There was a great French bishop, Doupanloup, who said to rectors of seminaries, "Be good with these (young men) who are to become priests, be fathers, be mothers." It is pleasant. Other truths, on the other hand, are difficult. God must punish if I really resist. He runs after me, He begs me, "Please be converted!" and I say, "No, no, no!" until the very last, it is as though I am the one forcing Him to punish me. This is not pleasant, but it is a truth of faith.

There is a final difficulty, the Church. St. Paul asked, "Who are you, Lord?" "I am that Jesus whom you are persecuting." A light, a flash of light went through his mind. "I am not persecuting Jesus. I don't even know Him. I am persecuting Christians." It is clear that Jesus and Christians, Jesus and the Church, are the same thing: indivisible, inseparable. Read St. Paul, Ephesians 1:22-23. Christ and the Church make up a single thing. Christ is the head, we, the Church, are His members. It is not possible to have faith and say, "I believe in Jesus, I accept Jesus, but I do not accept the Church." We must accept the Church, accept what she is. And what is she, this Church? Pope John said, *Mater et Magistra* — a teacher too! St. Paul said, "Everyone must accept us as helpers of Christ and stewards and dispensers of his mysteries" (I Cor. 4:1).

When the poor Pope, when the bishops, and the priests set forth a doctrine, they are not doing anything but helping Christ. It is not our doctrine. It is Christ's; we must only watch over it, we must only present it. I was present when Pope John opened the council. At one point he said, "Let us hope that with the council the Church will make a forward leap." That is what we all hoped; however, a forward leap on what road? He said it immediately, on the road of certain and unchangeable truths. Pope John did not even dream that it would be the truths that would travel, that would go forward, and that little by little, would change. No! The truths are the same. We must travel down the road of these truths, perfecting them, understanding them more and more fully, and updating them, by proposing them in a new form.

And also Pope Paul, the same thought. The first thing I did, as soon as I was elected Pope, was to enter the chapel (the private chapel of the papal household), and there in the back Pope Paul had two mosaics made, St. Peter and St. Paul — St. Peter dying, St. Paul dying. But there underneath St. Peter, he wrote, "I will pray for you, Peter, so that your faith will never fail" (cf. Lk 22:32).

And underneath St. Paul, as he received the blow from the sword, "I have run my course, I have kept the faith" (II Tim 4:7). You know that in his last address on June 29 he said, "I have spent fifteen years as Pope, I can thank the Lord that I have defended the faith, that I have kept my faith."

The Church is also a mother, if she is a continuation of Christ. Christ is good; the Church must also be good; she must be a mother to everyone. But what if by chance there should sometimes be some wicked people in the Church? But we have a mama. If our mamas are sick, if my mother, for example, were to become lame, I would still love her. Therefore, even if in the Church there are — and sometimes there are — some defects and some failings, our affection for the Church must never fail.

Yesterday — and I am finished — they sent me the issue of *Cittd Nuova,* and I saw that they had printed, by taping it, a very short talk of mine, and speaking to young people, I had told an anecdote. A certain preacher, McNabb, an Englishman, speaking at Hyde Park, had spoken about the Church. When he was finished, someone asked to speak and said, "Beautiful words, yours. However, I know certain Catholics who have been anything but with the poor, instead they have become rich. I know some Catholic husbands who have cheated on their wives; therefore, I don't like this Church which has sinners in it." And the Father said, "You are partly right, but may I make an objection?" "Let's hear it," he says. "Excuse me, am I mistaken, or is the collar of your shirt a little bit greasy?" "Well, yes," he says, "I admit it, it is, a bit." "But is it greasy because you didn't use soap, or because you used soap, but it didn't help at all?" "No," he says, "I didn't use soap."

There you are. The Church — the Catholic Church — also has some extraordinary soap, the gospel, the sacraments, and prayer. The gospel read and lived, the sacraments properly celebrated, and prayer would be a kind of soap capable of making us all saints. We are not all saints because we have not used enough of this soap. Let us see that we fulfill the hopes of the Popes who convened and applied the council, Pope John and Pope Paul. Let us seek to improve the Church, by becoming better ourselves.

Each one of us and the whole Church could recite the prayer that I recite, "Lord, take me as I am, with my defects and failings, but make me become what You want me to be."

I must say a word also to our dear sick people, whom I see over there. You know, Jesus said, "I am hidden behind them; what is done to them is done to me." Therefore, in the persons we are venerating the Lord Himself, and let us hope that the Lord will be close to them, help them, and sustain them.

Over on the right, on the other hand, are the newlyweds *(applause)*. They have received a great sacrament, let us wish for them that the sacrament of matrimony that they have received may truly be the bearer not only of the good things of this world, but especially of eternal graces. A century ago, there lived in France Frederic Ozanam, a great professor. He taught at the Sorbonne. How eloquent, how brilliant! His friend was Lacordaire, who said, "He is so intelligent, and so good, this man, he will become a priest and become a great bishop!" No! He met a nice girl, and they got married. Lacordaire was very disappointed, and he said, "Poor Ozanam! Even he has been caught in the snare!" *(laughter)* But two years later, *(applause)* two years later, Lacordaire came to Rome, and was received by Pius IX. "Come now, Father," he says. "Come. I have always heard it said that Jesus instituted seven sacraments, now you come along, you change the words on me, and say that He instituted six sacraments — and a snare!" *(laughter)* "No," he said, "marriage is not a snare, *(applause)* it is a great sacrament!" And, therefore, let's congratulate these dear newlyweds again; may the Lord bless them!

5

Hope

General Audience Talk, September 20, 1978

The "second lamp of sanctification," for Pope John, was hope. An obligatory virtue for every Christian. Dante Alighieri, in his *Paradise,* imagined submitting to an examination in Christianity. There was a distinguished exam board. "Do you have faith?" St. Peter asked him first. "Do you have hope?" continued St. James. "Do you have love?" St. John finished. "Yes!" he said. "I have faith, I have hope, and I have love," and he proved it and was passed with highest marks (Par. 24-26).

Hope, therefore, is also a necessary virtue; an obligatory one, but not because of this, an unpleasant one. Anything but! A person who has hope travels in a world and in an atmosphere of trust and abandonment to God. It is like when we read the Psalms. "Lord," we say with the psalmist, "you are my rock, my help, my lamp, my savior, my shepherd, my salvation. Even if a whole army is camped against me, my heart will not fear, and if a battle is fought against me, my trust will not fail."

Some will say, "But isn't this psalmist too much of an optimist?" Did things always go straight for him? No. They didn't always go straight for him. He knows it, and he says it, that in this world often the scoundrels are the most fortunate, and the poor are the most oppressed. And he complains about it to the Lord. He goes so far as to say, "Why are you sleeping, Lord? Why are you silent? Wake up Lord! Hear me, Lord!" But his hope remains firm and unshakable. To him and to all those who hope, we can apply what Paul said of Abraham: "He believed, hoping against every hope" (Rom 4:18).

It is He, the Lord, Who kindles this hope in us. It carries us forward in life. Someone will ask, "But how is this possible?" It is possible. It is possible if we cling to three firm convictions. First, God is all-powerful. Second, God loves me immensely. Third, God is faithful to His promises. Then once this trust has been kindled in me by Him, the merciful God, I no longer feel alone, or abandoned, or isolated; instead I feel myself involved in a plan of salvation which, carried out with the help of the Lord, will lead to the joy of heaven.

I spoke of the Psalms, but the same certainty also vibrates in the speeches and writings of the saints. I would like you to read a homily that St. Augustine gave at Hippo one Easter. He explains the Alleluia, and he says, "The true Alleluia is up there, in heaven, because we will say it with a glory kindled by a love that is fulfilled. Down here, the Alleluia that we sing is the Alleluia of a love that hungers." That is what hope is for Augustine, hunger for the love of God.

Some will say, "But what if I am a poor sinner? What if I have a great many sins?" I will answer them as I answered, many years ago, to an unknown lady who came to me in confession. She was discouraged by life because, she said, "I have a very stormy moral life behind me." "May I ask," I said, "how old you are?" "Thirty-five." "Thirty-five? But you still might live forty or fifty years. You can still do a great deal of good, *signora*. Let go of the past. Repentant as you are, look towards the future, change your life with God's help. You will live, and everything will be changed."

And, on that occasion, I quoted my favorite author, St. Francis de Sales, who speaks of our "dear imperfections." Imperfections, but dear ones. And I explained, "You see, *signora,* God detests faults inasmuch as they are faults. But, from another point of view, God loves our faults because they are opportunities for Him to show His mercy, and for us to remain lowly, to be humble, and to understand and sympathize with the failings of others."

So you can see that the Pope is somewhat of an enthusiast for, and has a great liking for, this virtue of hope. I know, however, that not everyone is in agreement with me. The German Nietzsche is not in agreement. To him, hope is the virtue of the weak. He thinks that it makes Christians into irresolute, uncertain, isolated people who renounce the battle for social progress. Others speak of alienation, which prevents them from contributing to the human advancement of mankind. The council, however, is not of this opinion. It said, "The Christian message not only does not exempt Christians from the building up of a better world, but it obliges them to it with an even more binding commitment" (*Gaudium et Spes*, 34, cf. 39 and 57 and the Message of the Council Fathers to the World, October 20, 1962). It is right. We are still more obliged than everyone else to commit ourselves to this.

I also know that in the past, in the course of history, there have emerged some situations and some statements by Christians, by Catholics, who were too pessimistic in regard to mankind. However, the Church has disowned them. These statements have gradually been forgotten, thanks to a long line of holy, joyful, and hardworking people. . . . [A book has been written about Don Bosco] called *Don Bosco Laughing,* and about St. Alphonsus di Liguori, another book called *Monsignor Enjoys Himself.* And this pessimism has also been forgotten thanks to a Christian humanism, and to a line of ascetic writers whom the Frenchman, Saint-Beuve, would have called *les-doux,* "the gentle ones." And especially thanks to Catholic theology, which is made precisely to the measure of man, and very understanding. St. Thomas Aquinas, for example, in speaking of the virtues, gives an important place to *jucunditas,* or cheerfulness. And, he says, it consists of this: it allows a Christian to find an occasion in what he sees, and in what he hears, to be merry, to smile cheerfully (*Summa Theologicae,* II-II, q. 168, a. 2).

When I taught school, I used to say to my students, cheerful is what that Irish mason was who fell from a second-story scaffolding. He broke his legs. They took him to the hospital. The doctor and the nursing Sister came. "You poor man!" the Sister said, "You hurt yourself when you fell." "No, Mother," he said, "not exactly when I fell; when I hit the ground, that's when I hurt myself" *(laughter, applause).* It is a great virtue to find occasion in his legs to smile, and to make others smile too.

St. Thomas, and all of theology, in making smiling and joking into a real virtue, are in agreement with Christ, who preached the "Good News," with St. Augustine, who so strongly recommended *hilaritas;* they have defeated pessimism; they have vested Christian life with joy; and above all, they have stimulated us to take courage from the joys of every day, the good ones, of course, that the Lord never allows to be lacking, even though intermixed with some sorrows in life.

When I was a boy, I read the life of a Scotchman who moved to the United States with his parents and became the richest man in the world. And he says, "I was born in misery; nevertheless, I would not change the memories of my childhood for those of the rich, of the children of millionaires. What do they know about the joys of a family, about a mother who unites at one and the same time the jobs of nursemaid, washerwoman, cook, teacher, angel and saint?" He was employed; his name was Carnegie. He was employed in Pittsburgh for only $1.20 a month, a very poor salary. One evening, the paymaster said to him, "Wait." Carnegie thought, "Now they are going to fire me." Instead, after the others had gone, the paymaster said to him, "Andrew, I have observed your work. You produce more than the others. I have decided to raise your salary from $1.20 to $1.45." "I ran home, and my mother wept for joy. You speak to me of millions. I have made millions, but I would exchange them for the 25-cent raise I earned that time."

Necessary, along with Christian hope, and fitting for us, are these purely human joys. However, the Church says, "Don't absolutize them. They are something; they are not everything. They last a little while, not forever. They are a means; they cannot be the main goal." Of them, St. Paul has said, "Use them, but as if you did not use them, for the scene of this world is passing away" (cf. I Cor 7:31). And first Jesus said, "Seek first the kingdom of God" . . . and afterwards the rest (Mt 6:33).

To finish, and I have almost finished, I would like to speak of a kind of hope that is called Christian by a number of people. Sometimes it is not really completely Christian. I will explain what I mean. At the council, I was there and I signed, in 1962, the "Message of the Council Fathers to the World." There it said, more or less, "The Church's main task of *divinizing* should not make us forget the other, of *humanizing.*" I also signed *Gaudium et Spes.*

When Paul VI issued *Populorum Progressio,* I was moved and enthusiastic, I spoke, I wrote, even today I am truly convinced that enough can never be done by the hierarchy, by the Magisterium, to insist on [the importance of], to recommend the great problems of liberty, justice, peace, and development. And lay people can never commit themselves enough to resolving these problems.

I am speaking about Catholic lay people. At this moment an example comes to us from Camp David in Maryland. The American Congress burst into applause, which we heard too, when President Carter quoted the words of Jesus, "Blessed are the peacemakers." From Maryland, may that applause, may those words enter the hearts of all Christians, especially we Catholics, and may they make us peacemakers and workers for peace.

However, for me, it is wrong to state that civil, social, and political liberation coincide exactly with the message of salvation in Christ, to say that the *Regnum Dei* is to be identified with the *regnum hominis,* to say, it's happened that *Ubi Lenin, ubi Jerusalem.* There is some coincidence, but we cannot make them exactly the same. We have above all a spiritual goal.

At Frieburg, in the last few days, the people of Germany have, with great success, celebrated their *Katholikentag,* entitled "The Future of Hope." The word "future" was very fitting there because they were talking about the world. If, however, from the world, from society, we come to individual souls because souls must be saved one by one, it is not enough to speak of the future. We must also speak of eternity. St. Augustine, in the ninth book of the *Confessions,* quotes his conversation with his mother at Ostia, on the seashore, and he says, "The past forgotten, and looking towards the future, we asked ourselves, Mama and I, what this eternal life is like" *(Confessions* IX, no. 10). This is Christian hope. This is the kind of hope that Pope John meant. This is also what we mean when, with the catechism, we say, "My God, I hope to receive from Your goodness eternal life, and the graces I need to merit it through the good works I ought to do and want to do."

6

Love

General Audience Talk, September 27, 1978

First the Pope greeted the bishops, among whom there was also an oriental patriarch, Maximos V. Hakim.

"It is difficult to be a bishop. We must all pray for them."

"Oh, my God, I love You with all my heart, above everything else, for You are infinite Good and our eternal happiness. For love of You, I love my neighbor as myself, and forgive those who have offended me. O Lord, make me love You more and more."

It is a very well-known prayer, a whole mosaic of biblical texts. My mama taught it to me when I was little *(applause)*. My mama taught it to me, but I still recite it several times a day. And I will try to explain it to you, word for word, as if I were a simple parish catechist. So I am beginning what Pope John called "the third lamp of sanctification," love.

"I love," the first word.

When I was going to philosophy classes, the professor said to me, "Do you know the campanile of San Marco [in Venice]?" "Yes." "Well then, listen carefully. It means that the campanile has made a kind of journey towards you. It has left inside of you a kind of mental picture of itself. On the other hand, do you love the campanile of San Marco? The situation is reversed. It is you who goes toward it, impelled by that little mental picture." So you see, to love means to go towards the object loved with your mind, with your heart. *The Imitation of Christ* says it too, a person who loves *currit, volat, laetatur.* "The one who loves, runs, flies, and is happy" (Book 3, no . 4). He wants to. So then, to love God means to go towards God with your heart. A very beautiful journey!

When I was a boy, I used to go into ecstasy when I read about the journeys described by Jules Verne: *Twenty Thousand Leagues Under the Sea, Around the World in Eighty Days, Journey to the Center of the Earth, From the Earth to the Moon,* and so many others. However, the journey towards God is much more interesting. We read about it not in the novels of Verne, but in the lives of the saints.

Today, for example, we have St. Vincent de Paul, a giant of charity, who loved God as no one loves a mama or papa. And he gave himself completely to the poor, the prisoners, the orphans, and the sick. About another saint, Peter Claver, I have been reading, or rather rereading, these past few days that on the day that he consecrated himself to God, he signed this way, "Peter Claver, slave of the blacks forever."

These are interesting journeys, a little difficult sometimes, of course. However, we must not let ourselves be stopped by the difficulties. Jesus is on the cross. Do you want to give a kiss to Jesus on the cross? Dear friend, you cannot do it without bending over the cross and letting yourself be pierced by one of the thorns that Jesus has around His head (cf. St. Francis de Sales, *Oeuvres*, 21:153). You cannot appear like good St. Peter, who was very good at saying, "Long live Jesus," on Mount Tabor, where there was glory and joy. On the other hand, he did not even let himself be seen on Mount Calvary, where there was risk and suffering (*Ibid,* 15:140).

A sometimes difficult journey. And also a mysterious one because I do not start out on this journey loving the Lord, unless the Lord himself takes the initiative. Jesus said, "No one can come to me, unless my Father in heaven draws him" (Jn 6:44). And here, St. Augustine asks himself, "But then, if He draws me, what happens to human liberty?" Never fear! It is God Himself Who has willed this human liberty, Who has made it, and Who has placed it in us. He knows very well how to respect this liberty, even if He wants to bring us to the point where He wishes us to come. Augustine wrote, *"Parum est voluntate, etiam voluptate, traheris."* He says He draws you, but in such a way that you not only want, but you take pleasure in, you enjoy being drawn. Liberty respected. A mysterious journey.

"I love you with all my heart." I want to stress that "all." Totalitarianism, in politics, is an ugly thing. In religion, on the other hand, a kind of totalitarianism on our part towards God is very fitting. It is written, "You shall love the Lord your God, with all your heart, with all your mind, and with all your strength. Let these commandments of mine be fixed in your heart. You shall repeat them to your children, you shall speak of them seated in your home, on the street, while you walk, when you lay down at night, and when you rise in the morning. You shall write them on the doorposts and the doors of your house" (Deut 6:59).

Do you understand? This "all" repeated insistently, adapted to all the circumstances of life; this "all" truly becomes the banner of Christian maximalism. We must love God not just a little bit, but very much. God is too great, He has done too much for us, He is too deserving, for us to throw to Him, every now and then, only the crumbs of our time and our hearts, as if He were a poor Lazarus! He is infinite Good. He will be our eternal happiness! Money, pleasure, all the careers in this world are only fragments of good, only fleeting moments of happiness. It is not wise to give so much of ourselves to these things, and on the other hand to give God little of ourselves.

Then, it says, "with all my heart, above everything else." Here a comparison is made between God and things. Let's be careful. We must not say, "... either God or man." We must say, "I must love both God and man," but in a different way, however. Man, never love him more than God, never against God, never on the same level as God. The Bible speaks of Jacob, it calls him holy and loved by God (Dn 3:35; Mal 1:2; Rom 9:13). It sees him working for seven years to win Rachel for his wife, and it says, "Seven years passed like a few days, so much did he love his girl" (cf. Gen. 29:30). Francis de Sales writes a little commentary on it, on these words. And he says, "Jacob loves Rachel with all his strength. But with all his strength he also loves God." However, "God as God, above all other things, and more than himself; Rachel as his wife, above all other women, and as himself. God, with a sovereign, absolutely supreme love; Rachel with a maritally supreme love" (Francis de Sales, *Oeuvres*, 5:175). In other words, a love that must not be exclusive, but however, prevalent and supreme. In short, it is possible to love many other things.

Next, "For love of you, I love my neighbor as myself." Here, as with Jesus, the two loves are joined together, the love of God and the love of neighbor. The French say, *ces sont les freres jumeaux!* They are like twins, these two loves, they go together. God has willed it thus. How can I love my neighbor, or better, a certain type of neighbor, if first I do not love God? Certain facets I don't find attractive. Certain people have hurt me, or they annoy me. But I must love them all the same. I will succeed only if I extend to them the great love that I already have for God. They may not deserve it, Lord, but they are Your children, they are brothers and sisters of Christ, even these people. How ... *(here a man in the audience shouts something and the Pope laughs, while the audience applauds).*

And how? Not only in our words, but in our actions. We will take an exam at the end of our lives, and Jesus has already said what the questions He will ask us will be. "I was hungry in the persons of the least of My brothers, did you give Me anything to eat? I was sick, I was a prisoner, did you come to visit Me?" These are the questions. Here we will have to give an answer (cf. Mt. 25:34).

Taking these words and some others from the Bible, the Church has made two lists, seven corporal works of mercy, and seven spiritual ones. They are not complete. We should update them. For example, hunger. Today it is no longer a question only of this or that individual. It is whole peoples who are hungry. We all remember the great words of the great Pope Paul VI. "The peoples who are hungry are making a dramatic appeal to the peoples who live in opulence. The Church shudders at this cry of anguish and calls on everyone to respond with love to his brother" (*Populorum progresssio*, 3). And then, here justice is united to love. Because the Pope says, still in *Populorum Progresio*, "Private property is not undeniable and absolute for anyone. No one has the right to be able to make use of his goods exclusively for his own benefit, when others are dying because they have nothing" (*Ibid.*, 22). These are great words that we are given. In the light of these words, we must ask ourselves, not only as nations, but as private individuals, especially we who are members of the Church, have we really carried out the plan of Jesus, Who has said, "Love your neighbor as yourself"?

And forgiveness is also in the plan of Jesus, and it is perhaps the most difficult thing. But it almost seems as if He prefers forgiveness to the worship of God. "If you are standing in front of the altar to make your offering, and you remember that your brother has something against you, leave your offering there, go first to reconcile yourself with your brother, then return and make your offering" (Mt 5:23-24).

The last words.... Why, am I mistaken, or is there a fifth grade class here too? Can one of the children come up to help the Pope? Just one *(applause).* Just one . . . one! I was saying... *(sees boy coming up).* Come up, come up! *(applause; the Pope invites the boy over to the microphone)*

Pope: What grade are you in?

Daniele: Fifth grade.

Pope: Good. Now, listen carefully. Do you want to stay in the fifth grade again, or do you want to go to another grade next year?

Daniele: Um, it's all the same to me. But, um, I would like to stay in the fifth grade because otherwise, when I go to the sixth, I will lose my teacher. But . . . .

Pope: Well then, do you want to stay in the fifth, or do you want to go to the sixth?

Daniele: I want to stay in the fifth again.

Pope: Oh! *(laughs with the audience).* Well, this boy is different from the Pope because when I was in fourth grade, I used to say, "Oh, if only I were in fifth!" and when I was in fifth grade, I would say, "Who knows if I'll go to sixth, if they promote me!" Do you understand? What's your name?

Daniele: Daniele.

Pope: You see, Daniele, the Lord has put inside us a strong desire to make progress, to advance. Someone in first grade says, "Just wait until I'm in second." Someone in second grade says, "I can't wait until I'm in third." And it's the same with grown-ups too, you know. I knew a captain who said, "Oh, when are they going to make me a lieutenant colonel?" He wanted to advance too *(laughter)*. Everyone wants to advance. And this . . .*(he is interrupted by applause)*.

(He continues, to Daniele) The Lord has given us this strong desire to make progress. Look. We began by living in caves, in lake-dwellings, then in huts, then we put up houses, then palaces, now there are skyscrapers. Always advancing. At first we went on foot, then on horseback, on camels, then in carriages, then by train, now by airplane. Always advancing. This is the law of progress. But not only progress in traveling. I said before, I don't know if you were listening, that the love of God is a kind of journey. We must make progress here too. "Lord, make me love You more and more." Never stop. The Lord has said to all Christians, "You are the light of the world," "You are the salt of the earth," "Become perfect as your heavenly Father is perfect.". . . Here, never stop. Make progress, with the help of God, in loving God. All right? There, I'll let you go now *(he pats Daniele on the cheek; to the audience)*. Did you see how he helped me? *(applause)*.

We have sick people present here. Let's hope they recover. But *(applause)* let's really urge those in their families, and those who are looking after them, to take very good care of them. The Pope who is speaking to you has been to the hospital eight times, and has had four operations. And . . . it's not the same to have one nurse as it is another. There are some people who do it wholeheartedly. We do not only appreciate the service, we appreciate the way we are served, the way we are taken care of. So let's beg very earnestly that they be helped with great love and kindness.

Next, there are the young married couples. . . *(applause)*. Last time I quoted the council on marriage. But in *Gaudium et Spes* there is a note in which some passages of the Bible are recalled. There is one which refers to the bride and it says, "May you always be for me my joy," says the husband. And it also says a very charming thing, "lovely doe, may you always be, as you were in your youth, the joy of my old age," something like that (cf. Prv

5:18-19). Let's hope that the love of these married couples will always be preserved intact, as it is now *(applause)*.

There is also a large group representing the airmen from the central school in Viterbo, with their commandant and officers. I don't know very much about the Air Force, but a nephew of mine, who came the other day to say hello to me, right after I was elected Pope, who has been a soldier for a short time... "What branch are you in?" "The Air Force!" he said — and he said it proudly! Obviously, being in the Air Force must be a very fine thing, *(laughs)* so let's give them our best wishes! *(applause)*.

To English-Speaking Pilgrims:

Dear Sons and Daughters:

Your presence is a great joy for me, because I love you all very much. And it is about love that I want to speak to you today. For Pope John, love was the third lamp of holiness. From our mothers, we all learned a prayer that goes more or less like this, "O my God, I love You with all my heart, above everything else. I love my neighbor as myself for love of You. I forgive all who have offended me. O Lord, make me love You ever more."

The words of this prayer help us to understand love. Love is like a journey, which we run towards the object of love. To love God is a wonderful journey! But sometimes it involves sacrifice. We cannot embrace Christ on the cross without being hurt by a thorn.

With all my heart, these words mean that God is too great for us to throw Him only the crumbs of our love. He desires all our heart.

And we must love God above all else. Love for God prevails, but it is not exclusive.

There is also love of neighbor. These two loves are twins and they go together. Jesus spoke about the importance of loving our neighbors when He said, "I was hungry and you gave me food." And Paul VI reminded us that there are whole peoples who are hungry and waiting for our fraternal love. Private property is not an absolute right, and the arms race is a scandal. From these things, we can see that as individuals and peoples we have still not fulfilled the command of Jesus, to love our neighbors as ourselves.

Christ tells us also how important it is to forgive. He seems to give forgiveness priority even over worship. Because love is a journey, we must not stop. Our heavenly Father wants us perfect like Himself. God wants us to make progress in love.

With my Apostolic Blessing.

7

The Lesson of the Christmas Donkey

December 24, 1977

Of the figures of the Christmas crib, the most humble is the donkey. Will a patriarch who brings him to the attention of readers cause a scandal? I hope not. As children, they presented us with Pinocchio transformed into a little donkey as a punishment; later we saw at the theater *Class de asen*, a comic trifle by Ferravilla, in which the standout was the composition written by Massinelli, so inventive that it seemed like a geometric line made up of length without breadth and depth, in which the connecting thread was the recurring phrase, "Oh, what a beautiful feast! Oh, what a beautiful feast!" Later still, to tell the truth, with little sensitivity towards our neighbors, we have heard so many times those presumed to be ignorant defined as "men with their brains in their backs" and as "donkeys." Let's confess it, we are unfavorably disposed to this figure. Christ, on the other hand, actually wanted to mount a gentle donkey on His entrance into Jerusalem, and Francis Jammes, the Pascoli of France, sang with love of the donkey in his poetry. St. Francis of Assisi, accustomed to calling his body "Brother Ass," asked its pardon at the point of death for having treated it too harshly.

Donkeys are tenacious workers. We don't see them very much in our country now, but in the past how many baskets we saw them carrying on their sides and how many dented cans on their backs; how many mountebanks' wagons they pulled and how many little carts. As a child, I met them with close-fitting pants put on their slender legs to hide the livid and purulent wounds from the flies that otherwise would have thrown themselves avidly on them in swarms. And they pulled the two-wheeled cart just the same, poor things!

Now I want to issue a warning that it seems to me that at this moment of serious crisis, we must all "pull the cart" without slacking off, without unjustified absenteeism at the office or the factory. If you are really sick, stay at home, but it is an ugly fact that nonexistent troubles or pretended illnesses are often covered up by the "trousers" of complacent medical certificates or pretended excuses, that exempt us from being at our jobs. A nation can only rise up from its ills with sacrifice and serious continued work, not work that is constantly interrupted by strikes. Nor can schools lift themselves up.

Today, we want schools that are "run democratically," "integrated," "full time," or "permanent," with parascholastic and extrascholastic activities, and subsidies. You can't have more scholastic work than this. Good, as long as the "new school" really makes students study more and work harder. But what if, instead, school is disturbed by too many student protest lines, demonstrations, and interventions by the police? What if on the pretext of "pluralism" there were to be a moral subjugation of the students and free-wheeling actions by the teachers? What if the very minute prescriptions of the law about the "card" imposes on the principals and teachers a disproportionate amount of work, which is not teaching and which doesn't help teaching?

The donkey has also always been the friend of poor people. A popular Greek legend says that Satan has been opposed to God from the beginning and whenever God created something, Satan would try to make another of his own to oppose it. Thus it was one day that Satan made a donkey. But he was not capable of giving it life. When he set out on the road, he went to the Lord and said to Him, "You give him life." God listened to him, but in His own way. "Get up, donkey," He said, "and from now on be the right arm of the poor." The legend continues that the poor people who cannot afford to keep a mule or a horse, own a donkey. They load him with bundles of wood and make him carry them home; they load him with grain and he carries it to the mill; they load him with manure and the donkey carries it to the fields. The donkey is the best help, and without him the life of the poor would be too harsh.

What can we say now about people of great worth who resolve to be nothing else in life but the "donkeys" of the poor? Ignazio Silone recounts on an unforgettable page how, as a child traveling from Rome to a boarding school in Liguria, he met Don Luigi Orione at the station. He saw an ordinary little priest there to look after him and other boys. He was irritated because the famous Don Orione had not come and [he] allowed the priest to load himself up with his suitcases and his bundles, without lifting a finger to help him. Once they were in the train, the little priest asked him if he wanted a newspaper. "Yes, *Avanti!* [the socialist newspaper]," Silone answered in a provocative tone. The priest got off the train. He reappeared a short time later and brought him *Avanti*. Later, still on the train, the boy asked, "Why didn't Don Orione come?" The priest answered, "I am Don Orione; forgive me for not introducing myself." "I was stunned," Silone confessed. "I felt despicable and vile.... I stammered my apologies for having let him transport my suitcases and the rest. He smiled and confided to me his happiness at being able to carry suitcases for impertinent boys like me.... I also made a confidence that my vocation would be to be able to live like an authentic donkey of God, like an authentic donkey of Providence."

It is beautiful, especially today, when there are so many poor people, so many also who speak or write for the "marginalized," but few authentic "donkeys" who agree to load themselves with other people's burdens. What a pain at times to find families who could keep their old people at home without great hardship, but instead get rid of them, "unloading" them on the nursing home. But then, it is a duty to remain close to these relatives with visits and affection often, but instead, they never, or almost never, go to visit them, leaving them sorrowful and feeling that they are forgotten.

The last lesson, which comes from the donkey, is patience and gentleness. Look at him. He lowers his head gently, and when he stops, he puts his little hooves together in such a meek way that it moves us to sympathy. Even when the horseflies, bees, and flies attack him, he defends himself only with a quick flick of his ears. Poor thing, he is not really made for the bold action necessary today to produce greater justice in the world, and much less for times in which the fashion is violence based on kidnappings, Molotov cocktails, threatening writings, and constant talk of revolution. He would certainly understand the good mama, who gets her little girl ready, neat, and clean and all dressed up for school and covers her textbook with flowered paper. But he would not understand what is written inside that textbook so lovingly covered: "Revolutions are a necessary consequence... if the oppressed proletariat ends up being driven to a revolution... we will defend the cause of the proletariat with action." It is up to us to know that these words printed in a fifth-grade textbook resemble, like one drop of water does another, others pronounced by Lafayette on February 20, 1790, before the French Constituent Assembly, "Insurrection is the holiest of duties." That time, insurrection really broke out and became the French Revolution. It resolved some problems, but created a good many others, causing rivers of blood to flow. There was a fashion during that time for what we call today *samizdat* (underground publications) and among them the work *Considerations on France* by Joseph de Maistre, printed three times in 1796, enjoyed a great success. It reads, "No despot gambled with the life of a people as the Jacobins did, and no people gave themselves up more passively to the slaughter... the Revolution, after having punished the sins of the monarchy and the aristocracy, punished its own and devoured itself.... Of the presidents of the Convention, 18 were guillotined, eight deported, and six imprisoned. Of the members, 70 were guillotined and 130 deported," and yet the intentions of those who had kindled insurrection and revolution at the beginning had been very good ones, and the slogan proclaimed constantly was "Liberty, Fraternity, Equality." But once the riverbanks are broken, who can control the waters any longer? Jeanne Roland, a major figure in the Revolution, understood this. It did not help her to be the wife of the minister Roland. The public did not allow her to defend herself before the Tribunal because though she was a revolutionary, she was a Girondin. When brought to the scaffold, she bowed to the Statue of Liberty and said, "O Liberty, how many crimes are committed in your name."

I return to the donkey and to Francis Jammes who sang of him. The poet even composed a "prayer to go to heaven with the donkeys." He writes in it, "When the time comes for me to come to You, my God, I will take my staff and on the highroad, I will say to my friends the donkeys, 'Come poor beasts, let me be yoked, my God, to these animals I love so much.'" I don't think I can make this prayer mine. It is enough for me to be able to go to heaven after learning the road from Jesus, from my Mother and His, from the saints, and why not? It may help also from the humble donkey of the Christmas crib.

8

Never Lose Heart

Liberation from Sin

Christmas Homily, December 25, 1972

*O*nce again it is Christmas. Once more in every church and in every home a Christmas crib has been prepared. Before it on this day, grown-ups and children, moved and contrite, repeat with St. Alphonsus Liguori:

> *You, the world's creator*
> *have no clothes or fire, O my Lord,*
> *O blessed God!*
> *Ah, how much it cost you*
> *To have loved us!*

These seem like naive words. But they faithfully translate the biblical words, on which we should meditate as we adore, "for your sake he became poor, although he was rich" (II Cor 8:9). "He has loved me and given himself up for me" (Gal 2:20). "God so loved the world that he sacrificed his only begotten Son, so that everyone who believes in him might not perish, but might have eternal life" (cf. Jn 3:16).

What is striking, first of all, in this love, is that God has loved us in spite of our sins. "It is rare that someone should wish to die for a just man," says St. Paul. And he continues, "Christ, on the other hand, died for us while we were still sinners" (cf. Rom 5:7-8). He has loved us without cherishing any illusion about our innocence. Once some people who came along while He was speaking told Him that a group of Galileans had been massacred by Pilate. And Jesus said, "Do you think that because these Galileans suffered this way, they were greater sinners than all other Galileans? By no means! But I tell you, unless you repent, you will all perish as they did" (Lk 13:2-3).

Therefore, we are all sinners. The apostles themselves, treated by Christ not as servants but as friends, were not loved by Him because they were innocent and holy; they had their faults and failings too, and Christ had to correct them. "Do you still not understand?" He said to them one time. "Are your hearts hardened? You have ears, do you not hear?" (Mk 8:17-18). Another time He said to good, generous Peter, "Get behind me, Satan; you are an obstacle to me. Your thoughts are not those of God, but those of human beings" (Mt 16:23).

The reality is that Christ knew about life and He knew human beings. There are dark depths within each of us, from which emerge every now and then outbursts and explosions of passion; and there are, even in the most wicked, luminous zones, from which come thoughtful and generous actions. Christ knew this. This is why His first sermon was "Repent" (Mk 4:17). This is why He kept repeating, "Do not judge that you might not be judged. . . . Why do you notice the splinter in your brother's eye but do not perceive the wooden beam in your own eye?" (Mt 7:13). This is why He stared down the accusers of the woman taken in adultery, those who wanted to condemn that poor woman at any cost, and then turning to her, said, "Woman . . . neither do I condemn you; go, and from now on, sin no more" (Jn 8:11).

Not only has He loved us, but He has loved us like a brother, putting Himself among us, trying to resemble us in everything, except for sin. Like the poorest of us, He worked and sweated; He knew hunger and thirst. He was persecuted by persistent and cruel adversaries. He wept for Jerusalem, His country, and for Lazarus His friend. After telling us to choose the last places and declaring that He had come to serve, He knelt like a slave and washed the feet of His apostles.

Yesterday, on Christmas Eve, the genealogy of Jesus was read at Mass. It contains the story of His ancestors. Usually people stress the glories of their house and modestly draw a veil over the less respectable events. Instead, Jesus wanted the story of His earthly family to be written without any veil. And so we find among His ancestors just men like the patriarchs and the pious Hezekiah; repentant sinners like David and Solomon; and outright criminals like Ahaz, Amon, and Manasseh. Of the four women named, the only one who makes something of a good impression is Ruth, a young widow and affectionate and faithful daughter-in-law, who remarries after a curious pastoral idyll. The other three, Rahab, Tamar, and Bathsheba, on the other hand, are stained respectively by prostitution, incest, and adultery. What graciousness and humility! The immaculate Lamb agrees — rather, orders — that things of this kind be written in His family history in order to hearten us, as though to say to us, "Never lose heart! You can become good, in spite of a wicked past, whether yours or your family's!"

A last consideration. He has loved us, because we are poor. For Christ, however, the poorest among the poor are sinners. They are the ones described in the great parables of the lost lamb, of the coin found again, of the prodigal son welcomed with jubilation in the arms of his father (cf. Lk 15). Before me are the words of St. Paul. "A teaching that is trustworthy and deserves full acceptance is this, Christ Jesus came into the world to save sinners, the greatest of whom am I" (I Tm 1:15). What strikes me still more are the words and actions of Jesus. He was at dinner in the house of Zaccheus, a sinner and a rich man. Everyone was whispering about it, but Christ said to the grumblers, "This man too is a descendant of Abraham . . . the Son of Man has come to seek out and save what was lost" (Lk 19:9-10). Of course, Jesus also taught us to ask the Father for our daily bread, but He said, "Man does not live on bread alone" (Mt 4:4); "Seek first the kingdom of God and his righteousness" (Mt 6:33).

Some people today try to maintain that Christ called human beings to fight against existing structures and preached social revolution. Oscar Cullman, a Protestant, has thoroughly and brilliantly refuted this thesis. Christ was too profound and saw too deeply to expect remedies for poverty from a revolution. "The poor," He said, "you will always have with you" (Jn 12:8). He never said, "With my religion I will make all the poor rich"! He never thought that to work hard for heaven was alienation and would disturb the work for human progress and liberty. He said, "Provide money bags for yourselves that do not wear out, an inexhaustible treasure in heaven that no thief can reach, and no moth can destroy, for where your treasure is, there will your heart be also" (Lk 12:33-34). He did love poverty, but why? Because it is the means for detaching hearts from the goods of this world and sharpening the desire for salvation. He did say "blessed are the poor," but because they are usually readier than the rich to listen to the Word of God, and to hunger and thirst for religious righteousness.

He was a fighter, who harshly reproved the Pharisees. It is true. "He was a political fighter," some hasten to say. At the trial of Jesus, the leaders were indeed moved by political aims. They did indeed exploit the religious positions of the Pharisees for their own ends, but the Pharisees were very little concerned with politics. In reality, they formed the party of religious legalism. They made religion consist solely of traditional, external observances. And Christ said to them, "You have nullified the word of God for the sake of your tradition" (cf. Mt 15:6). They despised the simple. They were proud, even in prayer, and Christ put them to shame by the parable of the Pharisee and the publican. The first exalts himself and is humbled, the second humbles himself and is exalted (Lk 18:9-14). Some still insist, "Christ pronounced a series of 'Woe to you's' against the Pharisees! Only a political or union agitator could pronounce them with so much force and vehemence!" But similar reproaches against fellow Jews are found in the prophet Isaiah, and they are all reproaches for religious reasons. The Essenes too were concerned solely with religion, and yet they reproved the Pharisees with the same words as Christ. [Jesus] called them "whitened sepulchers." The Essenes called them "those who cover themselves with whitewash."

In turn, the accusations of the Pharisees against Jesus are strictly religious ones. He forgives the paralytic's sins, and they say, "This man blasphemes. Who can forgive sins but God?" (Mk 2:7). Jesus says, "I am the Lord of the Sabbath," and they reproach Him for "making himself equal to God" (Jn 5:18). It is a perversion of both the gospel and Christ to say that those who refuse to support a violent social revolution are not Christian. Those who make Christianity consist completely and solely of changing social structures are "putting on shoes that are too tight," says German Bishop [now Cardinal] Franz Hengsbach. Even if we were to succeed in eliminating all social and economic miseries from the world, there would still be the problem of achieving the liberation of human beings from sin, the greatest misery in all human history.

———

My brothers and sisters!

This Christmas, I hear that many people are talking about bread, liberation, justice, and peace! And this is very good; we must associate ourselves with them. But Christ taught us to say "forgive us our trespasses . . . and lead us not into temptation, but deliver us from evil." May this humble and fervid prayer also well up from the depths of our hearts and be laid before God made man lying in the manger in Bethlehem!

9

Christ, the Physician of Souls

Christmas Homily 1976

The Savior has been born, this is the old and always new announcement of Christmas. But why was He born? So that we might be born again. It happened to us first at our baptism, which made us children of God. It happens on many other occasions. When, after having fallen into faults, sins, or vices, we get up again with a firm resolve, forewarned and accompanied by the grace of the Lord, this, for us, is to be born again.

During the past few days, in speaking with a number of different people, I have found them discouraged about the moral situation of the world. There is evil, unfortunately, but there also exists much good, which usually neither appears nor is allowed to appear in the press. But we who believe in a Christ Who is alive, close to us, and our Savior, can't lose faith in "Operation Rebirth," which has three aspects: the sick person, Christ the physician, and the proper therapy.

1. Morally sick, that is sinners, we all are, to some extent. "Father, forgive us our debts"; not being angels, we all often fall into some shortcoming, and we live in this world almost like people in some kind of "hospital for incurables." "On Jacob's ladder the angels have wings, but they do not fly, they climb up one rung at a time. The same with the soul [that] is climbing from sin towards the peak of devotion. It is like the dawn, it does drive away the darkness, but little by little; it is like illnesses which come riding on horseback, but which go slowly and on foot." "Often we waste too much time in trying to be good angels, but we neglect to be good men and women . . . we cannot walk without touching the ground; agreed, we shouldn't lay down or roll around on the ground, but neither should we think we can fly because we are

127

little birds who do not yet have wings." I am speaking, as you can see, of good people.

But also about the saints, if Father Grou [Jean Grou, S.J.] was able to write, "The greatest saints are not those who commit fewer sins; but rather those who have more courage and generosity; who make greater efforts to conquer themselves; who are not afraid of falling and also of dirtying themselves a little, as long as they go forward." "Those who never engage in battle," says St. John Chrysostom, "will never be wounded; those who throw themselves ardently into battle against their enemies, on the other hand, are often wounded."

About these moral battles de Maistre [Joseph de Maistre, Catholic apologist] wrote, "The only lost battle is one which we think we have lost." And St. Francis de Sales, in battles for goodness, "we are victors as long as we are ready to fight."

Turning to more serious cases, for example, to Christians who seem to be gangrenous with bad habits and vice, Paul VI says, "No case of human evil is desperate in the school of the gospel."

There is the vivid example of [Venerable] Matt Talbot, a simple English porter, who will be beatified within a short time. He belonged to a deeply Christian family, but, after he was sent to work when he was twelve years old in an environment that wasn't very good, he quickly began to give himself up to alcohol, and was ruined. He drank away all his salary; he would even pawn his clothes for a drink. Every now and then, when his brother and sister begged him, he would go to confession, and try to mend his ways, but he would quickly fall again; so it went for fifteen whole years. One Saturday evening at the pub, his companions, instead of paying for the usual drink for him, cruelly made fun of him. Humiliated and deeply depressed, he reflected on his wretched situation. The following morning he made up his mind. He went to confession and began his new life. He promised to abstain completely from all liquor; first for three months, then for a year, then forever.

He kept his promise. Not only that, as an honest worker, he sent home part of his salary. The rest he gave to those poorer than himself, keeping for himself merely what was necessary. And he prayed. And he became an apostle of harmony and solidarity, greatly loved by the workers. He died at the age of sixty-nine in 1925.

2. A physician for the morally sick is Jesus Christ, who declared, "People who are in good health do not need a doctor, but sick people do.... It is mercy I desire and not sacrifice ... and I have come to call not the self-righteous, but sinners" (Mt 9:12-13).

And He made it clear what kind of relationship He wanted to have with sinners. He became close to them and allowed them to become close to Him; if they did not have the courage, He invited Himself to their homes, as in the case of Zaccheus. The title attributed to Him by the Pharisees was "the friend of sinners" (Lk 7:34). He had an immense liking for the tax collector who, once he had repented, prayed, "Be merciful to me, a sinner" (Lk 18:13). It was enough for Him that the thief crucified with Him repented, and immediately He assured him, "This day you will be with me in paradise" (Lk 23:43). The adulterous woman and the other sinful woman were scorned and judged harshly. He not only forgave them, but, once they repented, He defended them. And He also defended all the sinners of this world from malicious barbs when He ordered, "If you want to avoid judgment, stop passing judgment.... Why look at the speck in your brother's eye, when you miss the plank in your own" (Mt 7:1, 3)? "Do not condemn, and you will not be condemned" (Lk 6:37). Because we are sinners, we are morally exhausted, and He encourages us, "Come to me all you who are weary ... and I will refresh you" (Mt 11:28).

St. Paul perhaps remembered this invitation when he wrote, "When I am powerless, it is then that I am strong" (II Cor 12:10), strong, of course, with the power of Christ, Whose power shows forth best in our weakness. With the same faith, although feeling poor and small, Paul was able to write, "In him who is the source of my strength, I have the strength for everything" (Phil 4:13).

3. The treatment or therapy for moral illnesses begins when the sick person recognizes that he needs God. St. Paul said, "By the grace of God, I am what I am" (I Cor 15:10). In the hospital, the sick people who are on the ground floor go up to the third or

fourth floor by means of the elevator. "My elevator," said Thérèse of the Child Jesus, "is the divine arms." Before her, the Bible, "Who will give me the wings of a dove to fly and find rest? (Ps 55:7)? Who but God? The Church has us pray like this, "Lord, precede our good actions by Your inspiration; continue them by helping them, so that all our prayers and our every work may begin and end with You." Let us act, therefore, as if everything depended on us; let us pray as if everything depended on God. Let us look at ourselves. Let us look at God. We will see a divine mercy wholly concerned with our misery and our misery as the constant object of divine mercy. Here we must have a serene and optimistic realism. A melancholy man, Faber said, will never be a cured man, but always a convalescent in the hospital of God. Have my efforts been successful? Good, it is an incentive to try greater things. Is there a failure instead? Good all the same, it is an invitation to begin again with fidelity. The best method of becoming good, in fact, is to always begin all over again and never think that we have done enough. Of course, it is better to die than to seriously offend the Lord; however, if we have fallen into serious sin, it is better to lose everything else rather than to lose hope and the decision to begin again. Has it happened? No use crying over spilt milk, on your feet immediately, and on your way again, with courage, as if the sin had never happened.

And know how to derive profit from your own sins. "All things work together to the good of those who love God" (Rom 8:28), St. Paul wrote. St. Augustine commented, everything, "even falling into sin because from sin we can rise again more humble, more cautious, and more fervent."

St. Francis de Sales went so far as to speak of our "beloved imperfections." Why "beloved?" Because they make us aware of our misery, they give us practice in humility, patience, and diligence. The saint insists, these imperfections should be regretted, of course, but they must not discourage us, not make an impression; "they should be hated insofar as they are imperfections; they are to be loved, since they allow us to experience firsthand our own nothingness and since they are matter for God's mercy."

Another fruit that we can derive from our sins is the ability to understand and sympathize with others. I think of the prophet Elijah. He is the most terrible of all the Old Testament prophets. He proclaims from on high that God is an "intransigent and universal" God; in the name of Yahweh he sends drought and rain, and he has hundreds of false priests killed. However, before the anger of Jezebel, a woman, he flees precipitously.

More emblematic is the case of Peter. He is generous, sincere, and attached to his teacher; and yet he denies Him three times. Why did Christ permit him to fall in this way and then put him at the head of the Church? In order to teach him, I think, to treat the apostles as his brothers and the faithful with mercy.

The *Imitation of Christ* says, "We are all frail, but you must think that there is no one more frail than you."

This is the thought of authentic Christian humility. It may do us some good on the day on which Christ lowered Himself from His throne in heaven to a stable in Bethlehem. With this I close, wishing all of you a holy Christmas.

10

The Way of the Magi

Homily for Epiphany, January 6, 1962

Today I will offer some reflections on the Magi and on the road they traveled.

1. Who were the Magi? princes? astrologers? philosophers? Very learned men? I can't say for sure. But I can say this for sure, the Magi were men "called by God." And I can also describe for you the mechanism of their call.

First there was an external element at work, the star, which brought them the message from God, through their eyes. Then there was an invisible, internal, divine aid at work, which shed light into their minds and exerted pressure on their wills. Finally, came their response to the message, "Yes, it's decided; let's start out."

A similar call and a similar mechanism are also operating for us, "Called by God" — to what? Perhaps what I say will seem new to you, but I assure you that it is as old as Christianity: we have been called to be true saints.

Some people are probably thinking, "I'll bet now our bishop is addressing the seminarians, who are up front in the first pews. Or he is probably talking to the Sisters, who are scattered throughout the cathedral."

No, I am talking to everyone. The Lord invites and obligates everyone to sanctity. "But I am married," some will say. Married people are also called. St. Louis IX was married and a king; St. Elizabeth of Hungary and St. Margaret of Scotland were married and queens. Marriage was elevated by Christ to the dignity of a sacrament precisely for this reason, so that it would not be a wall, an obstacle, but a ladder and a help to the sanctification of husbands and wives. When Frederick Ozanam was married, Lacordaire [Jean Baptiste, orator] commented, "He too has been caught in the snare." But Pope Pius IX said to Lacordaire, "Dear Father, I had always heard that Christ thought of seven sacraments. Now you are going around saying that he instituted six sacraments plus a snare."

Saints have come from all corners of the world: St. Aloysius Gonzaga; St. Wenceslaus; St. Canute and St. Edward from the royal and princely courts; St. Zita and St. Gemma Galgani from the kitchens, which they ruled as domestic servants; St. Sebastian and St. Martin of Tours from the army; St. Isidore and St. Maria Goretti from the fields. Even the businessmen have their saints, like St. Homobonus of Cremona. And even the lawyers. In fact, this humorous little stanza made the rounds in the Middle Ages:

> *Sanctus tvo erat Britto,*
> *Advocatus et non Iatro*
> *Res miranda populo.*
> *(St. Yves was from Brittany,*
> *A lawyer, yet not a thief.*
> *Something amazing and almost incredible.)*

I said this is not a question of a simple invitation, but an obligation. God must have reasoned more or less like this, "Lazy and dull as they are, they will never make up their minds; neither to take advantage of their opportunities, nor to be spiritually great and rich. I must impose it on them and make it an obligation. They are half deaf and half blind; they need thunder and lightning." And He made it an obligation. He sent thunder and lightning.

And, on the other hand, who is God? Someone Who is worth more than all the treasures, than all the worlds put together. What would He have looked like, if He had said, "Love me only a little bit?" No, He spoke strongly, He said the only thing that He could have said, "You shall love me with all your heart, with all your strength, and with all your soul." And He expects, as they would say today, a "responsible and irrevocable choice." "Whoever acknowledges me before men, I will acknowledge before my Father in heaven; whoever disowns me before men, I will disown before my Father in heaven" (Mt 10:32-33). And He continued, "Whoever loves father or mother, son or daughter, more than me is not worthy of me" (Mt 10:37).

He wants us, then, to love Him with all our hearts, above everything else, and anyone who does this is really already a saint. God knows that sanctity already possessed, held tightly in the hand, is an arduous thing, and while He demands it, He is happy with a sincere daily effort to arrive at sanctity. When we say in our prayers, "My God, I love You with all my heart above everything else," it is understood that, as a minimum, we are saying, "My God, I want to be a saint. I will try to be a saint." But let us beware. It must be a prayer, not a lie.

The mechanism [that] we saw working with the Magi also holds good for us. Instead of the star, the external element for us might be a sermon, a page, or a sentence from the gospel, a good example, even an illness or a period of mourning. A friend has died suddenly, our heart sinks, we say to ourselves, what if it happens to you? Think about it. Do something. Don't waste any more time. It is one of so many external messages, through which God calls us to sanctity.

More powerful, however, are the internal messages. God is a fisherman right in the middle of our souls. He throws the hook; He wants to catch a little fish, which is us. But nothing will happen, unless He pulls us. "No one," Jesus said, "can come to me unless the Father draws him" (Jn 6:44). For this reason, St. Augustine used to repeat, "Lord, first grant to me to do what You command me to do; then command me and I will do it."

We are actually at His mercy; without Him we can accomplish no supernatural good.

Our decision, however, also remains absolutely necessary. I suppose that the seminarians, who I have in front of me, have also risen this morning at the sound of the bell. It is still a bell of the old system. It interrupts our sleep. It recalls our duty to get out of bed. It also, at times, brings to mind the beautiful things that await us during the day that is beginning, but it stops there. It has not gotten so far as to gently "scoop" my seminarians up and put them on the floor of their rooms. They must get from the bed to the floor by themselves, but by a free decision and by making, let's also call it that, a "free and responsible choice."

God's help is like this. "Get up. Up from that bed of sins, blasphemies, and those bad habits," says God, and He helps us and makes it easy for us and accompanies us in the effort. But what if we turn on our other side and say, "Afterwards. Later. When it isn't too cold. When it isn't so dark." Nothing now happens, and a grace of the Lord is wasted. So keep an eye on the "choices." St. Thomas wrote to his sister, "To become saints? It takes only one thing, to want it." He knew that another thing is also necessary — the help of God — but he was quite certain that it is offered to everyone. Let's look to our "choices," and let's be people of good will.

2. And now, a few reflections on the way of the Magi. It was one road, traveled by all three together, not free from adventures. And, in fact at one point, the star could no longer be seen. Then they ran into Herod. Then they needed to have the Bible explained by the doctors of law in Jerusalem. Then they arrived at their goal.

The way of holiness is also one in its substance. It is true that the way the commandments and the virtues are practiced by a Carthusian in a monastery is one thing, and the way it is practiced by a married man at home or in a factory is another. One stamp impresses Franciscan spirituality on souls, another the spirituality of St. Ignatius. But these are quite incidental things. In Rome, when they proceed to "make" saints, whether they are young or old, bishops or Sisters, the rigorous, minutely detailed examination always revolves around the same outline, "Has this person practiced the virtues to a heroic degree or not? Especially the theological and cardinal ones?" If so, the cause for beatification goes ahead; if not, it stops. And neither do they go in search of tremendous deeds. One sentence, plus a second, plus a third, and so on, bring forth a book. One brick joined to another, a little at a time, produces a house. Little acts of virtue, joined to one another, without pause, for a period of years and years, mixed with great love of God and neighbor, produce the holiness of the altars.

We can say of many saints what Pius XI said of St. Benilde [Pierre Romançon] of the Brothers of the Christian Schools: "His life was all modesty and silence, completely ordinary and everyday. But how much that was not ordinary and not everyday in that everyday. The everyday which always turns out to be the same, which always has the same concerns, the same weaknesses, the same miseries, has rightly been called the 'terrible everyday'. . . . how much extraordinary virtue is necessary to accomplish the whole complex of ordinary things that fill our everyday life with extraordinary care, or rather, not with the ordinary and everyday and therefore frequent carelessness, negligence, and superficiality, but with attention, piety, and inner fervor of spirit."

On the way of holiness, everyone must make an effort; of course, it is a "narrow way." But to the effort is joined serene peace because the Lord has said, "My yoke is easy and my burden light" (Mt 11:30). Surliness and holiness therefore clash, and when someone said to me, "I too have seen holy people, but they were gloomy, grim, frowning, sour, and hypocritical." I answered, "Friend, I am afraid that you are mistaken; if anything, those were sick people, not saints. They either had liver trouble or stiff necks or heartburn." Saints are happy, even when they embrace a very severe life. Wasn't St. Romuald, the founder of the Camaldolese hermits? And yet he was humorous, as a young man and as an old man. Even when they were close to death, some martyrs have found the strength to make a joke. So it was with St. Lawrence, who said while roasting on a gridiron, "I think I have been cooked enough on this side now." So with St. Thomas More, who asked the executioner to respect his beard while the ax was falling. "It has done nothing wrong, poor thing, it is really innocent."

Just as on the way of the Magi, a Herod also appears on the way of the saints. It may be sin; it may be concupiscence.

The saints are subject to sin; venial, of course, but they are subject to it. When, saying the "Our Father," they say, "Forgive us our trespasses," it's not that they are paying a compliment or speaking out of humility, or thinking about their neighbor's sins. They must beat their breasts for their own sins, and go to confession. "But then, what's so great about that?" you will say.

This is what is great, that the saints trust in the grace of God, even when they find themselves flat on the ground. And they have the courage and humility to turn and continually begin again.

Dante wrote, "Here begins the new life," only once, at the beginning of a book. The saints say every morning, by their actions, "Today, Lord, begins the new life. It doesn't matter at all that yesterday I got into mischief and came up with some real disasters. We have a working agreement, You and I, Lord; no confidence in me, unlimited confidence in You," "When I am weak, then I am strong" (II Cor 12:10). In this way, they make progress. On the other hand, those who, after the first tumbles, start to whine and say that they did not believe they were so weak, so inconstant, remain there, still planted in their own spot.

Another tyranny, which everyone, saints included, must reckon with, is concupiscence. Even the saints are divided. They carry inside them the famous "old man," who, when he is bound, gagged, and soundly beaten, always finds a way to free himself and return to cause trouble. They too pray to be liberated from this constant annoyance, and they hear the answer, "My grace is enough for you" (II Cor 12:9).

This is the way. It is exactly like the way of the Magi. At every street corner, there may be a new adventure, a new danger. The struggle, the spiritual Herod, and the ancient serpent await us. But awaiting us also is the Lord Jesus, the invincible captain, Who covers us with His shield, nourishes us with His body and His blood, and washes us with confession.

Let's keep the appointment, let's make the true "responsible choice," let's become saints.

11

Proper Veneration of the Real Presence

Homily for the Feast of Corpus Christi, June 13, 1963

A few minutes ago, as a bishop and spiritual leader, I asked the Lord for this grace for me and for my faithful, *sacra mysteria venerari*; to be able to venerate properly the Most Holy Eucharist.

I know seven ways of honoring the Eucharist, and I will expound on them to all of you this evening.

The *first* way is the Holy Mass.

On the cross, on Good Friday, Jesus was not so much a great prophet, Who was killed by others; rather, He was the great priest Who presented Himself to God the Father in the name of all humanity and said, "No one takes my life from me, but I lay it down on my own" (Jn 10:18). And I give it for these ends; to say loudly that You alone, O God, are the Lord, You alone are the Most High; to thank You; to ask pardon and new benefits. This voluntary offering and death of Jesus has a name — "sacrifice" — and it is the greatest religious event in history, the most sublime prayer of all the centuries.

And yet, the Mass is that same event repeated, made present and visible in every moment and in every part of the earth. In the Mass Christ is still there, still a priest, still a victim, with the same emotions of adoration and love that He had on the cross. There is this difference, however; He is invisible and His death is repeated in a new and mysterious way, which eludes our understanding.

Many were present at the sacrifice of Calvary, but the people stood looking on without understanding anything, says St. Luke (Lk 23:35).

It shouldn't happen this way at the Mass! It is not only a matter of looking on, even though respectfully, but of participating.

We do not listen to the Mass; we live it actively. We are not present at it as spectators, but as actors and protagonists. We say, "Amen" when it is time, and it is our consent, our signature. We look at the celebrant, and it is understood that he acts and speaks in our name. We speak with Jesus and we say to Him, "You are our older brother, you pray and pray for us!"

The *second* way is by Holy Communion.

The deacon has just sung, "Whoever eats this bread will live forever" (Jn 6:51). And what if someone does not eat? He will never have the stature and perfection of a true Christian. The Body of Christ is for the soul what bread is for the body. We cannot do without bread. And this is an extraordinary bread, says St. Augustine, entering into you; it says clearly to you, "I have come to change you; from now on, new thoughts, new affections, new virtues; you will think as I think, you will desire what I desire!" Someone says to me, "It has been such a long time that I have been going to Communion, but I seem to still be the same, with the same old faults!" I answer, "Of course." Because we are still poor human beings and not angels. Communion does not act miraculously; making every imperfection disappear point-blank. It happens as it does when we send our children to school. It isn't that ignorance has completely disappeared after six months and that the child knows all languages and all the sciences. But it is still true that school is a great means for the acquisition of knowledge. It is still true that Communion well made is a very great aid for the acquisition of the virtues. Our cantors have sung it just now, "*Recedant vetera, nova sint omnia, corda, voces et opera!*" ("May the old recede, may all things be new, heart, voices and works!").

The *third* way is by spiritual Communion.

Sometimes I cannot make sacramental Communion. I make up for it by desire. I am at school or on the bus, in the factory or in an airplane. I take myself to church in my thoughts. I see the faithful coming up to the rail. Still in thought I associate myself with them and I try to find in my heart the same love, the same resolutions that I am accustomed to express at Communion, "I am here, Lord, as poor and needy as ever. I unite myself to these brothers and sisters of mine, better and more fortunate than me. Give me the help that You give them. Help us form together a true family of people who love each other and who try to love You!"

The Lord will not be deaf, and He will give us remarkable graces in proportion to our humility and our fervor.

The *fourth* way is by Benediction of the Blessed Sacrament.

Staying with the gospel, Jesus blessed not only the bread and the fish that were later multiplied (Mt 14:19; Mk 6:41; Lk 9:16), not only the bread and the wine at the Last Supper (Mt 26:26). He also blessed the children after laying His hands on them (Mk 10:16) and also the apostles and the disciples before ascending to heaven (Lk 24:50).

It is good to recall this when we receive the Eucharistic blessing. We bow our heads and say to the Lord, "Place your hands on my head, too, so that I may remain firm in the good! Grant that I too may return home 'filled with joy' (Lk 14:52) like the apostles, and that I might find a little relief for these '*anxietates, quae multiplicantur in corde*' ('anxieties that multiply in the heart') (Ps 93)."

The *fifth* way is by a visit to the Blessed Sacrament. It is not that the Lord limits Himself to only brushing by us; no, He has built His home in the middle of our homes and receives us at all hours and without any special ceremony. There are those who only listen to Him; others confess in front of Him in silence; others study Him in order to imitate Him; others speak with Him in the most varied ways. At a birthday celebration for the father of the house, the celebration goes like this: the smallest child recites a short poem from memory; his brother actually comes out with a little speech; his sister, already a young lady, presents a bouquet of red carnations and does not speak, but her blush speaks of her affection and her pleasure; lastly, the wife brings nothing and says nothing, she only looks at her husband, who, in his turn, reads everything in that look.

Something similar can happen in our visits to the Blessed Sacrament. The poem from memory is vocal prayer, the Our Father, the Hail Mary, the Glory Be. The little speech represents our meditation on our reading, or mental prayer. The bouquet of flowers with the blush is affective prayer, made up completely of acts of love, of holy resolutions. The simple look, on the other hand, is the so-called "prayer of simplicity" in which the soul places itself before its God, without so many words, but in this attitude, "Lord I am here, I know that You are looking at me, that You understand me, that is enough for me."

The *sixth* way is by the Eucharistic procession. Everyone knows that "*tota vita Christi crux fuit et martyrium*" ("the whole life of Christ was a cross and martyrdom"), but even He was pleased with a little public recognition. On Palm Sunday He willingly got on the donkey, He was glad to see that the people were spreading a carpet of cloaks and green, leafy branches on the road, cheering and waving palm branches.

This assures us that He is glad to see our procession this evening. It is an homage, a humble triumph, that we give Him with this feeling, "Lord, there have been moments in which we have offended You and caused You sorrow. Those were ugly moments, forgiven and forgotten. We are truly ourselves this evening, when we recognize You as our God, our King, our Brother, and we promise You love and fidelity."

The *seventh* way is by Viaticum.

The moments of our existence are not all the same, some are the saline or most important points. But the point of points is the passage between this short life and the other eternal one.

The Lord wants to be with us and to give us courage at that moment. Here comes the priest into our sickroom. He says, "Brother, receive the Viaticum of the Body of our Lord Jesus Christ, may it defend you from the evil enemy and lead you to eternal life!" Those who know what the passage means, those who believe in the very great love of Christ for us, are happy to receive the Viaticum. A few days ago, when Pope John learned from his doctor that he was in grave danger, he immediately wanted the Lord. And when the priest was in front of him, with the particle of the host raised, he paused first, made his profession of faith, asked forgiveness for his sins and for the offenses he might possibly have given anyone, then he received Communion. Still not content, he asked that the Blessed Sacrament be exposed in his room, and for a half hour, from his bed, he continued to contemplate and pray.

Here is the Eucharist! May it help us to die well after it has helped us to live well. From our First Communion to our Viaticum, may it influence our life as Christians.

Let us see that we do not stay away from this beneficial influence, and let us ask to venerate it always.

12

Education in the Family

March 1977

*E*ducation is a work of love. It may seem strange, but it is certain that parents begin to educate their children by their love for each other. If a child perceives that his parents have little love for each other, he feels disoriented, insecure, alone with his problems, and he starts out with a handicap on the long road of education. Pediatricians say that from the first few months, babies are furnished with very sensitive antennae for picking up their mother's psychic disturbances. Is she in a state of nervous tension because she is neglected by her husband, or quarreling with him? The nursing child notices it right away: he takes less food, sometimes he does not retain it, and he becomes restless and irritable. The most difficult cases in pediatrics sometimes depend not on the baby's organic deficiencies, but on the mother's constant state of anxiety.

By observing his parents' mutual affection, the child knows by intuition, even without reasoning, that his home is secure, and he is more serene and open to a good education. Wise parents know this, and if their child has been a chance witness of one of their bad-tempered moments, they make sure he is present at their affectionate reconciliation, in order to cancel the unfavorable impression made on his soul! Love for the child then, they say, should have an influence on education from the days of the pre-engagement period.

"What kind of father will he be for my children?" the fiancée-to-be should ask herself. And the candidate for engagement, "What kind of mother will she be?" Simone Weil said, "There is not a single thing in me that does not have its origin in the meeting between my father and my mother."

Miss Betsy Trotwood, David Copperfield's aunt, felt absolutely certain that her young sister-in-law would give birth to a girl. With her galloping imagination, she had already elected herself as her godmother, assigning her to her destiny. And she waited nervously in the first-floor parlor during the labor. But here, descending from the birthing room is the doctor, who innocently and gaily announces, "It's a boy!" Miss Betsy does not say a word, but seizes her hat by its long ribbons and wielding it like a slingshot, fetches the doctor a blow on the head with it, to punish him for the unhappy news. Then she puts her battered hat back on her head and runs furiously from the house.

There should not be reactions of this kind in the parents, when the birth of a child for this or that reason represents a disappointment!

This also happens, if a child is loved and feels that he is loved, he learns to love others more easily and lays the foundation of warm and trusting relationships with his neighbors. Not only this, but he is introduced to life's disappointments and helped to react to them serenely if he feels his mother and father very close to him in his small misfortunes. Let me make it clear: close to him, not with a love that claims always and only to pity, to defend everything in their children; rather, with a love that trains them in patience and tolerance.

A three-year-old boy was crying desperately, pointing to his foot. The nursemaid took him in her arms and took off his little shoe, in which she found a tiny pebble. "Ah," the woman then exclaimed. "You see? It's this bad thing that hurt you so much. Nasty! Well, throw it away." His mother, who had heard the shrieks, arrived at this point, and said to the nursemaid, "Put the shoe back on Nino with the pebble in it. I mean it, do as I tell you!" And she obeyed. The mother then went and stood at the other end of the room, turned, bent over, opened her arms, and with her most loving smile, called her little one, like this, "You who love me so much, come and give me a hug, without crying, with the pebble in your shoe!" And the child went, without crying, limping a little, into his mother's arms. Then she spoke to him words which at that time he did not understand, but which she would repeat later on: "You must always do as you're doing now. You will go on your way in spite of the obstacles and the sorrows that there always are in life. Remember your mother's words, 'You can only get to heaven with a pebble in your shoe!'"

People once said education is the work of authority! We should still say it now, but with some adaptation.

You do not command an adolescent, for example, in the same way you do a child. The adolescent in a crisis of development feels that he is maturing and wants to demonstrate it to himself and to others. Hence his desire to act on his own, his need for independence, and his irritation at apparent contradictions. "You aren't a baby anymore!" his father says to him, but the next day, "These things are not for you; you are still a child." "Choose, you are free!" but the child has the impression that deep down his parents are bending him towards what pleases them. "I came home last night a half hour late, and they made a tragedy out of it!" "They don't do anything but remind me about the other girls my age who do better than me. Look at this one, look at that one." In every home, it can be said, there are children who speak like this. In every home we have the two generations facing one another: the young people who distrust the experience of others; the old people who have had experience, and do not intend to bring up everything for discussion again.

What can we say? The parents need patience and indulgence, united with prudent firmness. The children should not lack respect and docility. The parents should accept discussion and become real friends to their children, taking a sincere and heartfelt interest in today's sports, fashions, and ideas. The children should make sure that they do not refuse dialogue and that they seek it together with their parents. When her mother shows her dissatisfaction with the company she keeps, the daughter should not say, "Mother, you don't understand anything!" but "What do you think, my friend Guliana is frivolous?"

Many things have changed in the world, and we must take note of them. "Young people," the council says, "exert a very substantial influence on modern society. There has been a complete change in the circumstances of their lives, their mental attitudes, and their

relationships with their own families. As they become more con-
scious of their own personality, they are impelled by a zest for life
and abounding energies to assume their own responsibility, and
they yearn to play their part in social and cultural life. Adults
ought to engage in friendly discussions with young people" (*Apostolicam Actuositatem*, 12).

The facts are before our eyes. Young people have contributed
to the overthrow of the governments of Korea, Turkey, and Indone-
sia and have brought about the "new course" in Czechoslovakia. For
years they have filled the newspaper columns, now impressing people, now firing them with enthusiasm, now causing them concern.
First supporters of Kennedy and the "New Frontier" and now of
Carter, drunk with liberty, spring, and heroism in Prague, got up
in beats, teddy boys, *blousons noirs*, and launched on improbable
invasions of beaches, and hysterical performances with electric gui-
tars and pop-songs in a number of European countries. They
showed exemplary civic spirit in the floods in Florence and Friuli.
Even the youth "protest movement," with its demands on schools
and society, is certainly exaggerated in the means and methods it
uses, but it often desires authentic "values" and is capable of stim-
ulating adults and government authorities.

It would not be wise to condemn everything at home. It is better to engage in the "friendly dialogue" the council suggests; to
accept the new, if it is good; to gradually introduce their sons and
daughters to share in responsibilities at home, to encourage them
to change their sterile protest into a realistic proposal, dialoguing
in a way that allows them to glimpse the terrible consequences of
movements that are uncontrolled or manipulated by people with
evil intentions. This is the kind of authority to use with young people today. It is better not even to recall the "strong" discipline of
yesterday. It is not wise to say, "My father did it this way, and this
is the way I'm going to do it with you!" It hasn't actually been
proved that your father used the better method.

In the end, education is a work of example. It not only means
pushing your children; it means leading them lovingly by the
hand. "Pierino, go to confession," his father says, and it creates
an effect. But if the father says "Pierino, let's go to confession

together," it has another effect! Carlo Bo has written about Pope John's letters to his family. "The fundamental values [of Pope John] remained that of his first years and the religious education that he received in his family. Nor could his long and valorous service as a priest have added anything really essential, anything that he had not already derived from the words and the example of his parents."

And what that example was we can understand from what Roncalli wrote from Constantinople in 1939 on the death of his mother: "On turning back in thought, in recalling what Mama Marianna Roncalli was — what a conscience she had, what faith, what holy and just love of her dear ones, what spirit of piety and generosity, what serenity of soul towards the Lord in everything — ah, we must really be moved. And what a heart, what a heart she had, poor woman, for everyone! I remember her and weep with you, but at the same time I experience a tenderness and gentleness that seems to me to be the most certain sign that she is already among the blessed heavenly choirs...."

Children who can write like this about their parents will turn out badly in life only by voluntarily and disastrously straying from the right path!

The reality of the good family ... is very rich. In this family, the brothers and sisters teach each other, the parents teach each other, and the children teach the parents. If there are five brothers and sisters, the cake that Mother prepares is divided into five pieces, and each child then learns that he is not everything and that he must leave a little something for others. If one of a child's little brothers or sisters is in bed with tonsillitis, he sees that everyone in the house is worried about the sick child, and he becomes convinced that he alone cannot be the center of the world, nor that everyone in the house bows to him. Rather, he will be attracted into becoming altruistically involved in the wave of sympathy and love flowing towards the sick child during those days. Obviously, I am supposing that there are not only one or two children, and that the thought that Pope John expressed several times in his letters to his family is true, "The Lord blesses the largest cooking pots most, that is, large families."

But the parents also teach each other, the council says. "They increasingly advance their own sanctification and together give glory to God." In fact, they must now travel forever in the same boat, together they sanctify and elevate each other. St. Monica, by her patience and meekness, brought her husband, Patricius, to God. By her sincere religiosity and her governing of her household, St. Margaret of Scotland conquered her husband, the illiterate King Malcolm, who used to kiss the queen's prayer book, saying, "Here is where my wife learned the art of management, and the wisdom and strength to carry it out!" St. Louis of France, in turn, tried to bring his Margaret with him to spiritual heights, even though she was far, far behind him. But this idea did not seem to be working in the household where, when the wife died, the parish priest entered with a word of comfort. He said to the new widower, "Courage, the Lord has taken her from you!" "Yes," the widower answered, without thinking, "but the Lord will find out what kind of woman he has taken!"

Péguy wrote, "Every cradle is the meeting place of the Magi." Their child's cradle too. The husband and wife themselves are Magi, who deposit their gifts at the foot of that cradle every day: privations, anxieties, nightlong vigils, detachment. They receive other gifts in return, new impulses to live and become holy, a joy purified by sacrifice, the renewal of their mutual affection, and a fuller communion of souls. Perhaps the father used to be authoritarian and absent-minded. "Daddy," his child says to him, "don't open the door all of a sudden anymore, there might be a little child playing behind it. Moderate many of your gestures, curb many of your impulses, don't say anymore with absolute certainty on such and such a day, I will do so and so!" Wasn't Socrates seen playing with his children? Wasn't Agesilaus, the king of Sparta, found one day playing hobby horse with his little son? Don't I know some fathers who have stopped swearing in front of the crystal-clear innocence of their little girls? "I can't disturb such enchanting innocence!" they said to themselves. It happens, in short, that "the goslings often lead the geese to drink," or better, as the council says, that the children, as living members of the family, contribute in their way to the sanctification of their parents.

13

You Too Must Do the Same

Mass For Holy Thursday, 1975

This evening the liturgy wants us to meditate on the Eucharist, on the priesthood, and on fraternal love. In A.D. 165 Justin, a martyr of Christ, died in Rome. A pagan philosopher, he had converted to Christianity after much seeking. He had traveled at length in the Middle East, then he established himself in Rome. His is the oldest description of the Mass that we possess.

"Every Sunday," he writes to the emperor and the Roman Senate, "those of us who live in the city or the country all gather together in the same place." First there are readings, then "the one who presides speaks, admonishing and exhorting." Then "we all rise and pray together . . . bread and wine are brought forth and in the same way the one who presides raises his prayer and actions with all his soul . . . then [the bread and wine] are distributed" (1 Apology, 67).

"The food thus distributed among us," Justin explains, "is called the Eucharist. . . . It is not licit for anyone else to share in it but those who have been washed in the purifying bath set apart for the forgiveness of sins and regeneration, and those who live as Christ has taught. For we do not take this as a common drink; but as our Savior Jesus Christ, possessed flesh and blood for our salvation, so it is our teaching that the food over which thanksgiving is celebrated is the flesh and blood of Christ" (1 Apology, 66).

But who willed and commanded this rite? Christ himself. "Indeed," Justin continues to write, "the apostles, in the memoirs that they wrote, which are called gospels, taught that this commandment had been given to them. That is, that Jesus, after He took bread and gave thanks, said, 'Do this in memory of me, this is my body.' And in the same way, after taking the cup and giving thanks, He shared it with them alone" (1 Apology, 66).

Justin is clear. Christ gave a command, the Apostles transmitted it, the Christians received it. For this reason we celebrate the Mass. So Justin believed; so it was believed in Rome; so too in the Middle East. This was one-hundred-fifty years after Christ.

But the passage of St. Paul, which has just been read to us, actually goes back to fifty years after Christ. Paul too speaks of a command. He says that Christ repeated it twice. He adds — Justin is silent about this — that the order was given during the supper. And he states, "I have received from the Lord what I in turn have transmitted to you."

In what way would Paul have received it "from the Lord"? It is thought to have been through the Christian communities to which Paul belonged immediately after his conversion, the one in Damascus, and the one in Antioch, both closely bound to the community in Jerusalem. From the very first years, therefore, a Eucharist was celebrated in Jerusalem, Damascus, and Antioch, which, like that in Corinth, was bound to a meal, signified the love and unity of the faithful (cf. I Cor 11:21-22), and required specific moral dispositions in the participants. With documents in our hands, therefore, we can state that our Eucharist comes from the Last Supper, and it was willed by Christ. Those who, in the name of a pseudotheology, go around fantasizing that it was a late invention are lying. The Eucharist is the greatest treasure personally left by Christ to His Church.

The second mystery, which we recall this evening, is the Catholic priesthood. Christ, the true priest, said to the apostles, "Do this (that is, the Eucharist) in memory of me." And later, "Those whose sins you forgive will be forgiven" (Jn 20:23). And still later, "All power has been given to me . . . go, therefore, and make disciples of all nations, baptize the people and instruct them to observe all that I have commanded you" (Mt 28:18-20). In this way Christ shared with others His own powers, to which He held the original claim, and gave us a great gift.

Do we appreciate it enough? I'm afraid not. I hear some people say, for example, that confession of sins is no longer necessary.

Oh dear! If there were a hundred stairways offered to those who have serious sins to climb to heaven, we might be able to "skip" confession. Instead, only one stairway has been offered — repentance, and that is precisely through confession made in reality or at least desired. The Church, in the name of Christ, has always asked her children to recognize their own sins, to feel sorry for them, and to ask for forgiveness from God, by confiding them to the priest authorized to represent Christ and to speak in His name. Agreed, this is something that costs a little effort. But it permits us to know ourselves for what we are (it is so easy to forget our wretchedness and to think ourselves near-saints!). And then it constitutes in itself a useful act of humility. Some people say, "I confess personally to God, and that's enough." I ask, but does this person really confess to God? And if he does confess, Who will guarantee him forgiveness? Who will give him the sign of inner liberation, which gives him peace in his heart? I always think of the case of Chesterton, converted from the Anglican Church to Catholicism. "Why did you do it?" he was asked. He answered, "Because only the Catholic Church, with sacramental absolution, gave me the certainty that my sins had been forgiven."

The last teaching this evening, love for our neighbor. Christ knelt at the feet of His apostles and washed their feet; when He got up, He commanded, "You too must do the same!"

But do we do this seriously? All the divisions which exist among us and within the Church itself, are they love?

Everyone is good at preaching love, and they talk about brotherhood, solidarity, union, communion, and community spirit. Many people, however, claim that it is the other people who must give way, adapt themselves, bend, renounce. As for themselves, they refuse even the duties that they are obligated to perform. There comes to my mind Paul's sad lament, "Everyone seeks his own interest" (Phil 2:21). We seem to have regressed to the time of the ferocious medieval struggles between the Guelphs and Ghibellines. If he were here, Dante would have to repeat again with bitter irony, "Come and see how the people love one another" (Purg 6:116). My Florence, continued the poet, elsewhere, people are reluctant to accept public office, with you the contrary happens, there is a race for small and great seats "...Your people solicitously respond without being called and cry, 'I'll take it on!'" (Purg 6:134-35).

In this aspect, Italy today seems like a new "Florence"! This living in a continuous state of pitiless struggle without truce, to the sound of speeches and slogans, to the blows of newspapers, posters, insults written on all the walls, pamphlets, Molotov cocktails; this struggle which often degenerates into brawls between opposed ranks, in shootings, killings, and even in terrorist massacres — [these] are truly not things worthy of Christians and fellow citizens! Where are we going to end up? At few times has it been as necessary as it is today to listen to Christ as He says, "Wash one another's feet, love one another as I have loved you!" St. Paul comments, "Love is patient, love is kind. It is not jealous, it is not pompous, it is not inflated, it is not rude, it does not seek its own interests, it is not quick-tempered, it does not brood over injury, it does not rejoice over wrongdoing.... It bears all things, believes all things, hopes all things, endures all things" (I Cor 13:4-6). These works form a program, a model of life.

How close are we to it? Let us think seriously about it, and each one, in his own little way, resolve to do something.

14

Crosses

Homily at the Good Friday Liturgy, 1974

*D*uring the reading of John's deeply compassionate account, I have contemplated Him together with you, full of sorrows, nailed in His hands and suspended; nailed in His feet and immobilized. There I was, facing Him; I, who cannot bear obstacles; I, who shrug off every annoyance; I, who am drowning in ease. And yet I profess to be His disciple.

I have a beautiful crucifix hanging on the wall of my study; another crucifix at the end of the rosary that I carry in my pocket. I make the sign of the cross I don't know how many times a day. Every day I celebrate the Mass, the sacrifice of the cross represented on the altar. In spite of all this, I am so afraid of crosses.

Reflecting on crosses, I have made a distinction. There are some that do not make us tremble; for example, the pain that is heavy, but which you have the strength to bear. Competition, which exhausts you and leaves you breathless, which makes you thirsty and wears you out, but at the same time, stimulates you to overcome your opponent and reach the finish line in glory. These are very small crosses.

The cross is a beam fastened to a crossbeam. It is, therefore, the road blocked in front of me. I thought I would be able to go on and someone stops me, unjustly blocking all of my hopes. I cherished legitimate desires and I see them destroyed from beginning to end. I wanted to keep my feet on the ground and I find myself separated from the earth, lifted up and nailed where I really didn't want to be. And without any glory; the same people who sympathize with me outwardly for propriety's sake, deep down are laughing at me. This really is a cross, this wounds the depths of the heart, it twists the soul, and makes this cry rise spontaneously to the lips, "This I really didn't want, Lord! Let this cup pass from me, Lord!"

Jesus too experienced this. In the garden He felt prostrated, annihilated, sorrowful unto death. He too, said, "Father, if it is possible let this cup pass from me." Afterwards, however, He accepted it heroically. Afterwards, He said, "let not my will, but yours be done" (Lk 22:42).

My brothers and sisters! Let us also try to say our *Fiat* and carry our daily cross. To us too, as to Christ, a little bit of strength will come from the Father. On our painful journey, there will also be some Simon of Cyrene to help us, a mother to suffer along with us and console us.

In any case, every cross is a passing thing; it is the road, not the goal, and no crosses without heaven in view. St. Peter wrote, "Rejoice in the measure that you share Christ's sufferings. When His glory is revealed, you will rejoice exultantly" (I Pt 4:13).

15

We Bring Love

Homily at the Easter Vigil, 1976

St. Augustine used to say that this is the queen of vigils, a night holy among all nights. Everything we have seen, heard, or sung in the course of this liturgy is Easter: the lighted candle, the Easter proclamation, the readings that spoke about the crossing of the Red Sea, waters that quench the thirst of the deer, hearts of flesh replacing hearts of stone, the "Gloria" that has awakened the organ with all its stops out and has unleashed all the bells of Venice — everything has been Easter. One word, however, has always been Easter *par excellence*, in the highest way, *Alleluia*. When we sang a short time ago, it placed us in the full atmosphere of the Christian Easter; it says delight, happiness and joy, internal joy, naturally, joy of the heart. It says, put hate and envy out of your hearts, and make room for love, a great love for God and your neighbor.

St. Augustine said, "We do not go to God by walking, but by loving." I like this loving, spiritual, weekend trip. Without it, there is no true Easter. Unfortunately, it is not an easy trip. There is opposition: "the flesh has desires against the Spirit . . . so that you may not do what you want" (Gal 5:17). St. Paul said this, and how many times we experience it! We start out towards the heights with good resolutions, but then our bad habits and passions, our old friends, "pull at us," says Augustine," by our garment of flesh." They try to frighten us — "Just think, you will no longer be allowed to do this or this." On the other hand, God and His goods are invisible and seem far away, while the other goods are clearly visible and close at hand. It takes a [lot] to detach ourselves from those things that attract us so much, and head for a beyond, which we do not see, but only glimpse.

In addition to faith, we need a power that only God can grant. "No one can come to me unless the Father who sent me draws him" (Jn 6:44). At times, I find myself like a sick person, who has no desire to eat, and says, Lord, send me a little bit of appetite. That is, give me at least the desire to love You! Once in possession of this desire, I change my prayer and say with St. Peter, "Lord if it is you, command me to come to you on the water" (cf. Mt 14:28). "God is the one who, for His good purpose, works in you both to desire and to work" (Phil 2:13). "No one can say 'Jesus is Lord' except by the Holy Spirit" (I Cor 12:3). With St. Augustine I pray, "*Da, Domine, quod iubes et iubes quod vis*" ("Give, Lord, what You order, and order what You will").

In order to be able to love God, in short, I need two things. His grace and my free participation, but even my participation needs divine help. In the case of the little girl who went to eat the cherries in her father's orchard, what happened? First, thanks to her father, the ripe cherries were available in the orchard of the house; second, the father aroused in the little girl a strong desire, by extolling the sweetness and color of the cherries; third, when they arrived at the tree, the father lifted the little girl under her arms to the height of the first branch. In this case, what did the child's contribution amount to? With the help of her father, she desired to go in the orchard. In the orchard, she saw the cherries extolled by her father. Her mouth watered. When she was held up by her father's arms, she held out her hand and ate. But what if her father had not been there? This is our story, what if, from the first step to the last, we did not have the help of God?

Some people think of a love of God made up of sighs, tears, and sweet prayers. No, it is not a weak and effeminate love, but a virile and dynamic one, that carries us to God. "Not everyone who says to me, 'Lord, Lord,' will enter the kingdom of heaven, but only the one who does the will of my Father in heaven" (Mt 7:21). "A man had two sons. He went to the first and said, 'Son, go out and work in the vineyard today.' He said in reply, 'I will not,' but afterwards he changed his mind and went. The man came to the other son and gave the same order. He said in reply, 'Yes, sir,' but did not go. Which of the two did his father's will? They answered 'the first.'

Jesus said to them 'Amen, I say to you, the tax collectors and prostitutes are entering the kingdom of God before you'" (Mt 21:28-
31). There is no love, then, in those who have an easy "yes" on their
lips, but refuse God the work of their arms. As far as the work is
concerned, we need to understand, however, it is not that God
needs our labor or needs our good works. He is more interested in
quality than quantity, *non quaerit donum amantis ... amorem donan-
tis* — He does not ask for the gift of the one loving, but the love
of the one giving. A person fasts to save money, gives great offerings, writes, speaks in order to make himself known — all that does
not interest God. Jesus Christ once said to His apostles that the poor
widow with the single small coin had given more than all the others, who had offered large amounts of money (cf. Mk 12:41-44).
With what heart, with what love, with how much purity of heart
is it done or given? This is what He is most interested in. The
quantity of works comes afterwards.

I won't speak to you for long. I will only stress that it is not
easy if we need to love even our enemies, and do some good even
to those who have done us wrong. All the more so because God
has repeatedly prescribed the measure of this love, "You shall love
your neighbor as yourself" (Mt 5:43; 19:19; 22:39; Mk 12:31; Lk
12:27).

There is only one way to fully face up to this commandment:
by accustoming ourselves to seeing God in our neighbor according to the advice of Jesus Himself, Who said that He hides Himself in the person of the poor, the imprisoned, and the sick, and
that He considers anything that is done for any of these little ones
is done for Him (cf. Mt 25).

When Tobias, accompanied by the angel Raphael, arrived in
Ecbatana and entered the house of Raguel, their host asked them
who they were and where they had come from. After hearing that
they were Hebrews deported to Nineveh, Raguel asked, "Do you
know Tobit?" "He is my father," Tobias answered. At these words,
Raguel leapt to his feet, kissed him and wept. Then he said, "Blessings on you child! You are the son of a noble father" (Tob 7:4-7).

Here is the system, so many people come to us. Are they good,
are they deserving? We don't know, or maybe we know that they

are not at all deserving. One thing only do we know, these people are children of a noble Father — God. For love of God we must jump to our feet, love them, help them, and bear with them. To many the system seems absurd, and yet it is the specifically Christian system, as Sienkiewicz says in his novel *Quo Vadis?* People asked Paul, "What did Greece bring? Art. What did Rome bring? Law? And you Christians, what do you bring?" The answer, "We bring love."

16

Our Lady of the People

Luciani gave this homily at the conclusion of the novena to the "Madonna del Popolo" (Our Lady of the People) in Verona on September 8, 1970.

*O*ur *Lady of the People* is an expression I like very much. It means, it seems to me, that the people feel that our Lady is close to them, both as a mother who takes care of her children, and as a sister who has traveled in part the same road we are traveling.

Properly speaking, Our Lady is the Mother of Christ and the Mother of God. But Christ is our older Brother, the head of the whole Christian family; we too, then, can call her Mother, Mother of the Church, Mother of each one of us.

And as a Mother, she is higher than we are. She was preserved from original sin through the merits of her Son applied in anticipation. She conceived miraculously and, intact in her virginal glory, radiates eternal light on the world. She was assumed, body and soul, into heaven. From up there she constantly helps us. The council has stressed that Christ is the sole and unique mediator between God and humanity: He alone gives graces and works miracles (*Lumen Gentium*, 60). But He has made for Himself, in a way, this law, to make use . . . of His Mother, who becomes for us (in a secondary way), an advocate, helper, aid, and mediatrix (*Lumen Gentium*, 62).

Pius XII said, "If Peter has the keys of the Church, Mary has the keys to the heart of God; if Peter binds and looses, Mary too binds with the chains of love; she too looses with the art of forgiving. If Peter is the keeper and the minister of the indulgence, Mary is the wise and bountiful keeper of the treasury of divine favors" (Discourse, April 21, 1940). Dante expressed the same concept, saying to Our Lady, "Lady, you are so great and of so high a worth, that if anyone wants grace and does not turn to you, his desire wants to fly without wings" (Paradiso, 33:13-15).

We should explain it to our children like this, "It is as if the king were seated on his throne and had his mother seated next to him. Here comes a poor man asking for help. The king smiles at him and turns to his mother, 'Shall we give him this help?' His mother is already looking at the poor man and smiling at him with great sweetness. At her son's words, she gets up, goes to the chest, opens it and, still smiling, brings the poor man the help he asked for."

We should, then, invoke her with confidence, and I am very pleased to see that our centenary celebration has included, every evening throughout the octave, the recitation of the holy rosary. It is a humble form of prayer, but one so dear to the people. Some people today consider it out of date, not adapted to our time, which demands, they say, a Church that is all spirit and charisms. History and psychology are against them. For human beings, even when they believe in very high values, tend by instinct to concretize them, to seek simple words and simple means to express the sacred. And then too, Christianity is not a religion made up of all colonels, but is intended for all of humanity, which is also made up of simple people and those of little culture. So, a small number of the faithful will perhaps arrive at the point where they can live a Christianity that is completely interiorized, without need of external aids, but the great mass will always feel the need for their faith to be protected and helped by a setting, formed according to the circumstances, of popular music, processions, and sacred images and objects. Among these objects is the rosary.

Several years ago, a missionary was accused in China, "You hold a gadget in your hand." They say, "you move the beads through your fingers, and at the same time, you speak mysterious words. It must be a radio transmitter!" In a way they were right. The rosary, if said well, can become a kind of radio transmitting to heaven!

Our Lady is also our sister. The council says that she lived on the earth "a life common to everyone, full of family cares and work" (*Apostolicam Actuositatem*, 5). She swept floors, she prepared meals, she washed dishes and clothes and this too helped her become the greatest of all the saints. "Do common things," she seems to be admonishing us, "but in an uncommon way, ordinary actions, but pervaded with extraordinary love for God and our brothers and sisters, and you will achieve holiness!"

Even Our Lady, the council adds, "made progress in her pilgrimage of faith" (*Lumen Gentium,* 58) and had to have an attitude of listening, seeking, self-sacrifice, since, after finding Jesus in the temple, she and Joseph "did not understand the words of the Son" (*Lumen Gentium,* 57). In her suffering faith, she encourages us in the difficulties we experience facing the truths revealed by God. We do not see them; we only glimpse them. It is like when the earth is covered with fog and we cannot see the sun. We see only a little light in the part where it is. We see it, so to say, without seeing it. But we must say, "I have been told this by God, who cannot err, nor lead us astray. I trust in Him and I want to hear Him say to me what Our Lady heard Elizabeth say to her, 'Blessed are you for having believed'" (Lk 1:45).

But today some people find it difficult to even admit that God exists. We have set foot on the moon, and now we have the whole world in our hands! We no longer need God! But is it true? Today we are still subject to death. Our progress is marvelous but has some limits in missiles, in the pollution of the air and water, and in atomic, bacterial, and chemical weapons. And let us not be under the illusion that the future, which has already begun in the present, will be more beautiful; it will be more beautiful on one hand, but it will be similar to the present on the other. We still need God.

Others ask, "How can we reconcile God and evil?" I have no answer to give, so difficult is the problem. One element of the answer might be the one given by St. Francis de Sales. "I was a child," he said, "and on the bank of a stream I had built little houses and streets of sand. And a mischievous boy came by and with a few kicks, knocked everything down. How I cried! I thought I was the unhappiest person in the world. Now that I am old, I smile at my tears; that misfortune was a very small one!"

Something similar will happen to us. If heaven exists (and it does exist), if we go there (and it is our duty to hope that we will go there), we will come to smile at the evils of this world that seemed enormous and that now will be infinitely far away!

But Our Lady is presented to us not only as a model of faith, but a model of obedience. "The knot of Eve's disobedience," the council says, "was untied by the obedience of Mary!"

The subject of obedience concerns not only the subjects, but the superiors. The superiors, in fact, while commanding, must do it for the benefit of their subjects, with a spirit of service, respecting their dignity. The subjects too must recall that it is not possible to obey without sacrifice. Christ Himself found obedience to the Father painful. Today, people desire an obedience illuminated by explanations and dialogue, an obedience that respects group psychology, that respects competence.

And that is as it should be. But it will always cost an effort. Philip Neri used to say, "Holiness is all in three fingers!" He meant the three fingers that are enough to cover your forehead and bow saying yes to God and to those who represent him: parents, teachers, and superiors. This is what Mary did, she bowed her head when she answered the angel. "Behold the handmaid of the Lord, let it be done to me according to your word" (Lk 1:38). It is in this way, as the council says, that is, "by obeying," that "she became the cause of salvation for herself and for the whole human race" (*Lumen Gentium*, 56). The heart of our religious faith is in obedience to God. Our position can only be the following, "Lord, You are very great; compared to You, I am very small. I am not ashamed to say it. And I will gladly do what You ask of me. All the more since You do not ask in order to take, but in order to give; You do not ask for Your own profit, but for my advantage!"

17

The Gifts of the Spirit

Homily for the Feast of the Sacred Heart, June 21, 1974

The following homily was given to the Dorothean Sisters, Daughters of the Sacred Heart, in Mestre, and to the White Sisters, Daughters of the Sacred Heart at the Lido.

The readings we have listened to (Ez 34: 11-16; Rom 5:5-11; Lk 15:3-7) have presented Christ to us as the shepherd of our souls; they have told us how much care and how much love He has for us. Readings that are well suited for the feast of the Sacred Heart and for Sisters who are Daughters of the Sacred Heart.

There comes to my mind what St. Paul says, "For those who are led by the Spirit of God are children of God" (cf. Rom 8:14). Since you are about to renew your profession, I want to recall to you in an elementary way the doctrine of the gifts or movements, by which the Holy Spirit guides us.

1. There is the gift of *wisdom*, the supernatural enjoyment of divine things. You all recall how, at a certain period of her life, St. Thérèse of the Child Jesus said that she found delight in saying the Our Father. Bremon[1] narrates a similar case. One day, the mother of Ponçonas, then still a young woman, met a girl who was keeping sheep. She took her aside to teach her something of religion. The girl was very grateful, and with tears brimming in her eyes, begged her to explain to her how she might be able to finish the Our Father. "Because," she said, "I am never able to get to the end. For five years now, I have been saying the word "Father" and when I think that He is up there . . . that He is truly my Father, I start crying, and I stay all day like that, while I am watching my sheep." It is an enjoyment of this kind, which is alluded to in the

prayer "give us in the same Spirit true knowledge and allow us always to enjoy its consolation."

2. The gift of *understanding*, on the other hand, consists of a penetrating intuition of revealed truths. Some of these are veiled in mystery, instead of seeing them, we can only glimpse them; nevertheless, being able to gaze a little inside them carries a great advantage.[2] Other truths are not obscure in themselves, but only if we squeeze out their profound essence do they give help to the soul. At times, it is from a single phrase truly possessed and embraced as a program of life that the saints set out resolutely on their journey towards holiness. Blessed Marie of the Incarnation, who introduced Carmel into France and who, after she was widowed, became a Carmelite herself, along with her three daughters, was given in marriage at the age of sixteen to [Viscount] Pierre Acarie. One day, her husband, who was pious in his own way, found his young wife intent on reading a romance which one of her young women friends had lent her. "I don't want you to ruin yourself with romances," he said. And he immediately ran to the Abbé Roussel, his confessor, to consult with him. He returned home with a pile of books of devotion for his wife. She read them quickly and returned them. Then it was the Abbé Roussel's turn to come to the Acarie house with a new pile of books of devotion. The good priest had, in addition, underlined the salient passages with a pencil. One of these said, *The one for whom God is not enough is too avaricious*. For the young woman, this was a revelation. Her affections, convictions, heart, and soul suddenly seemed to be turned upside down. "God must be enough for me, God is worth more than all the rest" was the thought which from then on dominated all her life as a spouse, a widow, a Carmelite, and which stimulated her to works that had an immense influence on all of religious France in the first part of the seventeenth century.

We encounter something similar when we pray with St. Augustine, "Let us try with our desire to find, and let us find with our desire to try again!"

3. The gift of *counsel* helps us to judge with prudence the fitting thing to do, especially in difficult cases. We are accustomed

to invoke the Holy Spirit as "the right forefinger of the Father." Exactly, it is the finger that points, and that says at the right moment, "Take this road and avoid that one." Those who have read the autobiography and the letters of St. Teresa of Ávila seem to experience directly the presence of this finger in the activity, at once dynamic and prudent, of this great saint. Her ecstasies alternate with everyday material concerns, quarrels, threatened lawsuits, protests about rights, disputes, contracts, and differences of opinion with the parents of novices over their dowries, gathering of crops, travels. And yet, she moves in the midst of all these activities as secure and serene as a fish in water. At one moment a battle even breaks out, no less a person than the papal nuncio accuses her of being a "restless, vagabond, disobedient, and contumacious woman, who teaches wicked doctrines, who wants to do so as a teacher" against the prohibition, he says, of St. Paul, who imposed silence on women! Teresa is not afraid, her letters to Rome, the messengers she sent to Philip II, her interventions with princes and prelates succeed in unraveling every difficulty; but she is convinced above all that all that is a gift: "Teresa alone is worth nothing. Teresa plus a penny are worth less than nothing. Teresa, plus a penny, plus God, can do everything!"

4. The gift of *fortitude* allows our weak will to accomplish great things intrepidly and joyously, overcoming the obstacles, that in one way or another, everyone finds on their path. I spoke of weakness. Alas! In a way, we are all in the situation of that poor lazy man described by the Bible, "The lazy man says, there is a lion there outside; I would be killed in the middle of the road" (Prov 22:13). It is laziness that makes us see the difficulties as greater than they are. A cat on the road becomes a lion through the imagination of the lazy man, who is afraid of every risk. The same lazy people seem to expect to always travel flat roads, without obstacles, something which can happen only in heaven. On this earth, along with good, there is evil; along with rest, effort; along with money, the fear of losing it and concern for protecting and investing it. In the spiritual life things go now straight, now crooked; today there is fervor, tomorrow weakness and apathy; today there is joy, light, and enthusiasm — tomorrow, pain, darkness, and

anguish. "When Our Lady brings forth her Son, the angels announce His birth, the shepherds and the Wise Men come to adore Him; who knows how much grace and consolation Mary and Joseph felt. But behold, a short time passes and the angel comes to Joseph in a dream to say, 'Take the child and his mother and flee into Egypt.' Their joy is changed into sorrow." Christian fortitude obliges us, through a gift of the Spirit, to preserve a lovable equanimity of spirit and to pull ahead, in spite of our every external and internal change. The Spirit, however, also works with ordinary means. "We must do as two people who walk on the ice," says St. Francis de Sales. "They take each other by the hand and hold each other by the arm to support each other, if one of them slips. In this life it is as though we are on the ice, because at every moment we encounter occasions that are likely to make us stumble.[3] On Who, then, are we to lean in our weakness? On our superiors, in fact. For me, the practice of considering our superiors as oppressors of our personality is a grave evil. This personality, though it is rich in many gifts, has its incomplete areas, its moments of discouragement, of confusion and weakness. To lean on someone, by confiding and even by only obeying, is a great help. Our superiors were placed here precisely in order to serve us.

Recently, a Sister said to me, "What is the bishop's delegate to the Sisters supposed to do for us? Are we women religious perhaps underage children?" "Sister," I answered, "it seems that you think that the bishops need and desire to exercise power over the sisters. Don't you think that the Sisters rather need to lean on the bishop in order to have help and directives? Do you think that to loosen the bonds with one who has been placed as a means and guarantee of unity in the Church can damage your congregation or the Church itself? I know that you teach literature, allow me to summarize a little English poem:

> *There was a little screw; it was together with a thousand other screws and they kept bound and fixed the steel plates of a gigantic ship.*
> *But in the middle of the Indian Ocean, the little screw began to come loose and threatened to fall into the water.*

The nearest screws said, "If you fall, we are coming too."
And the nails in the body of the ship, "We too feel a little con-
fined, we want to come loose a little bit."

But the great iron framework cried, "For the love of heaven,
stay; unless you hold firm, we are finished."

The notice of what the little screw was about to do spread
like lightning throughout the immense body of the iron colos-
sus, which began to shake and to tremble in all its joints.

Then the girders, the plates, the screws, even the smallest
nail, sent a collective embassy to the screw to say, "Stay with
us; if you don't, everything will fall to pieces."

"That screw, Sister," I continued, "is you. That ship is the Church. One begins to leave, to give way, to go away, and her neighbors move. The word spreads, in short many find themselves too confined; there is danger of collapse. It is true, the Holy Spirit, which guides the ship of the Church, will steer it to the final port. What responsibility, however, for the one who has caused or allowed collapse and damage while the ship is on course!"

5. The gift of *knowledge* allows us to know created things as they are ordered by God. The world is beautiful. We are happy to see and admire it. It is not enough, however, to stop here; we must lift ourselves from the world to God. The beauty here must make us think of the much greater perfections of the One Who produced them.

St. Francis, on seeing a mountain crag, said, "You, O Lord, are the rock, on which my weakness leans." When he saw the flowers of the field, "You, Lord are still more pure, beautiful, and delicate than the flowers." When he saw the baby birds, "How tender You are, Lord, to send food to these poor little beings!" Francis followed the line of ascent; he had the gift of wonder, a sacred wonder.

The Russian, who, on returning from a trip into space reported that he had not come across God there, followed instead the way of descent, of a wonder that is now secularized. Many people follow him. In love only with human progress, they praise the beautiful things that man has produced, using the intelligence they have received from God to say that there is no need for God. They do not notice how prodigious is the earth willed by God, all charged and quivering with life, in the middle of a universe of lifeless planets and gaseous stars. One who came from Sirius or another star and saw this earth of ours so green, so flowering, so populated with billions of living beings, would say, "Thank you, Lord, for granting to me a chance to see all this." Without coming from Sirius, let us become used to saying to ourselves a constant "thank you" to God with the gift of *knowledge*.

6. The gift of *piety* communicates to us a filial affection for God. St. Paul wrote, ". . . for you did not receive a spirit of slavery to fall back into fear, but . . . a spirit of adoption, through which we cry: Abba, Father" (Rom 8:14). And it is not only a sentiment; it is also an impulse to act in order to please God as His children. Jesus said, "I always do what is pleasing to him" (Jn 8:29). Things, if we are full of affection and tenderness for the Father, appear different to us. The Bible becomes a paternal letter, which God has sent expressly to me, to help me and save me. Christ becomes my older brother (Rom 8:29) beside whom, that is, after the example of whom, I must grow and journey.

The institutions of the Church, the rules themselves, are a help placed at my disposal by a paternal goodness. "It is a waste of time to dream of castles in Spain, if I must live in France," said St. Francis de Sales. And I say to you, "You are wasting time, if you think that you will become a holy Sister, when the congregation has removed this or that structure. Until the new structures are put in place, try to become saints within those that exist; if you don't, you will run the risk of trying to live in a state of restlessness and of not becoming a saint, now or ever."

7. The fear of God, more than anything else, is the fear of offending God. The soul says, "I have offended You too much, Lord, in the past; help me at least not to offend You in the future!" Let me make it clear. Avoiding all sin for long, in this poor world, is not possible without a special privilege of God. Trying to avoid it and getting up again immediately after possible falls is already a great deal. Benedict XIV, not as Pope, but as a private theologian and examiner of the causes of the saints, used to say, "When I find myself before a servant of God, who committed venial sins,

I am accustomed to make a distinction. Are the sins few, deliberate, but immediately retraced with an effort to improve? I do not block the cause; such a person might deserve to be proclaimed a saint. On the other hand, do the venial sins turn out to be many, and frequently repeated and not retracted with sufficient penitence? Then I stop the cause."

This is a famous text, written by a specialist. It gives us courage. A Sister, who falls into venial sin, but who gets up again right away and tries constantly to avoid them, can be canonized! Canonization apart, I hope that you all find yourselves in this disposition of holy fear, doing everything in order not to offend God; if sometimes it happens, getting up again and taking up your journey again with humble and trusting courage.

Notes

1. H. Bremond, *Histoire litteraire du sentiment religieux en France*, Paris, 1967, II, p. 6.

2. St. Thomas Aquinas, "The knowledge, however imperfect of truly noble things, confers the greatest perfection on the soul" (*Contra gentes*, 1:3). "Reason, enlightened by faith . . . God willing, grants a mysterious understanding, and a very fruitful one" (Vatican Council I,: DS, 3016).

3. St. Francis de Sales, *Trattenimenti* (Milan, 1945), p. 34.

18

⌾⌾⌾

Presiding in Charity

Homily Inaugurating His Pontificate, September 3, 1978

Venerable Brothers, and dear Sons and Daughters:

In this sacred celebration, which is the solemn beginning of the ministry which has been placed on our shoulders, the ministry of Supreme Pastor of the Church, we first turn our mind in adoration and prayer to the infinite and eternal God Who, by His decision, inexplicable to human reasoning, and by His most gracious kindness, has raised us to the See of Blessed Peter. Spontaneously we burst forth, in the words of St. Paul the apostle, "Oh, how deep are the riches, the wisdom, and the knowledge of God! How inscrutable his judgments, how unsearchable his ways!" (Rom 11:33).

Next, we embrace in our thoughts, and salute with paternal love, the whole Church of Christ, this assembly which represents it, and which is gathered here in this place full of piety, religion, and works of art, which jealously guards the tomb of the Prince of the Apostles. Next we greet the Church that is watching and listening to us at this moment through the modern means of social communication.

We greet all the members of the People of God: cardinals, bishops, priests, men and women religious, missionaries, seminary students, lay people carrying out the apostolate and employed in various professions, men and women expert in politics, culture, art, and economics, fathers and mothers of families, migrants, workers, young men and women, children, the sick, the suffering, and the poor.

We also wish to greet, with respect and affection, all men and women in the world, who we think of and love as brothers and sisters because they are all sons and daughters of the same heavenly Father and brothers and sisters in Christ Jesus (cf. Mt 23:8f).

————

We decided to begin this homily of ours in Latin because, as is well-known, it is the official language of the Church, and it expresses, in a clear and effective way, its universality and unity.

The word of God, to which we have just been listening, has presented to us, as though in a crescendo, the whole Church, prefigured and glimpsed by the prophet Isaiah (cf. Is 2:2-5) as the new temple, to which people stream from all directions, wishing to know the law of God and to observe it docilely, while the terrible arms of war are transformed into instruments of peace. But this mysterious new temple, the pole of attraction for the new humanity, St. Peter reminds us, has its living, chosen, and precious cornerstone, and it is Jesus Christ, Who founded His Church on the apostles and built it on blessed Peter, their head (cf. *Lumen Gentium*, 19).

"You are Peter, and upon this rock I will build my Church" (Mt 16:18). These are the weighty words which Jesus, at Caesarea Philippi, addressed to Simon, son of John, after his profession of faith. This profession was not the product of human logic by the fisherman of Bethsaida, or the expression of his special keeness of perception, or the effect of a psychological impulse, but the unique and mysterious fruit of an authentic revelation of the heavenly Father. And Jesus changes Simon's name to Peter, signifying by this the conferring of a special mission. He promises to build on him His Church, which will not be overcome by the forces of evil or death. He confers on him the keys to the kingdom of God, thus naming him to the post of greatest responsibility in His Church, and gives him the power to interpret authentically the divine law.

In considering (these privileges or rather) these superhuman tasks entrusted to Peter, St. Augustine tells us, "Peter, by nature, was simply a man; by grace a Christian; by a special and still more abundant grace, one of and at the same time the first of the apostles" (St. Augustine: 124, 5: *Patrologia Latina* 35, 1973).

With astonished and understandable trepidation, but also with immense trust in the powerful grace of God and in the ardent prayer of the Church, we have agreed to become the successor of Peter in the See of Rome, taking on the "yoke" that Christ has wished to place on our frail shoulders. And we seem to hear, as though addressed to us, the words that St. Ephraim . . . has Christ address to St. Peter, "Simon, my apostle, I have constituted you as the foundation of the Holy Church. I have called you Peter because you will hold up all the buildings; you are the superintendent of all those who will build the Church on earth; you are the source of the spring from which my doctrine is drawn; you are the leader of my apostles. . . . I have given you the keys of my kingdom."

From the moment of our election and in the days immediately following, we were deeply impressed and encouraged by the demonstrations of affection by our sons and daughters in Rome and also by those who throughout the world have sent (*applause*) us expressions of their uncontrollable joy at the fact that God has once again given the Church its visible head. Our soul spontaneously re-echoes the emotional words that our great and holy predecessor, St. Leo the Great, addressed to the faithful of Rome: "Blessed Peter has not ceased presiding over his See, and he is bound to the eternal priest in a unity that will never fail . . . and therefore you should know that all of the demonstrations of affection that you have addressed to us, out of fraternal kindness or filial piety, have really been addressed by you along with me, with greater devotion and truth, to the One over whose See we rejoice not so much to preside over as to serve."

––––––––––

. . . Our presiding in charity is a service, and in saying this we are thinking not only of our Catholic brothers and sisters and sons and daughters, but of all those who try to be disciples of Jesus Christ, to love God, and to work for the good of humanity.

In this sense, we address a grateful and affectionate greeting to the delegations from the other churches and ecclesial communities who are present here. Brothers and sisters not yet in full communion, let us turn together to Christ the Savior, each progressing in the holiness He desires of us, and progressing together in the mutual love without which there is no Christianity, preparing the paths of unity in faith, with respect for His truth and for the ministry which He has conferred, for the good of His Church, on the apostles and on their successors.

In addition, we owe a special greeting to the heads of state and to the members of the extraordinary missions. We are very touched by your presence, whether you preside yourselves over the destinies of your countries, or whether you represent your governments or international organizations, to which we offer our warm thanks. We see in this participation the respect and trust you have for the Holy See and for the Church, the humble messenger of the gospel to all the people in the world, to help in creating a climate of justice, fraternity, solidarity, and hope, without which the world could not live.

May all here, great and small, be assured of our readiness to serve them according to the Spirit of the Lord!

———

Surrounded by your love, and sustained by your prayers, we begin our apostolic service by invoking as a splendid star upon our way, Mary the Mother of God, "the health of the Roman people," and Mother of the Church, whom the liturgy venerates in a special way during this month of September. May the Virgin Mary, who has guided our life as a child, a seminarian, a priest, and a bishop, with delicate tenderness, continue to enlighten and guide our steps, so that with our eyes and mind fixed on her Son, Jesus, we may proclaim to the world with joyful firmness, our own profession of faith, "You are Christ, the Son of the living God!" (Mt 16:16). Amen.

19

The Three Levels of the Pyramid

Notes for the Clergy on the Church, May 9, 1963

*A*mong the many titles that are given to the Lord, that of "Shepherd and guardian of souls" stands out (I Pt 2:25). He Himself showed that He prefers it, when He said, "I am the good shepherd" (Jn 10:14).

His desire as a shepherd was to have a flock, or souls gathered together in a chosen group to be saved. He is heard to say, "I will give my life for my sheep" (Jn 10:15). And again, "I must lead them" (Jn 10:16). On His last night He prayed like this: "I pray for those who will believe in me, that they all may be one" (Jn 17:20).

He willed that the realization of His desire should take place in three movements:

First of all, He wanted there to be a group, the "one" whole, the Church, and He said, "There will be one flock" (Jn 10:16). Then He wanted the flock to be served and guided by a stable group of pastors, the college of the apostles, which is perpetuated and continued in the college of bishops. He entrusted His own powers to the one and the other, saying, "As the Father has sent me, so I send you" (Jn 20:21).

Finally, in the interest of the flock, He wanted the college to be solid and united. He chose Peter from the college and put him at the head of the college. He put the Pope at the service of the bishops as well as the faithful, saying, "Strengthen your brothers" (Lk 22:32) and "Feed my sheep" (John 21:16).

It is a kind of pyramid that Our Lord saw, willed, and brought into being, but the top and the base are reversed, they are not as many people think of them.

At the top, the peak, and the goal of everything else, are the souls that are so greatly loved and that are to be saved. Further down, at the service of the souls, there is the episcopal college, furnished with the necessary powers. Still further down, at the service of the souls and the bishops, as a guarantee of unity, there is the Pope, endowed with higher powers, so that he truly can be *servus servorum Dei* ("the servant of the servants of God").

It is these three levels of the pyramid that I want to discuss.

1. The Faithful in the Church
a. They Are the People of God

At the top, therefore, are the souls, and the souls united together in a given way are the Church.

Here our catechism says, "the Church is the society of the baptized, who profess faith in Jesus Christ, participate in His sacraments and obey the pastors established by Him." What it says is correct, but it says it a little coldly, and is silent about some rich realities. Those who want to understand better and bring warmth to their hearts, need to open the Bible along with the catechism and read there a few pages regarding the Church.

Here, for example, is one of Daniel's famous dreams, painted in scenes with vivid brush strokes.

In the first scene, four huge beasts emerge from the sea, a winged lion, a bear, a leopard, and a horrible nameless beast, with fearful iron teeth and ten horns. In the second picture, a tribunal is set up, an Ancient One is seated on a throne made of flames of fire, and surrounded by thousands of servants. He is God, the Eternal One, the Ancient of Days. In the third scene, the horrible beasts are disposed of, and Daniel learns that they represent the kingdoms of this world, destined to collapse one after another. In the final scene, "one like a son of man" advances towards the throne on the clouds of heaven, and as soon as he arrives, the Ancient One hands over to Him "dominion and glory and kingship" (Dn 7:1-27).

This "one like a son of man" who rides through the heavens, who remains when the kingdoms pass away, who is loaded with gifts, is not a single individual, but a collective personality, made up of a number of people. They are, says Daniel, the "Holy Ones of the Most High" who "shall receive the kingship, to possess it forever and ever." In other words, it represents the Church, seen by Daniel long before its foundation, as a privileged and fortunate people, with eternal dimensions and an eternal destiny. The theme of the privileged and fortunate people is taken up again by Christ and continued by the apostles. One day, in the temple, Christ tells the high priests and the elders the parable of the wicked tenants of the vineyard who kill the owner's son. He gives them to understand that they are those tenants, and concludes, "The kingdom of God will be taken away from you and given to a people who will yield a rich harvest" (Mt 21:43). St. Paul says that, in giving Himself, the Lord had this goal, "to cleanse for himself a people of his own, eager to do what is good" (Titus 2:14). St. Peter wrote to the faithful, "You are . . . a holy nation, a people he claims for his own. . . . Once you were no people, but now you are God's people" (I Pt 2:9-10). Finally, St. John shows the people now gathered in the heavenly city after life on earth. A city, which "had no need of sun or moon, for the glory of God gave it light, and its lamp was the Lamb. The nations will walk by its light; to it the kings of the earth will bring their treasures. . . . Nothing accursed will be found there. The throne of God and of the Lamb will be there, and his servants will worship him. They shall see him face to face and bear his name on their foreheads . . . and they shall reign forever" (Rv 21:23-34, 22:3-4).

b. They Are the Bride of Christ

It is, therefore, a good fortune to belong to the Church. When we become part of it, we become something so great that Christ Himself calls Himself fortunate to have us as His own. We of the Church, indeed, are for Christ a reward, a longed-for thing that has been won, a bride ardently desired and tenderly loved. In the books that we read as children, there was often a prince who performed prodigies and underwent trials, dangers, and adventures in order to have a princess as a reward. Christ is the prince. We are the princess. We are the Church which St. John contemplated — "a new Jerusalem, the holy city coming down out of heaven . . . beautiful as a bride prepared to meet her husband" (Rv 21:2).

St. Paul said to the Christians of Corinth, "I have given you in marriage to one husband, presenting you as a chaste virgin to Christ" (II Cor 11:2).

c. They Are the Mystical Body of Christ

Inasmuch as we are the bride or betrothed of Christ, we are in a sense facing Christ. Under another aspect, however, says St. Paul (I Cor 12:27), we are intimately united to Him. We are His members and His Mystical Body. We are a body because each of us is in the Church not as any part is to any whole, but as each organ with its own function is to a living body. Every square piece in a marble table is part of the table, but it does not have a special service to carry out for the table. An eye, on the other hand, and a hand, and an arm contribute to the good of the whole body, and each in its own way, with different resources. Thus a bishop, a Sister, a father of a family, and a member of Catholic Action each bring to the Church a different individual contribution.

We are of Christ because He has founded the Church. He is its Head, forming one whole with it and sharing its fate, He gives it life, permeating it with His Spirit.

Finally, we are a "Mystical" Body, that is, a mysterious and unusual one. In the usual physical bodies, the members exist because of the existence of the whole. In the Church, on the other hand, each member is a distinct person with his own existence. Other moral or social bodies have for their end the common good. The Church, on the other hand, intends the good of each individual soul. In the Church, we know that Christ influences souls together with the Holy Spirit and all of the Holy Trinity, but how this influence works is a mystery. In the Church, some things can be seen, but other things can only be believed. We can see, for example, the social apparatus of the Church, but that this external society is the extension of Jesus in time, that inside it, a supernatural life circulates in each and every soul, cannot be seen. It is an object of faith. The more we know the Church, the more it is revealed as something very lofty, with multiple facets, and the more we see that those who are part of the Mystical Body are exalted and endowed with mysterious gifts.

d. They Are in a Certain Sense Priests

Psalm 133 speaks of a very fine oil, which first is poured on the head of Aaron, then spreads to his beard, then flows down over the front of his garments to scent everything with its perfume. Something similar happens in the Church. Christ, the High Priest and the only priest, has the priestly anointing before everyone else. Then the bishops have it, deriving it in fullness from Him. Then ordinary priests participate in it in abundance, but in another capacity. Finally, the ordinary faithful have it in a more restricted measure and by power of their baptism and confirmation.

So the faithful too have a cultic power, a special right to be heard by the Lord. At Holy Mass they too offer to God along with the priest the Body of the Lord, which the priest alone has transubstantiated from the bread. They administer baptism in extraordinary cases. In the Sacrament of Matrimony they alone [the man and woman] are the ministers. The faithful too are invested with responsibility and must do something for souls. St. Paul did not want them to be dead weights and "infants, tossed by waves, and swept along by every wind of teaching" (Eph 4:14). St. Peter recommended, "Always be ready to give an explanation to everyone who asks you the reason for your hope, but do it with gentleness and reverence" (I Pt 3:15-16). Before St. Paul and St. Peter, the Lord had said to the faithful, "You are the light of the world" (Mt 5:14).

Now, what kind of light is the "light of the world," if it does not try to bring a little brightness where there is darkness? And there is so much darkness. Out of three billion people on earth, two billion are pagan. Of a billion Christians, half are not Catholic. Out of a half billion Catholics there are many who do not practice their faith. And these are men and women who are closer to us now than ever before. Once it took months and a great deal of money to go to America or Africa. Now you might say we can touch the Americans; we rub elbows with the Africans. Now the problem is urgent and anguishing, and it is not going to be resolved by saying, "Let the Pope, the bishops, and the missionaries think about it!" Instead, we must say, "Here, it is time for all of us to act at least a little bit as missionaries!"

e. They Have a Magnificent Task in a Magnificent Work

I said "at least a little bit as missionaries" because there are three different degrees of activity and commitment by Catholic lay people. The first is the so-called *consecratio mundi,* consecration of the world. What I am calling "world" here is the whole of creation and humankind: art, industry, politics, technology, science, commerce, agriculture, professional work, husband, wife, fiancé, children, and a hundred other things. I say, do you feel an inclination, love, enthusiasm for one or more of these things? Nothing wrong with that. Go ahead and immerse yourself in your work; become a great politician or a great industrialist. Create, if you can, true and great art. Invent, obtain patents. Love your wife or your fiancé. Don't be afraid of being too much of a politician, too much of a worker, too much of an artist, too loving a spouse, because you are a Christian. Do not say that the progress of science and technology have no meaning for the Christian faith. It is very important for the faith that the world should make progress. God Himself has commanded progress and conquest, saying to men and women, "Subdue the earth!" (Gn 1:29).

Faith has no need for little, static human beings with atrophied brains, but great human beings, co-workers of God, who intervene at the invitation of God to develop God's creation by their discoveries and works of genius. And don't think that you have to call on the Church to dominate this or that, or that you have to put a whole external religious ceremony on top of everything. Only try not to forget your Christianity and not to put yourself in conflict with it. You are at one and the same time inseparable, a politician and a Christian, a spouse and a Christian, an industrialist and a Christian. May it never happen that in you the first consumes the second.

The famous hare of Baron Munchhausen ran for an hour with the four legs that he had underneath his stomach; during the following hour, he put those to rest, and ran with the legs that he had above his back. But you cannot divide yourself in two. You do not have hours during which you are only a Christian and hours in which you are only an artist or an industrialist or a lawyer. There is not a single minute in which you can forget the salvation of your soul. If you succeed in putting aside some savings, do not attach yourself to them as the avaricious do. If you have had success in industry, do not be unjust and heartless with your employees. If you are a statesman and you perform for me the "Italian economic miracle," see to it that all Italians can participate in it. If you write a novel or produce a film for me, try to make one that causes no harm to the readers or the audience. In short, try to put a Christian spirit and intention into your human activities and then also carry out these activities with all the intelligence, with all the diligence, skill, and passion you are capable of, and you will have performed a good missionary activity.

The second degree of missionary activity consists of this, contributing to create a social atmosphere favorable to the practice of religion. An example, I refuse my vote to a party that favors divorce. I support a law that puts a brake on licentious films. I fight for a more equal distribution of goods. These actions of mine are in the social and political field, but they have repercussions in the religious field. When divorce is impeded, films uplifted morally, and the situation of those who have less is improved, in fact, it will be easier for certain sins to be avoided and for people to remain good.

The third degree consists of giving a direct aid to religion. I am thinking of teachers and catechists who break for children the bread of Christian doctrine. I think of the lay writers who write for Catholic newspapers and the advertisers who distribute them. I am thinking of parents who are really committed to a concern for the children's education. I am thinking of the constant and effective preaching that is done in schools, factories, and playing fields by the modest, exemplary, and courageous life of not a few of the faithful. I am thinking of so many consecrated souls, who are now dedicating their whole life and all of their energies to the salvation of souls. I am thinking of this, and by thinking of all this, I find something that consoles me.

But, as soon as I think of the needs that are not satisfied, of the problems still unsolved, of the energies that are not committed, I feel like saying, "How much remains to be done!" The faithful, who are the Church, must make a greater commitment of themselves to the Church! Their activity is necessary and urgent. May it not be refused or given with an eyedropper! No other activity gives honor and returns a profit, as this one does — it is done here but it will be rewarded beyond! It seems like a little thing, but it has immense dimensions! It is part of the process of salvation. The process that began with creation was taken up again by Christ, and is continued by us together with Christ. The process that will be perfected with the second coming of the Lord and will be perpetuated in an eternally triumphant Church!

2. The College of Bishops

a. What the Apostles Began

All the members of the Church must aid the Church, but the bishops in a very special way. The Lord has invented them for this end, and for this end He has given them both a special configuration and directives and limits.

Let's begin with the configuration. Recall that Christ did not only call around Him apostles, but apostles fused into a united group, gathered in a family or community. They had come to Him one by one, with the other disciples, but at one point, from among the many, "he chose twelve to whom he gave the name of apostles" (Lk 6:13). From this moment the college is in operation. We see the powers of binding and loosing, pardoning and consecrating, descend on the college, one after another (Mt 18:18; Jn 20:21; Lk 22:19). It is the college that receives the order to go into all the world, to teach all peoples and to baptize (Mt 28:18-20). It is awareness of the college, that the Lord re-awakes in the apostles by saying, "You will be seated on twelve thrones to judge the twelve tribes of Israel" (Mt 19:28). It is the entire college which waits in the upper room for the coming of the Holy Spirit (Acts 1:9). The first proclamation of the gospel to the world is made on the morning of Pentecost by "Peter together with the eleven" (Acts 2:24), that is, by the college. The form of the college was planned for the good of the Church that was to be founded and guided. If this Church was to remain united, it was fitting that the leaders, dispersed here and there, should feel bound to one another by ties of brotherhood and be obliged, at least in part, to a common action. If then the leaders of the Church were to be directed by a superior, his interventions would be better if he were included in the community, set up over the family and at the same time a member of the family, a head and at the same time a brother.

Once the college was set up, it had to be made effective. Here Christ showed Himself munificent and splendid. He says, "All that you will bind on earth, will be bound in heaven; and all that you will loose on earth will be loosed in heaven" (Mt 18:18). He did not mean physical cords or bonds, but moral and juridical bonds by which the power to enact binding religious laws, to pronounce judicial sentences, and to inflect penalties was conferred on the college. After consecrating the bread and wine, He says, "Do this in memory of me" (Lk 22:19). The members of the college receive the power to celebrate Mass and to ordain priests. On the evening of the Resurrection, he says, "Those whose sins you forgive are forgiven, and those whose sins you retain shall be retained" (Jn 20:23). Finally on the eve of the Ascension, He says "all power in heaven and on earth has been given to me. Go therefore and make disciples of all nations.... I am with you always, until the end of the world" (Mt 28:19-20). We must stress that "therefore" it links the powers of the apostles to those Christ has received from God. If the members of the college teach and baptize, it is because Christ, endowed with divine powers, transmits to them His own powers. By baptizing and preaching, they are His ambassadors, His visible extension in time.

b. The Bishops Continue

But not they alone. By extending Himself in time through the apostles, Christ wanted the apostolic college in its turn to be extended, substantially, with the same powers. In fact, He commanded, "Make disciples of all nations." One of the college might have objected, "Lord, how are we to 'make disciples of the nations' if we must die within a few decades?" The answer, implied, is evident "The college will do it! It doesn't matter if it is composed of you or of your successors; the college will make disciples of all nations!" He promised, "I will be with you . . . until the end of the world." We must recall the preceding words which complete it, "I will be with you . . . teaching and baptizing . . . until the end of the world," with you, as long as you are alive; when you die, with the others who, one by one, will teach and baptize in your place!

Thus it results that the college of bishops by the will of Christ succeeds as a group to the college of the apostles, and has, still as a group, substantially the same powers. It results that the bishop must be above all, the man who is concerned with extending and propagating the Church, in agreement with the others of the college. Others will become saints by obedience and poverty; the bishop must become a saint above all by working and sacrificing himself for souls. There results, finally, the eminent dignity of the bishops. As successors of the apostles, and lieutenants of Christ, they continue the service of Christ, the service of the word, of sanctification, of governing.

The dignity and the powers, however, can constitute a danger. In fact, when they are divided among several subjects, two dangers: first, that these subjects might become proud and harsh leaders; second, that contention, disorders, and confusion might occur. Jesus Christ knew this and has provided for it.

c. True Powers, but of a Special Kind!

Harsh and dominating leaders? It is the reverse that Christ wants. If He has given powers, He has also repeatedly explained the way and the style in which the powers must be exercised.

The apostles had been discussing their greatness while they were on the road. He stops, calls a child, places him in the midst of them and says, "The one who makes himself humble like this child, will be the greatest" (Mt 18:4). The mother of James and John asks for the first place for her sons. Jesus makes it understood that they are not to command like masters and to make their own power felt and that they must overturn the usual patterns of greatness. "Whoever wishes to be great among you shall be your servant; whoever wishes to be first among you, he shall be your slave. Just so, the Son of Man did not come to be served, but to serve, to give his life as a ransom for many" (Mt 20:26-27). On the evening of the Last Supper He insists on this again. He washes the feet of the apostles and then says, "I have given you the example so that you may also do as I have done" (Jn 13:12-17). And later, "The kings of the gentiles lord it over them and those in authority over them are called benefactors. But among you it shall not be so; rather, let the greatest among you be like the youngest and the leader as the servant. I am in the midst of you like one who serves" (Lk 22:25-27). In short, a "sweet new style" of power *ante litteram*, but so penetrating, so far from superficial, that it confers a special nature on the power itself and transforms it. It does not mean dominating, but serving; you do not climb, but descend; you are not first, but last; you do not have personal advantages or profits, but troubles, difficulties, and, if necessary, even death. A new and unheard-of style.

The apostles learned the lesson. "As for us," St. Paul writes, "we are your slaves for love of Jesus" (II Cor 4:5). "I have become a slave for all in order to gain many" (I Cor 9:19). And he said to the bishop Timothy, "A servant of the Lord must not quarrel, but be gentle with everyone, ready to teach, patient in suffering" (II Tim 2:24). St. Peter also exhorted the elders "not to lord it over those assigned to you, but be examples to your flock" (I Pt 5:3).

All this, naturally, must not encourage insubordination in the subjects or empty the powers of the superiors, putting their authority in danger. St. Paul called himself "slave of all"; but when necessary he was also able to claim energetically his title and authority as an apostle. He was also able to keep his staff in hand and make it flash when necessary before the eyes of the Corinthians. "What do you want? That I come to you with the rod, or with love and the spirit of meekness?" (I Cor 4:3 1). He also wrote to the faithful, "Obey your leaders and defer to them, for they keep watch over you and will have to give an account, that they may fulfill their task with joy and not with sorrow, for that would be of no advantage to you" (Heb 13:17).

Christ Himself, the most gentle shepherd, was forced at one point to "turn and look with anger" (Mk 3:5) at those who were impeding the good of souls; he also gave some rather strong statements. He chased the merchants from the temple, and he said of Herod, "Go and tell that fox . . ." (Lk 13:320). The gentleness, the spirit of service, must always remain, but at least one eye should remain open in the superior to check on those who abuse his gentleness, his prudence, and his duty.

d. "Under Peter!"

There remains, we have said, the danger of having bishops in conflict among themselves and subjects disturbed and uncertain which bishop they should obey. Christ provided for this, giving the college a head, choosing him from the college itself, in order to discipline the actions of the members of the college. All of you can bind and loose, he said to the apostles and bishops, but note well! — united to your head and placed under him. Your head, on the other hand, although not separated from you, will be able to bind and loose without depending on you! Note, in fact, that in the gospel of St. Matthew the discourse on binding and loosing is given by Christ first to Peter alone, and then to all the apostles united to Peter. In chapter 16 (Mt 16:13-19) Christ says, You will bind and loose!" in Chapter 18 (Mt 18:18) he says; "All of you will bind and loose!" And thus we can, in a sense, speak of a double primacy, of the Pope over all the Church, and of the Pope over the college of bishops. It has not only been said, "Feed my sheep" (Jn 21:15-18). It has also been said, "Strengthen your brothers" (Lk 22:31).

3. The "Humble Service" of the Pope

And notice that we are speaking about the service that the Pope renders to the Church. Chesterton, in one of his books, has described a group of children placed on a little island. All day long they jumped, ran, threw balls, danced, and had no fear and no worries because all around the island ran a high wall. One day some strange men landed on the island and began to spread propaganda against the wall. "But don't you see that it limits you? Don't you see that it takes away your liberty? Tear it down." Their orders were heeded, but if you go to the island today, you will find those children disoriented, no longer daring to run or throw balls — they are afraid of falling into the sea!

The bishops do not act like those children; they do not see in the primacy of the Pope a wall that limits their power and their work, but rather a help and a defense so that they can work with more order and concord.

Several times in Europe the episcopate found themselves in trouble; in order to get out of "difficult straits" several times, it has had need of the Pope, who, by intervening and centralizing, has renewed it, accomplishing its destiny and its prestige.

This centralization of the government of the Church has caused a number of superficial people to say that the bishops in their dioceses are nothing but functionaries of the Pope. Bismarck even had it written after the First Vatican Council, but the response of the German episcopate and of Pius IX was strong and immediate. It can be read in the *New Denzinger*, nn. 3112-3117, and in substance, it says, although subject to the Pope, the bishops are in their dioceses, the representatives of Christ, not of the Pope; willed by Christ as successors to the apostles, they have the power of the apostles; thus it has always been and thus it will always be, because that is part of the untouchable structure of the Church.

Along with the service given by the Pope by governing, there is the service of teaching, endowed, in certain cases, with infallibility. Some people are afraid of this infallibility, but wrongly; it too is nothing but a means granted by God to better serve the truth and the Church. The Pope is not master of the revealed truths, but the servant. The work of God is above him, directs him, and dominates him. It is not dominated by him and bent to say what he wants. It is so that it might be understood better, so that the same thing might not happen to it that happens to human theories, which, after starting with a certain face a hundred years ago, arrive today with their meaning completely changed, that the Lord assists the Pope. Only this divine assistance produces infallibility. And only under certain conditions, that the Pope speaks as pastor and teacher of all the faithful, using the fullness of his power, with the intention of deciding definitively a question of faith and morals.

We are, therefore, far from papal omniscience, even in matters of faith. The Pope is so little omniscient that although certain of divine assistance, before defining, he is obliged to study, and to have others study, to listen, to listen also to the thought of the Church. The "consensus ecclesiae" is not the cause of an infallible definition, even though it usually accompanies the definition and though, in practice, it never happens that a point is defined on which there is no consensus in the Church.

Papal infallibility, in addition to being a service of the word of God, is a service to us, because it gives us the secure and tranquil possession of the faith. The Protestant listens to the preaching of his pastor, then goes to compare it with the Bible. He must in some way, make the faith for himself because he does not have a single clear definition from his pastor. We have one, God has spoken in the past. God assists the Pope in the present, so that he might not err. What the Pope says in the name of God, we can receive in all tranquility!

4. Conclusion

These short notes require one conclusion, let us love the Church at all its levels!

Let us love our brothers and sisters, who are along with us a people chosen by God, Christ's body and His extension in time, invested with the highest dignity. By our conduct and profound convictions, let us act to form a climate in which the Church, its life and its destiny, can be close to the hearts of everyone.

Let us obey the bishops, fathers and servants of souls. The pastoral staff that they hold, now caresses and now pushes and goads, but it does good in every case. Like Cardinal Federigo, the bishops consider every opportunity offered them to help souls [with] a "banquet of grace." With St. Augustine, before their faithful, they feel at once *praepositi,* or "superiors," and *conservi,* or "fellow servants." Inasmuch as they are given to a diocese, they are fathers, and bishops. Inasmuch as they are frail beings, subject to evil, they are fellow servants and our brothers. When the unnamed, a hardened criminal comes along, he rests his head on their shoulder and weeps; they feel they are fathers. Valjean, the escaped man, the thief hunted by the police that Victor Hugo describes with such power, comes along. The bishop throws his arms around his neck. "But do you know who I am?" asked the wretched man, whom no one would receive. "Yes, my brother in Christ!" answered Bishop Myriel. Let us try to understand and help the work of these *praepositi-conservi!*

But above all, let us follow the Pope and help that work which the present Pope loves to call a "humble service." He is "sweet Christ on earth," the pilot of the bark of Peter. Every so often an order is given from the ship; a signal is launched. It is a service for us! Let us listen to it and follow it!

20

∽∾∿

You Have Been Sent

Homily at the Mass for Priestly Ordinations, June 26, 1976

In this ceremony, a link is being added to a marvelous chain that stretches across the centuries; each of these links is a person who is sent, and who, in turn, sends others. The first link was Christ. He constantly said that He had been sent by the Father. "He has sent me to bring glad tidings to the poor" (Lk 4:18). "God has sent His Son into the world . . . so that the world might be saved through him" (Jn 3:17). "My food is to do the will of the One who sent me" (Jn 4:34). "I do not seek my own will, but the will of the One who sent me" (Jn 5:30). "I have been sent, I have been sent," in the mouth of Christ it appears like a refrain: cf. Jn 1:33; 3:34; 5:23; 5:24; 5:36; 5:37; 5:38; 6:29; 6:39; 6:44; 6:58; 7:10; 7:18; 7:28; 7:29; 7:33; 8:16; 8:26; 8:9; 8:42; 9:4; 10:36; 12:45; 12:49; 13:20; 14:24; 15:21.

At one point, as one Who has been sent, Christ makes Himself a person Who sends. They hear Him say, "As the Father has sent me, so I send you"(Jn 20:21). In sending, He transmits the powers He has received, "Those whose sins you forgive shall be forgiven . . . baptize them . . . teach them" (cf. Mt 28:19). This is the second link.

The apostles too, in turn, send others. Paul sends Timothy, Timothy the elders of Ephesus. Peter writes to the presbyters, "Tend the flock of God" (1 Pt 5:2). This is the third link. And then come the fourth, and the fifth; then the links can no longer be counted, and after almost two thousand years it arrives at us.

It seems like yesterday to me when, in St. Peter's Basilica, Pope John had the open gospels placed on my shoulders, then, aided by the two consecrating bishops, he entrusted the gospel to me, saying, "Receive the gospel, and go, preach to the people who

189

have been assigned to you; God is powerful and will make *His grace grow in you.*" I too, therefore, am someone who has been sent.

And within a few short moments, I too will send. I will entrust the gospel to the lectors saying, "Believe in what you read; teach what you see; practice what you teach." To the deacons and priests I will say, "Preach!" But [teach] what? Christ, as interpreted by the Magisterium, in response to the religious problems of our time. Not a Christ sweetened and falsified to accommodate the fashion of the day, but "crucified" like Paul's Christ (I Cor 1:23). Paul's Greek listeners scorned a religion which did not present itself as a *sophia,* or philosophical system. His Jewish listeners thought only of wonders, demanding a God Who would manifest Himself with astounding stage effects, like the Exodus. And Paul says, I preach Christ as He is, crucified, even if it is folly to the Greeks and a scandal to the Jews (cf. I Cor 1:23).

That took a lot of guts! The fact is that Paul used a special strategy. His preaching was not "in sublimity of words or of wisdom" (I Cor 2:1). It was not based on "persuasive wisdom" but on the manifestation of the Spirit and His power (I Cor 2:4). Paul did not feel great or clever, but small, foolish, and stupefied. I am the least of all, he writes, and yet it is to me that the grace of bringing the Good News to the people has been given (cf. Eph 3:8). He was preaching to some women along the river near Philippi. One of them, Lydia, was converted, but why? Because "the Lord opened her heart" (Acts 16:14). Paul's pride was the church in Corinth, which had grown miraculously in a heavily populated and corrupt city, but what was the story of this great church? Paul sums it up in three words, "I planted, Apollos watered, but God caused the growth" (I Cor 3:6). You too, my dear young men, must put all your faith in God. It is He Who works on souls; we only lend Him our poor service.

That does not mean that preparation is not necessary. This is demanded by respect for the word of God and for our listeners. The lesson is worth as much, said the old teacher, as the preparation is worth. In evangelization this rule springs forth only in part, but it does. God does not usually work miracles; what He rewards in the priest is humble prayers, commitment, effort, not superficiality, improvisation, or only a smattering of knowledge. People, in turn, want to feel that their priest is completely penetrated by the truth that he states. It was once asked, why are people very attentive in the theater, while they are distracted and yawn at sermons? The answer was, perhaps because in the theater the actors say with verve, stupid things as if they were important. In church preachers say important things without verve, and as if they were trifles. And the conviction refers not only [to] what they preach, but the office of preaching itself. "Preaching the gospel is a duty for me: woe to me if I do not preach the gospel" (cf. I Cor 9:16). In these words we feel a conviction.

In the following we also feel the impassioned man. "To Greeks and non-Greeks alike, to the wise and the ignorant, I am under obligation; that is why I am eager to preach the gospel also to you in Rome" (Rom 1:14-15). "Some preach Christ from envy or rivalry . . . not from pure motives, thinking that they will cause me trouble in my imprisonment. What difference does it make, as long as in every way, whether in pretension or in truth, Christ is being proclaimed? And in that I rejoice" (Phil 1:15-18).

I will also give the chalice to the new priests and anoint their hands with the holy chrism. This is especially in view of the Holy Mass. At the Last Supper, Our Lord commanded, "Do this in memory of me." He decided at that moment that, after supper and the cross, He would continue to represent Himself in a liturgical sacrifice every day for us to the Father, and He wanted this to take place through the gestures and words of the priests. He, the high priest, would associate himself with secondary priests. The sacrifice would still be that of the cross, still His, but it would also be a sacrifice by the Church. Our limited merits would be added to the infinite and superabundant merits of Jesus, in order to fill up "what is lacking in the sufferings of Christ" to the benefit of the Church (cf. Col 1:24). You will not only be evangelizers, then, you will also be sacrificers and you will allow yourselves to have within you the same feelings as Christ. He constantly had His eyes fixed on His own sacrifice. "I am the Good Shepherd," He said, ". . . and I will lay down my life for my sheep. . . . I lay down my life . . . no one takes it from me, but I lay it down on my own" (Jn 10:14-18).

Five times, in the synoptics, He foretells His passion to the apostles. He preached, acted, journeyed, but His gaze was directed there, to the sacrifice, which is the center and the culmination of His work of liberation and salvation. Holy priests imitate Him; the Mass is the center of their apostolate and their lives. Francis de Sales, in the resolutions he made during the retreat before his priestly ordination, wrote, "My day will be totally made up of preparation for Mass and thanksgiving after celebrating it." He also wrote, the "Mass is the sun of the spiritual exercises," "the center of the Christian religion, the heart of devotion," "the soul of piety." These expressions explain his commitment, his resolution, and his fervor. How do we explain, on the other hand, the slovenliness, haste, and frivolity of priests who celebrate Mass rarely, sometimes without vestments, skipping formulas, changing prayers, tampering with the canon itself as if they were the masters? A wise man, godfather of a certain Don Giuseppe, present at a Mass bungled by his godson, could not keep himself (as Cavigioli wrote) from sighing, "Poor Christ, in the hands of Beppe." But shortly after that Mass, the godson died in an accident, and the good man said, spontaneously, "Poor Beppe, in the hands of Christ!"

My dear young men. Vatican II has emphasized the priesthood of the faithful, while stressing that it is a priesthood of another type. Let us honor it and value it as well. Do not speak, however, of declericalizing the Church. In the midst of the people of God, you will live like "brothers among brothers," but without forgetting that to the people, you are their spiritual guides. "Tend the flock," said St. Peter to the elders. "Do not lord it over those assigned to you, but be examples to the flock" (I Pt 5:3). To be of help to his brothers, St. Paul went so far as to desire to be separated from Christ (Rom 9:13), but he never renounced guiding his brothers. He was energetic with the Corinthians, and to the young Timothy he wrote, "be persistent, whether it is convenient or inconvenient; convince, reprimand, encourage . . . be self-possessed in all circumstances" (II Tm 4:2-5).

St. Augustine and St. Bernard summed up everything in one phrase, *praesint ut prosint*. Since bishops of priests have been placed in front of the others, let them stay at their post, in front; if they are there not for their own interests and convenience, but only for the good of others, no sensible person will have anything to say against it. Besides, it is the system of Christ. On one hand, He says, "All power in heaven and on earth has been given to me" (Mt 28:18). On the other, "The Son of Man did not come to be served but to serve and to give his life as a ransom for many" (Mt 20:28). Here is a beautiful program for priests. After his first Mass, Antonio Chevrier wrote, "I want to be good bread, eaten by the faithful." I hope you will become true guides, but in a style of humble service.

21

The Bishop, the Keeper of the Faith, the Man of Charity

First Homily in the Cathedral, Vittorio Veneto,
January 11, 1959

The very cordial and spontaneous welcome you have shown me moves me deeply. In entering the diocese, I have received the impression that I am meeting a people who still feel their religion very deeply and who have very warm hearts. The words of the most reverend and venerated archdeacon of the cathedral have struck me in this, that they have given the assurance that I will have at my side a good, disciplined, and faithful clergy. It is this above all that I am counting on, and therefore, your welcome, the very heartfelt obedience given me by my priests, and the words of the archdeacon give me assurance and hope that I will have cooperation and also affection from you.

I feel the need to give my warm thanks again to the government, civil, military, and political authorities who have been pleased to honor my coming among you by their presence. In the presence of His Honor the Mayor, I have seen the whole city. This city, so great because of its historic past, so industrious because of a fervent work, and now a city very dear to me because it has been assigned by the Supreme Pontiff as the center and heart of the diocese. It is for this reason that the Mayor's words have brought me great pleasure. Through them I have been placed in contact with the people of the city.

I thank again my priests and all the faithful present here this evening. I also thank the delegation from Belluno which, with illustrious and deserving men from my hometown at its head, has wanted to give me a last sign of kindness by accompanying me

here. I liked very much the gesture of the organizers of this ceremony, who have decided that shortly after entering the cathedral,
I should descend to venerate the body of the patron saint of the
diocese, St. Tiziano. For me, to pray before that venerable and very
ancient urn, also was to give a glance back through the centuries;
and so I saw myself meeting a long line of bishops from St. Flo-
riano, from St. Tiziano, from St. Magno, all the way down to Zaf-
fonato, to Carraro, and to me. I am the last of this glorious line.
I am one of them, and at this moment I ask the Lord from the
bottom of my heart for the grace not to be unworthy of them, and
the grace to be able to truly be in your midst, the keeper of the
faith and a man of charity.

Keeper of the Faith

You know from the catechism what faith is. When God speaks
on one hand and on the other a man says, "Yes, oh Lord, I believe,
it is just as You say, for me now there is no doubt," then we have
faith, a yes, an assent of the intellect, a bowing of the mind to God.
It seems to be a meeting of two people; instead it is a meeting of
three because the Lord has willed that a third element should come
into play in faith, the Church. And with the act of faith, we say
daily, "My God, I firmly believe what You, infallible truth, have
revealed, and what the Holy Church proposes that we believe." I,
all of you, and the Holy Church, three characters, the believer, the
Lord, and the bishop, the Holy Church united with the Pope. It
is a very serious responsibility for me to find myself mixed up
along with the Pope in your act of faith. With this I come to be,
in the diocese, the sole official teacher. My priests and I know that
there are some here who are more capable and intelligent than I
am. From this moment on, my priests are only delegated and substitute teachers. From this moment on, my teaching comes down
to you not plain, not naked, but clothed in divine authority. The
bishop does not only propose ideas to the mind, but he also
imposes them on the conscience; if you are a believer, you are
obliged to say "yes" to the bishop. The force of my words, of my
writings from here on will not be in their reasoning, in their eloquence, or in their style; it will be in the fact that behind me is

Christ, Who says to me, "As the Father has sent me, so I send you." Yet with all this, your faith, my dear ones, will always remain an exclusive gift of God.

One of the most brilliant bishops was St. Paul the apostle, who said of his own sermons preached at Corinth, "I sowed the seed, but nothing would have happened if God had not made it grow and bloom" (cf. I Cor 3:6). It is not a question of running; it is only a question of the mercy and the gentleness of God. I as a bishop and my priests can instruct, enlighten, and even convince you, but no more; only God can touch your heart and convert you.

In one of his novels, Cronin [A. J. Cronin] tells of a famous professor who had always been an unbeliever, always an atheist. As he approached his death, however, something in him broke down and it could be seen, but he found it difficult to admit it, and he said to his daughter, who was nursing him, "I am not yet capable of believing in God." And his good daughter, filled with joy when she saw the work that grace was accomplishing, said to him, "Don't worry, Papa, don't worry, it is not you who believes in God; it is God Who has confidence in you." And this is a true thought. If someone comes to believe in God, it means that God has first believed in him, drawing him to Himself by the sweet power of His grace.

Knowing this, and I say it frankly, I will never say to my children, especially to those who are farthest in the faith, I will never say, "I am here to convert you and conquer you." It is not a matter of conquest. It is only a matter of a modest and caring service. "Dear friend, I am here at your disposal, and I will be very happy if you will let yourself be conquered by the Lord Who loves you and believes in you."

The Man of Charity

I would like to be a bishop who is a teacher and servant. I would also like to be inspired by the example of St. John the apostle and Bishop of Ephesus, who as a feeble old man had himself carried into the assembly of his faithful and when he arrived there, always preached the same sermon, "My little children, love one another." "But Father," they said to him one day, "it is always the same sermon can't you change it?" And the old bishop said, "It is the commandment of God it is enough to put this into practice, there is no need for anything else!"

And in fact, the Lord has said, "This is how all will know you for my disciples, by your love for one another" (Jn 13:35).

Loving your neighbor, sympathizing, helping, supporting, forgiving, here is a beautiful program, suited to us bishops, to all priests, but also to all those who want to be truly Christian.

A program that is difficult to carry out, but very possible if our love for our neighbor exists along with true love of God. I will try to help you understand this with a modest example: There is a young man who has his eye on a good young girl. One day he meets her on the street and lets her know that he would like very much to marry her. "No, not here," she says. "You know where I live. My father and mother are there, come, and we will see." One fine evening he presents himself and knocks at the door of the famous house, and she herself opens it and he understands right away from the way she looks and acts that things are going to go well. His heart expands and he enters very happily.

Here is a modest, unassuming woman, the young lady's mother. He has met her any number of times in the street, and he has never thought to look at her. But now she actually seems to him to be a fine woman, a very nice lady.

And here is a man, it is her papa. He too is modest and unassuming, but he too seems to him to be truly likeable. Two young men knock and enter, her brothers. He would actually like to throw his arms around their necks, he is so glad to see them. What is happening, how many loves are multiplying in that young man's heart?

Don't worry, it's very simple, there is only one love; he loves her, and his love for the girl he hopes to marry spreads over all the others because they are close to her. And so it is for us, if we truly love the Lord. We will be able to love even those who have hurt us, to love even irritating people, to love those who do not seem to us to be attractive in themselves. Everything comes down to this: loving the Lord and meaning it, and then extending this love of God to everyone else.

The bishop asks the Lord not only to be able to teach this most important thing to you during the mission that the Lord will allow him to carry out among you, but also to be able to precede you by his example, and it is for this reason that I wrote to you.[1] And I am truly convinced that the Lord has made a law, and it is this: anyone who wants to do good to others must above all love others.

I would truly be the most unfortunate of all bishops if I did not begin my ministry above all with this, with loving your souls, loving them very much.

Notes

1. On January 3, Luciani had written to the people of his new diocese, "St. Pius X, on entering as the new patriarch of Venice, said to his people, 'What would become of me if I didn't love you?' My dear priests, my dear faithful, I would truly be an unfortunate bishop if I didn't love you. On the contrary, I can assure you that I love you, that I desire only to enter into your service and put at your disposal all of my poor strengths, the little that I have and that I am" (*Opera* 2:11). He repeated these exact words to the people of Rome after becoming Pope, in his sermon at St. John Lateran on September 23, 1978.

22

Sunday, the Lord's Day

September 17, 1977

*O*tto von Bismarck, when he was not yet chancellor of the
German Empire, once went for a short vacation in England.
Getting off the boat and walking down the street, he began to
whistle merrily. Behind him a gentleman said to him, "Pray sir,
do not whistle." "Why?" asked Bismarck. "Is it against the law?"
"It's not against the law, but today is Sunday." Bismarck, in his own
way, was deeply religious; he felt that Sunday should be respected,
but not in that way, by condemning some innocent whistling that
was doing no harm to anyone. He asked the way to the station
and took the first train for Scotland to escape from the net of an
exaggerated Puritanism and to be able to spend a Sunday full of
Christian and human joy.

It's a funny story, but a useful one. It warns us not to present
Sunday under its purely moral and juridical aspect; go to Mass and
abstain from servile work and that's all. Families might get from
this an impression of burden and annoyance, as though it were a
tax to be paid to God's Ministry of Finance. There is something
better to be proposed: the theology of Sunday, the theology of joy,
and the way that these two theologies can be lived in the family.

The Theology of Sunday

The theology of Sunday can be summed up in these words:
"the day of the Lord," "the day consecrated to God," "the day of
the Christian community."

"The Day of the Lord." And the Lord is Jesus, Who saved us
by instituting the New Covenant, with the Eucharist to seal it, by
suffering, dying, and rising on the very days on which Israel celebrated the Passover. For this reason we say that Jesus is our paschal

sacrifice, that it is the paschal mysteries which save us, and that at the center of these is the Eucharist, the sacrifice of the New Covenant, mysteriously renewed and represented, placed in the hands of the Church, so that by it the fruits of the Redemption may be applied. The Passover of the Jews was only an annual, festive memorial of an event in the past; the Christian Paschal celebration, on the other hand, is much more. It is a past event that is repeated today, every day. But the daily repetition threatens to lead to habit and monotony. So that we might live Easter and the Covenant more intensely, from the daily repetition emerges the Sunday of Sundays, the annual Easter celebration.

Every Sunday, therefore, is the Easter of the week, and the annual Easter celebration is the Sunday of the whole year.

The dominant note of Easter and of Sunday is joy. Christ, in rising and reassuring us, saying, "Death has been conquered, and in ascending to heaven I am only the first; after me will come all of you in a long line" cannot help but give joy to brothers and sisters who participate in so great a destiny.

"We spend this day in joy." An Egyptian Jew who converted to Christianity wrote in the year 1352, "On Sunday, we are always happy; anyone who is sad on Sunday commits a sin," says the *Teaching of the Twelve Apostles*. And Tertullian, "On Sunday we do not kneel, we do not fast, to do so would be wrong." But why pray on your feet and not on your knees? "As a sign of the Resurrection," explains St. Augustine. And St. Basil adds, ". . . and because Sunday is a reflection of the world to come."

In addition to being a memorial of a past event and a participation in a mystery in the present, therefore, Sunday is also the affirmation of a joyous future certainty. Today's temporary Sunday actually proclaims the definitive Sunday that will arise beyond time and history, when the world has finished living the present week. Someone who showed this sense of the "Lord's Day" was St. Thérèse of Lisieux, who enjoyed Sunday immensely as a little girl, and wanted it never to end. "Toward sunset," she wrote, "a veil of melancholy would be spread over my joy"; then Thérèse's heart would think of heavenly rest and the Sunday without end in our homeland.

Our Manzoni [Alessandro Manzoni] had the very same sense of "the Lord's day," when he wrote in his poem "The Resurrection,"

Far away the shouts and the tempest
Of immodest rejoicing:
This is not the type of merriment
With which the just are joyful.
But quiet in its bearing
But heavenly, as a sign of the joy to come . . .
Oh, blessed ones!
for them more beautifully
Rises the sun of the holy days.

"Day consecrated to God." Why consecrated? God has created us to know Him, love Him, and serve Him in this life and then to enjoy Him in the other life in heaven. We must constantly remain united to Him, to adore Him, thank Him, and ask Him for help. Since it is possible to do this continually at the level of inspiration, but impossible at the level of external actions and of worship, one day is taken out from the days of the week and dedicated to God in a special way. Let me make it clear: dedicated not because it alone is the day of God, but because it must confer such a religious impulse to the other days that it will give them their sense, their flavor, and their fragrance. Even our Sunday rest is not the Sabbath inactivity as conceived by the Pharisees (Mk 2:23-28; 3:1-6; Lk 13:10-17; 14:1-6; Jn 5:1-18; 9:1-41). It does not make Sunday a day to empty, but a day to fill, not only with Holy Mass, but with serene amusements, pious and joyful reading and reflections, prayers, and works of charity. A day of rest for the body but also rest for the heart in God, with time given to a silence that is true silence and not only an absence of noise.

"Day of the Christian community." It always has been, "On the day which is named after the Sun," writes St. Justin, "all of us who live in the town and in the country gather together in the same place."

The Teaching of the Twelve Apostles, written in the third century, told the bishops to "enjoin the people to be faithful gathering in the Church (or community) so that no one may diminish the body of Christ by one member." And, once they were gathered, the first Christians did not think only of themselves, but also of the other communities. Earlier, St. Paul used to ask that at the Sunday meeting an offering be taken up for the poor of Jerusalem (cf. I Cor 16:1). Dionysius, the bishop of Corinth, writes to Pope Soter, "Today we have celebrated the holy day of Sunday, during the course of which we have read your letter." We are in line with this hunger and thirst for community spirit, when during Mass we ask for prayers for Friuli, which has been hit by an earthquake, or for a hospital for the poorest countries, or take up our collection.... On the same line we find both the Code of Canon Law, which declares that Masses heard in private oratories do not fulfill the Sunday obligation, and the post-conciliar documents which favor Sunday and Holy Day Masses in the parish and ask that the number of Masses be reduced, to avoid those for groups, in order to have large and full assemblies.

The Theology of Joy

And now, excuse me if, in dedicating a few thoughts to a minitheology of joy, I cite Andrew Carnegie, one of the richest men in the world.

"I was born in extreme poverty, but I would not exchange the memories of my childhood with those of the children of millionaires. What do they know about family joys, about the gentle figure of a mother who combines in herself the jobs of nursemaid, washerwoman, cook, teacher, angel, and saint?"

When he was employed at a very young age in a cotton mill in Pittsburgh for a miserable $1.20 weekly wage, the cashier told him to wait one evening, instead of giving him his pay. Carnegie thought, "I'll bet now they're going to fire me," and he trembled. Instead, after the others had been paid, the cashier said to him, "Andrew, I have been watching your work closely. I have decided that it's worth more than the others; I'm raising your pay to $1.45." Carnegie ran home, where his mother wept for joy at her son's promotion. "You talk of millionaires," he said. "All my millions put together have not given me as much joy as that 25-cent raise did."

Many joys are similar to this, purely human, but healthy: the joy of a student who passes an exam, of a mother who can finally provide a home for her children, of a [graduate] who quickly finds a steady job. These joys can be a great help to a good life and are in harmony with the desires of Christ, Who has called His message the gospel, that is, the "good news" (Mt 24:18, Mk 14:9); whose birth was announced as a "great joy"; whose apostles wrote, "Rejoice in the Lord always... dismiss all anxiety from your minds" (Phil 4:4-6). "The reign of God is... justice, peace, and joy" (Rom 14:17). "The fruit of the Spirit is love, joy, and peace" (Gal 5:22).

However, we must not absolutize these joys. They are something; they are not everything. They can be a useful means; they are not the supreme goal. They last for a little time, but not forever. St. Paul admonished the Corinthians to "make use of them as if they were not using them, for the world as we know it is passing away" (I Cor 7:31). We must also distinguish and choose — joy is one thing; pleasure is another. The joy connected with our good passions, like pardoning and helping others, is one thing. The joy connected with our evil passions, like enjoying the failure of others or insolence in using power, is another.

Should joy also be sought, cultivated, and defended from sadness? Yes, and useful towards this end is a special virtue, which Aristotle called *eutrapeleia* and St. Thomas *jucunditas*. "Be *eutrapelic*," St. Thomas recommended, "that is, capable of turning the things you see and hear into laughter in a suitable measure and proper way."

Eutrapelic was that Irish mason who, when he fell from a second-story scaffolding on which he was working, was carried on a stretcher to the hospital. The Sister came running and, "Poor man," she said. "You hurt yourself when you fell." And the mason, "Sister, I hurt myself like this not when I fell, but when I hit the ground." Truly eutrapelic even from the fact of his "hitting the ground" and the Sister's work, he managed to find matter for smiling and making others smile.

Therefore, according to St. Thomas, Mark Twain, with his newspapers and his humorous books, Charlie Chaplin, with his farces, lighthearted and human at the same time, and Goldoni, with his comical plays, could have become saints, if they had added to their art and their genius the right intention and the practice of the other Christian virtues. We would have had in them attractive, smiling, and holy patron saints to teach Christians how they can and should smile and laugh. There seems to be a need for it, if it is true, as Tommaseo [Niccoló Tommaseo] says, "The Italians are like toothless old women; they don't know how to laugh without spitting."

Jucunditas, therefore, blossoms in an outer smile. The young Bismarck whistled; Tarantin de Tarascon, like a good exuberant southern Italian, expressed his internal joy by vivacious gestures and noisy exclamations; an English gentleman just barely shows it, in a contained and measured way. To each his style; even by smiling a showing joy, a Christian exercises the apostolate. St. Peter wrote, "Fear not and do not be troubled . . . should anyone ask you the reason for this hope of yours, be ever ready to reply" (I Pt 3:15). He was speaking of hope; but this is the twin sister of joy. Hope actually has for its object the good to be won, joy the good already possessed.

The saints understood this. St. Philip Neri was reprimanded one day by his friend Zernobi because, while reading *Father Arlotto's Joke Book,* he laughed heartily. "A priest of Our Lord shouldn't laugh like that," said Brother Zenobi. "But the Lord is good," Philip retorted. "Why shouldn't He be happy to see His children laugh? It is sadness that makes us bow our heads and does not let us look up to heaven. We must fight against sadness, not merriment."

But what if suffering comes along? Enlightened believers are not scandalized that misfortune and suffering happen in the world. They know that God is good, that He only permits evil; that He is capable of bringing good out of evil; that we are only here in passing, that we have been damaged by original sin. They do not know what more to say. They do not know how to answer the numerous and anguishing "whys" about the evil in the world. They can, however, answer one question, how to act in suffering. How . . . as Jesus Christ did. He was innocent and holy. He had done good to everyone; nevertheless, they persecuted Him, condemned Him to death and hung Him on the cross. And yet, He abandoned Himself, although with an effort, to the will of the Father (Mt 26:39, Lk 24:16). He suffered for the salvation of others (Lk 22:19-20). He prayed for those Who crucified Him (Lk 23:28-31). He acted like a lamb being led to slaughter, making no resistance, silent before His shearers (Is 53:7).

After doing this, He recommended to us, "Pray like this, 'Father, may Your will be done.'" Done of course, by us, and not as some understand it — "I will love You, my Jesus, as long as You do my will." St. Philip Neri, on the other hand, used to pray, "I thank You, my Jesus, that things are not going my way." This prayer of St. Philip takes us at one leap to a supernatural level of joy. At this level the apostles "left the Sanhedrin full of joy that they had been judged worthy of ill-treatment for the sake of the name of Jesus" (Acts 5:41). St. Paul calls himself "afflicted" but also "always rejoicing" (II Cor 6:10). St. Thérèse of the Child Jesus declared, "In my childhood I suffered in sadness; now I still suffer, but in a different way; in joy and peace, and I am truly happy to suffer."

Sunday in the Family

Now, how to make these mini-theologies penetrate the domestic reality of today's family? In other words, how to immerse today's family in such an atmosphere of joy that it is in harmony with the authentic Easter joy and is nourished by it?

It isn't easy. The atmosphere in which we live is consumer oriented; having and enjoying every convenience often becomes the goal to which everything else is sacrificed.

A great part of the time on Sunday is already taken up with noisy sports events, long trips, meetings, and entertainment of every kind. A few scraps, if anything, are left over for God. We call the weekend "Sunday rest," but often it is not rest, but rather a weekend exertion which is added to the weekday labors, wearing out people's nerves on streets jammed with interminable lines of cars going no faster than a person can walk, and bringing them to Monday more tired than they were on Saturday evening.

Then there is a new mentality of the family. I am not talking about exaggerated and radical feminism, which wants a struggle of women against men and the end of religious and civil marriage, and which makes young girls sing in protest lines, "Tremble, tremble, the witches have returned!" I am talking about the ideal type of family that advertising is constantly promoting. In this family, the children grow up healthy, plump, and intelligent by eating this brand of processed cheese and that brand of bread. Girls find suitable husbands quickly by using the soap with the delicate scent of French perfume and the brand of toothpaste that "makes your breath kissing sweet," which makes the boys gather around and the men turn to look. Students, even if they don't study, will find success in their careers by dressing in these brand-name designer clothes. The love of husband and wife will be protected against every danger if during the day they warm themselves with this brand of liquor, and at night with that brand of sheets and blankets. All nonsense, aiming at people's wallets. But it is believed and it makes people forget the need for work, sacrifice, and the painful realities that hit their eyes as soon as they enter hospitals, prisons, and the houses of the poor. It also makes a proper sense of "the Lord's Day" impossible.

It would be wrong, however, to accept this situation passively and neglect the necessary efforts to introduce another mentality, another climate. General rules aren't possible. Sundays are different, but above all, families are different, and then in the same family, the situations change as the children grow from babies and toddlers to school-age children, pre-teens, teenagers, and young adults. I will try to establish some principles.

1. The atmosphere of a Christian Sunday is not improvised in the home, it cannot be an island, a short interval preceded and followed by weeks of agnostic and secularly minded life. Nor do long faces that sulk all through the week light up as soon as they are kissed by the Sunday sun.

They say that the first seven years are the golden age of intelligence in children; that they absorb whatever they see and hear like a sponge. You can put a three-month-old Italian child in a Chinese family. When he is four years old, he will speak Chinese with a perfect accent without even wondering whether it was difficult to learn. You don't teach your children to speak; you keep them at home — they see, they hear, they answer, they speak. What will we do to have them learn to pray and be smiling people? We won't do anything but this; let them see their parents and brothers and sisters praying, loving one another, being happy and smiling.

Much, therefore, depends on how birthdays and saints' days are celebrated, on how the dead are remembered, on how teachers and priests are honored. Is the language at home noble or vulgar? Are the daily sufferings borne with Christian resignation? Knowing that they are "watched" by their children, how will the parents overcome the inevitable moments of exhaustion and bad moods? Is she able to light up with gentleness when he is angry and gloomy? Does he keep calm and wait for things to clear up when she is nervous and tired? And what is the interior design of the house like? Is everything there only a demonstration of material well-being and luxury? Or is everything there only in relation to utility? Or is there something in the furniture, in the pictures, in the books, in the magazines that reveal the refined and religious spirit of those who head the family? Each one of these elements acts day after day, year after year. They are impressed deeply on souls, influencing the future of their inner life and at the same time influencing the style of Sunday.

2. We have seen a life of joy alone is not possible for anyone. Since all of us have to take suffering into account it is wise to introduce your children to the disappointments in life from the time they are very small and help them react serenely to them. Children always need to feel that their father and mother are close to them, but with an intelligent love, which helps and encourages them, but without claiming everything, deploring everything, and shielding them from everything.

A three-year-old boy was crying desperately, pointing to his foot. The nursemaid took him in her arms and took off his little shoe, in which she found a tiny pebble. "Ah," the woman then exclaimed. "You see? It's this bad thing that hurt you so much. Nasty! We'll throw it away." His mother, who had heard the shrieks, arrived at this point, and said to the nursemaid, "Put the shoe back on Nino with the pebble in it. I mean it, do as I tell you!" And she obeyed. The mother then went and stood at the other end of the room, turned, bent over, opened her arms, and with her most loving smile, called her little one like this: "You who love me so much, come and give me a hug, without crying, with the pebble in your shoe!" And the child went, without crying, limping a little, into his mother's arms, and she spoke to him words which at that time he did not understand, but which she would repeat later on: "You must always do as you're doing now. You will go on your way in spite of the obstacles and the sorrows that there always are in life. Remember your mother's words, you can only get to heaven with a pebble in your shoe."

There are parents who don't want any pebbles in their children's shoes, they satisfy them always and in everything, and always give money in abundance for their whims. They are forming bad habits in them, they forget that life is not intended to be a burden for many and a holiday for a few, but a job for everyone, of which everyone will have to give an account. When this is done every day, these children will not feel that Sunday is a special day.

3. There will be no truly successful Sunday unless it is studied and programmed first. The principle programmer should be the father, the head of the family, better still in cooperation with his wife and the oldest children. He is an abdicator if he does not take advantage of Sunday at least, to be a little while with his family. He is being selfish if he thinks only about "his" card game, "his" bowling, without worrying about how his wife and children are amusing themselves. If he considers the tavern, the bar, and the sports field as "calm" after the "storm" of the family, the opposite should be true calm is in the family.

4. When programming, make sure that Sunday is something different from the other days, even externally. Already on Saturday afternoon, the youngest children observe with satisfaction a great sweeping or cleaning in the apartment; piles of linen pulled out of drawers and closets, a lot of shoes shined and then lined up as though in battle formation, supplies for the day stocked in advance, the cake for tomorrow is put away in the cupboard. After dinner, the good tablecloth, laid on the table, already by itself seems to welcome the coming Sunday. Even the children who aren't so little breathe the air of freedom and liberation on Saturday night. "Tomorrow there's no school; tomorrow Papa doesn't

work, under orders, in the pay of others during the week, yes, but tomorrow belongs entirely to us; it is the same too with the neighbor families and with our friends. Tomorrow, freedom for everyone. The atmosphere of Sunday is good, as good as the bread we all eat."

5. And here is Sunday in essence. It should be celebrated as much as possible as a family unit. Ordinarily it is good for the whole family to participate in the same Mass. St. Thérèse of Lisieux was very happy to give her hand to her father and to go with him and her sisters to Holy Mass. Little as she was, she understood little of the sermons, but she looked at her father more often than she did the preacher. Her father's face told her so many things. About the Mass, Pope John said, "Oh, the Mass! The book and the chalice!" The reading and the homily are the "book," but for the smallest children their parents' faces and their behavior in church can be a living book or gospel.

6. And then dinner. Those who have programmed it should have provided something on the table for everyone's taste, ice cream for the little children and the more grown-up ones, Mama's favorite dessert, cigar and after-dinner drink for Papa. And a conversation that involves everyone a little.

Manzoni's tailor from Vercurago commented with enthusiasm at the table on the sermon that Cardinal Federigo Borromeo had given that day. This cannot always be expected, but some unobtrusive connection between the Lord's table and the table at home wouldn't be a bad idea. The parents then should take a sympathetic and understanding interest in the problems that their children bring to the table, even if they seem of little importance, even if they have to do with sports, fashion, or school. And see to it that the conversation is moderately animated. And at times focus everyone's attention on the younger children. These children pose some problem on Sunday afternoon after dinner. Getting rid of them by planting them for hours at a time in front of the television or always sending them to the movies is neither wise nor prudent. Reducing their lively activity by multiplying prohibitions (don't do this, don't do that) may make it look as if you want to suffocate them. For parents to worry only about them and nothing else would take away from them the only time that they have to cultivate themselves intellectually and spiritually.

So it is obvious that a little inventiveness is necessary in order to vary the routine and to see to it that all family members spend a little time with one another. It also takes a spirit of adaptation and an effort. Didn't the great Darwin one day receive a delegation from his children? "Papa," said one of them, "we have decided to pay you four shillings every time you come and play with us and tell us one of your wonderful stories." Good for Darwin, who, in order to say yes to his children, often suspended his lofty studies and his scientific research, but better still if our Catholic parents, after having dialogued with their children, older and younger, find the time to read some good book or good newspaper or some serious magazine or attend Catholic adult education courses. Today, you keep only as much of the faith as you defend, and you don't defend anything at all, given the enormous propaganda being directed against the Church, unless you constantly educate yourself and keep yourself up-to-date.

7. Fifteen years ago there were some German bishops who asked their parish priests to suspend the celebration of Sunday vespers once a month; it was in order to allow even the most Christian families to go together on an excursion or to some honest entertainment.

Today something similar should be asked of the various formal Christian associations or spontaneous groups. Yes, take our older children, who feel the need to see each other and to form themselves in charity and the apostolate with those of their own age; but every now and then leave them to their families. It is also important for them to be able to spend a Sunday with their parents and brothers and sisters. Forming a community outside the home is in fashion today. But shouldn't the home also have its part?

I have before me an evening within one family as described by Andre Maurois. "Father, stretched out in an easy chair, reads the newspaper and dozes off. Mother works at her knitting and reviews, with her oldest daughter, the three or four problems that make her life as a housewife heavy. One of the boys reads a detective novel in a sing-song voice, another is taking apart an electrical outlet, another, lacerating the well-constructed ears of the others, is trying out on his radio the different types of music being transmitted from European capitols. The result is a fine cacophony, the noise from the radio ruins Father's reading or sleeping; her husband's silence saddens the wife; the conversation between mother and daughter exasperates the boys, who complain; someone is sulking; someone does not answer questions, others explode in shouts of unmotivated joy."

Avoiding situations of this kind by harmonizing, unifying, and persuading each person to take on a little bit of sacrifice for the good of everyone is also a goal to be reached on Sunday.

8. Another goal, to relieve Mama, who is usually the most put-upon person in the home. "Queen of the hearth," they once said. Alas! she is really "the slave of the hearth." At least on Sunday, the mother should be relieved a little of her cares. Her children or even her husband should offer to substitute for her in some duties. "On Sunday, Mama, we will wash the dishes." "On Sunday night, Mama doesn't cook supper; when we return from our walk together or from visiting our grandparents or aunt and uncle, we have a cold supper, taking it, already prepared ahead of time, from the cupboard."

9. And, after supper, and a little television, the Christian family should say a short prayer together.

I cite for the third time St. Thérèse of the Child Jesus; on Sunday evening after the games of checkers, after the songs that Papa sang, "we went upstairs to say our prayers together.... I only had to look at Papa to understand how saints pray."

It is things like this that Christian families should strive for, if they want to regain the Christian Sunday. I said families, but I am thinking above all of husbands and wives, if they want to give themselves in the fullness of Easter joy to Christ, Who they find at home in the person of the children that God has entrusted to them, they should try to recover the habit of praying together.

23

We Are Running Dry

Dear Dickens,

I am a bishop who has taken on the unusual job of writing a letter every month to some famous person for the *Messenger of St. Anthony.*

With only a short time, so close to Christmas, I really didn't know whom to choose, when all at once I found in a newspaper an advertisement for your "Christmas Books." Right away, I said to myself, I read them as a boy and I liked them immensely because they were completely pervaded by a feeling of love for the poor and a sense of social regeneration, all warm with imagination and humanity. I will write to him, and so here I am disturbing you.

I recalled just now your love for the poor. You felt it and expressed it magnificently because you had lived among the poor when you were a child.

At the age of ten, with your father in prison for debt, you went to work in a polish factory to help your mother and younger brothers and sisters. From morning to night your little hands packed boxes of shoe polish under the eyes of a pitiless employer; at night, you slept in an attic room. You spent your Sundays along with the whole family in prison in order to keep your father company; there your wide, alert, bewildered child's eyes gazed with emotion at dozens and dozens of piteous cases.

For this reason, all your novels are peopled by the poor, living in a scarring misery: women and children pressed into labor in factories or shops, without distinction, even children under six; no labor union to protect them, no protection against illness and accidents; starvation wages, work lasting up to fifteen hours a day, which, with distressing monotony, binds the most frail creatures to powerful and noisy machines in a physically and morally unhealthy environment, which often pushes them to seek oblivion in alcohol or to try to escape through prostitution.

These are the oppressed; to them goes all your sympathy. Facing them are the oppressors, whom you stigmatize with a pen wielded by the genius of anger and irony, a pen capable of etching character types as though in bronze.

One of these characters is the moneylender Scrooge, the protagonist of your *A Christmas Carol.*

Two gentlemen, arriving in his study, pens in hand, entreat him, "It is Christmas . . . many thousands are in want of common necessaries, sir."

"Are there no prisons? And the union workhouses, are they still in operation?"

"They exist, they are in operation, but they scarcely furnish Christian cheer of mind or body to the multitude. A few of us are endeavoring to raise a fund to buy the poor some meat, drink, and means of warmth. What shall I put you down for?"

"Nothing . . . I wish to be left alone. I don't make merry myself at Christmas and I can't afford to make idle people merry. I help to support the establishments I have mentioned — they cost enough, and those who are badly off must go there."

"Many can't go there, and many would rather die."

"If they would rather die, they had better do so, and reduce the surplus population. Besides . . . it's not my business."

This is how you described the moneylender Scrooge; concerned only with money and business. But when he speaks about business to the ghost of his "twin spirit," his deceased partner in moneylending, Marley, the latter laments sorrowfully, "Business! Mankind was my business, the common welfare was my business, charity, mercy, forebearance, and benevolence, were all my business . . . why did I walk through crowds of fellow beings with my eyes turned down, and never raise them to that blessed Star which led the Wise Men to a poor abode? Were there no poor houses to which its light would have conducted me?"

Since the time you wrote these words (1843), more than a hundred and thirty years have passed. You are probably curious to know if and how a remedy has been found for the situation of misery and injustice you denounced.

I will tell you right away. In your England and in an industrialized Europe, the workers have greatly improved their position. The only power available to them was their numbers. They employed it to their advantage.

The old socialist orators said, "A camel was going through the desert; his hooves trampled the grains of sand and he said, proud and triumphant, 'I am crushing you, I am crushing you!' The little grains let themselves be crushed, but then the wind came up, the terrible simoom. 'Up, grains,' it said, 'unite, join with me, and together we will whip the great beast and bury him under mountains of sand!'"

The workers have gone from being divided and scattered grains of sand to a cloud united in unions and in the various forms of socialism, which have the undeniable merit of having been nearly everywhere the principal cause of the promotion of the workers that has taken place.

From your time onwards, they have advanced and made conquests on the levels of economy, social security, and culture. And today through the unions, they often succeed in making themselves heard even up in the high spheres of the state, where in reality their fate is decided. All this, at the price of very heavy sacrifices, as they overcame opposition and obstacles.

The uniting of the workers for the defense of their rights, in fact, was at first declared illegal, then tolerated, then recognized in law. At first the state was a "policeman state"; it declared that labor contracts were a purely private matter, and prohibited collective bargaining; the employer was in control, unrestrained "free competition" prevailed. "Are two employers running after one worker? The worker's wages will increase. Are two workers tugging on one employer's coat? The wages will fall." This is the law, it was said; it works automatically to bring a balance of power! Instead it led to the abuses of a capitalism that was, and in some cases still is, a "wicked system."

And now? Alas! In your time the social injustices were in only one direction, against the workers, who could point their finger at the employers. Today, there is an immense crowd of people pointing their fingers—agricultural workers, who complain that they are much worse off than the industrial workers; here in Italy, the South points at the North; in Africa, in Asia, in Latin America, the nations of the "Third World" point at the wealthy nations.

But even in these wealthy nations there are numerous pockets of misery and insecurity. Many workers are unemployed or uncertain of their jobs; they are not sufficiently protected everywhere against accidents. Often they feel that they are being treated only as instruments of production and not as protagonists.

What's more, the frenetic race for creature comforts, the exaggerated and crazy use of unnecessary things has jeopardized the indispensable goods, pure air and water, silence, inner peace, and rest.

People used to think that the oil wells were like the well of St. Patrick, bottomless. All at once we are realizing that we are almost running dry. People used to have confidence that, when in the distant future, the oil had run out, we could count on nuclear energy, but now they come and tell us that in the production of this energy there is danger of radioactive waste, harmful to people and their environment.

The fear and concern are great. For many, the great beast of the desert to be attacked and buried is no longer only capitalism, but the whole present "system," which is to be overthrown by a total revolution. For others the overturning process is already beginning.

The poor Third World of today, they say, will soon be rich, thanks to the oil wells, which it will exploit for itself alone; consumer society, forced to count its oil with an eye dropper, will have to limit its industries and consumption and undergo a recession.

As the problems, worries, and tensions grow heavier, the principles that you, dear Dickens, supported so warmly (though a bit sentimentally), are still valid, though they should be enlarged and adapted.

Love for the poor, and not so much for the individual poor person as for the poor who, rejected as individuals as well as peoples, feel that they are a class and feel solidarity among themselves. It

is to them, without hesitation, that the sincere and open preference of Christians should be given, after the example of Christ.

Solidarity . . . we are a single boat full of people who have now
become closer together in space and in customs, but who are in a
turbulent sea. If we do not want to meet with serious difficulties,
the rule is this, all for one and one for all; we must insist on what
unites and let go of what divides.

Trust in God, through the mouth of your Marley, you hoped
that the star of the Magi would illuminate the houses of the poor.
Today the whole world is a poor house that has such great need
of God!

24

Joy, Exquisite Love

Letter to St. Thérèse of Lisieux

Dear little Thérèse,

I was seventeen years old when I read your autobiography. For me it was a lightning bolt. You had called it, *The Story of a Little May Flower.* To me it seemed like the story of an "iron bar" because of the sparks of strength of will, courage, and decision that shot from it. Once you had chosen the road of complete devotion to God, nothing could have barred your way, neither sickness, nor outward contradictions, nor inner clouds and darkness.

I recalled this when they brought me ill to the sanatorium, at a time when penicillin and antibiotics had not yet been invented, and when the patient had to expect death sooner or later.

I was ashamed at feeling some fear. "Thérèse, at twenty-three, up until then healthy and full of vitality, was flooded with joy and hope when she felt the first access of blood from tuberculosis rise into her mouth. Not only that, but when her illness subsided, she obtained permission to finish her fast on a diet of dry bread and water, and you want to start trembling? You are a priest, wake up, don't be a fool!"

When I read you again on the occasion of the centenary of your death, on the other hand, I was struck by the way you loved God and your neighbor. St. Augustine had written, "We go to God not by walking, but by loving." You too call your road the "way of love." Christ had said, "No one can come to me, unless my Father draws him." Perfectly in line with these words, you felt like a "little bird without strength and without wings," while you saw God as the eagle, coming down to take you to the heights on His own wings. You called divine grace the "elevator" which raised you to

God quickly and without effort, since you were "too little to climb the steep ladder of perfection."

I wrote above, "without effort." Let me make it clear, that is true in one way, but in another . . . we are in the last months; your soul is going down a kind of dark tunnel; it sees nothing of what it first saw so clearly. "Faith," you write, "is no longer a veil, but a wall!" Your physical sufferings are such that you say, "If I had not had faith, I would have given myself death!" Nevertheless, you continue to say to the Lord with your will that you love Him, "I sing the happiness of heaven, but without feeling joy; I sing merely that I will to believe." Your last words were "My God, I love You!"

You offered yourself as a victim to the merciful love of God. All that did not stop you from enjoying good and beautiful things. Before your last illness you loved to paint. You wrote poems and little sacred dramas, playing some of the parts with the taste of a fine actress.

During your last illness, when you had recovered for a moment, you asked for some chocolate pastry. You were not afraid of your own imperfections, not even of having fallen asleep at times during your meditation ("Mothers love their children even when they are asleep").

In loving your neighbor, you tried to perform small but useful services without being seen, and to prefer, if anything, people who annoyed you and were less compatible with you. Behind their not very lovable faces, you sought the most lovable face of Christ. And no one noticed what you were trying to do and what effort it took. "As mystical as she is in chapel and at work," the prioress wrote about you, "she is every bit as comical at recreation, and so full of witty remarks that she makes us burst out laughing!"

These few lines, which I have traced out, are very far from containing your complete message to Christians. They are enough, however, to point out some directives for us.

True love of God is married to firm decision, taken, and when necessary, renewed.

The indecisive Aeneas of Metastasio, who says, "Meanwhile confused / in terrible doubt / I do not leave, I do not stay," was not the stuff from which true love of God is made.

If anyone is like you, it was your fellow countryman Marshal Foch, who during the Battle of the Marne, telegraphed, "The center of our army is giving way, the left is retreating, but I am attacking all the same!" A little bit of combativeness and love of risk never does any harm in the love of the Lord. You had it; it was not for nothing that you sensed in Joan of Arc a "sister in arms."

In the opera "The Elixir of Love" by Donizetti, one "furtive tear" appearing on Adina's eyelashes is enough to reassure her lover Nemorino and to make him happy. God is not content with only furtive tears. An external tear pleases Him only insofar as it corresponds to a decision inside, in the will. So it is also in external works. They please the Lord only if they correspond to an inner love. Religious fasting had actually ravaged the faces of the Pharisees, but Christ did not like those gaunt faces because He found that the Pharisees' hearts were far from God. You wrote, "Love must not consist of feelings but of works." But you added, "God does not need our works, but only our love." Perfect!

Along with loving God, we can love a great many other beautiful things. On one condition: nothing is to be loved against or above or in the same measure as God. In other words, it is not necessary for the love of God to be exclusive, it is enough for it to be prevalent, at least in the value we place on it.

One day Jacob fell in love with Rachel; in order to have her he spent a good seven years in service, which "seemed to him," the Bible says, "like a few days, so great was his love for her." And God had nothing to object to; rather He gave His approval and His blessing.

But it is another thing to sprinkle with holy water and bless all the loves in this world. Unfortunately, today, some theologians, influenced by Freud, Kinsey and Marcuse, try to do so, they sing hymns to the "new sexual morality." If they do not want confusion and a decrease in population, Christians should look not to these theologians, but to the teaching office of the Church, which enjoys a special assistance both in preserving the teaching of Christ intact and in adapting it in a suitable way to new times.

Seeking the face of Christ in the face of our neighbor is the only criterion that guarantees that we love everyone in earnest, overcoming antipathies, ideologies, and mere philanthropy.

A young man, old Archbishop Perini [Norberto Perini] wrote, knocks one day on the door of a house. He is dressed in his best, a flower in his buttonhole, but inside, his heart is beating hard; how the girl and her family will welcome the proposal of marriage he is timidly coming to make.

The girl herself comes to open the door. The young lady's glance, her blush, and her evident pleasure (only the "furtive tear" is missing) reassure him, his heart expands. He enters, the girl's mother is there. She seems to him a most lovable lady; he actually feels like embracing her. There is her father, he has met him a hundred times, but tonight he seems to him transfigured by a special light. Later on, her two brothers arrive; hugs, warm greetings.

Perini asks himself, "What is happening in this young man? What are all these loves which have sprung up suddenly like mushrooms?" The answer: there are not many loves, but only one; he loves the girl, and his love for her spreads to all her relatives. Anyone who really loves Christ cannot refuse to love the men and women who are brothers of Christ. Even if they are ugly, bad, and boring, love must transfigure them a little.

Everyday love. Sometimes it is the only kind possible. I have never had the chance to throw myself into the waters of a rushing river to save someone in danger. Very often I have been asked to lend something, to write letters, to give modest and simple directions. I have never met a rabid dog on the road, but I have met a great many annoying flies and mosquitoes. I have never had persecutors beat me, but I have had many people disturb me by speaking loudly in the street, by having their television turned up too loud, or perhaps by the noise they make eating their soup.

To help as much as we are able, not to get angry, to be understanding, to remain calm and smiling (as much as possible!) on these occasions, is to love our neighbors without fancy words, but in a practical way. Christ practiced this kind of love a great deal. How much patience He showed in putting up with the apostles who were always quarreling among themselves! How much attention to encouraging and praising! "Never has such faith been found in Israel," He says of the centurion and the Canaanite woman. "You have remained with me even in difficult times," He says to the apostles. And one time He asks Peter to please lend Him his boat.

"Lord of every courtesy," Dante calls Him. He was able to put Himself in other people's shoes; He suffered with them. He not only forgave sinners, but protected and defended them as well, so with Zaccheus, so with the adulteress, and so with Mary Magdalene. You followed His example in Lisieux; we must do the same in the world.

Carnegie tells the story of that woman who one day presents her men, husband, and son, with a well-prepared table, complete with flowers, but with a handful of hay on every plate. "What? You're giving us hay today?" they say. "Oh no," she answers, "I will bring your dinner right away. But let me tell you one thing: for years I have cooked for you, tried to vary the menu, one time rice, another time broth, now roast, now stew, etc. Never have you said, 'We like it,' 'You did a good job!' Say just one word, please, I'm not made of stone! We cannot work without recognition, encouragement, for someone who doesn't even notice!"

Deprivatized or social love can be practiced in a small way too. There is a just strike in progress, it may cause some inconvenience to me, though I am not directly involved in the dispute. To accept the inconvenience, not to complain, to feel that I am in solidarity with my brothers who are struggling for the defense of their rights, is also Christian love. Little noticed, but no less exquisite for that.

A joy is mixed with Christian love. It appears already in the song of the angels in Bethlehem. It is part of the essence of the gospel, which is "good news." It is characteristic of the great saints, "A saint who is sad," said St. Teresa of Ávila, "is a sad excuse for a saint." "Here, among us," added St. Dominic Savio, "we became saints with gaiety."

Joy can become exquisite charity, if we communicate it to others, just as you did at Carmel during recreation.

The Irishman in the legend who, on dying suddenly, approached the divine tribunal, was more than a little worried, the balance sheet of his life seemed rather meager to him. There was a line in front of him. He stood watching and listening. After consulting His great record book, Christ said to the first person in line, "I find that I was hungry and you gave Me to eat. Good! Enter into heaven!" To the second, "I was thirsty and you gave Me to drink." To a third, "I was in prison, and you visited Me." And so on.

For each person who was dispatched to Heaven, the Irishman made an examination and found something to fear. He had not given either to eat or drink, nor had he visited the sick and imprisoned. His turn came, he trembled, looking at Christ, who was examining the record book. But suddenly Christ raised His eyes and said to Him, "There isn't much written here. But you have done something: I was sad, discouraged, disheartened; you told Me some funny stories, you made Me laugh and gave Me heart again. heaven!"

All right, it is a joke, but it does emphasize that no form of love should be neglected or undervalued.

Thérèse, the love you had for God (and for your neighbor for love of God) was truly worthy of God. So our love must be a flame that is fed, nourished on all that is great and good in us; renunciation of all that is rebellious in us; a victory that takes us on its own wings and bears us as a gift to the feet of God.

25

We Are the Astonishment of God

Letter to Charles Péguy

Dear Péguy,

I have always liked your enthusiastic spirit, your passion for rousing souls and leading them into battle. Less certain are your literary excesses, now bitter, now ironic, now too impassioned, in the struggles you carried on against the erring men of your time.

In the pages you wrote on religion, there are some poetically (I will not say theologically) felicitous passages; the one, for example, where you introduce God to talk about hope.

"The faith of human beings does not astonish me," says God. "It isn't anything surprising. I shine so in my creation that in order not to see me, these poor people would have to be blind. The charity of men does not surprise me," says God, "it is not anything surprising. These poor creatures are so unhappy that unless they have hearts of stone, they cannot help but love one another. Hope — that is what astonishes me!"

I agree with you, dear Péguy, that hope is astonishing. I agree with Dante that it is *"uno attender certo,"* an awaiting with certainty. I agree with what the Bible says about those who hope.

Abraham did not really know why God had ordered him to kill his only son; he could not see where the numerous posterity that had been promised him was to come from when Isaac was dead, and yet he awaited with certainty.

David, advancing against Goliath, knew very well that five stones were too little against an iron-clad giant. And yet he awaited with certainty and summoned the armored colossus to fight, with the words, "I come on behalf of God. In a little while I will cut your head from your body."

When I pray with the Psalms, dear Péguy, I too feel myself transformed into a man who awaits with certainty. "God is my light and my salvation, whom then shall I fear? . . . Even if an army is camped against me, my heart will not fear. Even if a battle is raised against me, even then will I trust!"

———

How mistaken they are, dear Péguy, those who do not hope! Judas made an enormous mistake the day he sold Christ for thirty pieces of silver, but he made a bigger one when he thought that his sin was too great to be forgiven. No sin is too great; a finite misery, however great, can always be covered by an infinite mercy.

And it is never too late. God is not only called Father, but Father of the prodigal son, a Father who perceives us when we are still a long ways off, whose heart is moved, and who runs to throw His arms around our neck and kiss us tenderly.

And a possible stormy past must not cause fear. The storms, which were evil in the past, become good in the present if they stimulate us to put things right and to change. They become a jewel, if we give them to God so that He might have the consolation of forgiving them.

The gospel recalls among the ancestors of Christ four women, three of them not wholly commendable. Rahab had been a harlot, Tamar had borne her son Phares to her father-in-law Judah, and Bathsheba had committed adultery with David. It is a mystery of humility that these relatives were accepted by Christ, that they are included in His genealogy, but I also think that in God's hands it also becomes a means of assuring us [that] you can become saints, whatever your family history, temperament, heredity, or past life!

But, dear Péguy, it would be wrong to keep on waiting and putting things off. Those who set out on the road of *later* end up on the road of *never*. I know a man who seems to make life into a perpetual "waiting room." The trains come and go, and he says, "I'll depart another time! I will confess at the end of my life!"

Visconti-Venosta wrote about "valiant Anselmo,"

One day passes, then another,
But valiant Anselmo never returns.

Here we have the opposite, an Anselm who *never departs*. The thing is not without risk. Suppose, dear Péguy, that the barbarians are invading Italy and that they advance, destroying and slaughtering. Everyone is fleeing: airplanes, cars, and trains are besieged. "Come on!" I shout to Anselmo, "there is still a seat on the train, get on, quick!" And he, "But is it really certain that the barbarians will do me in, if I stay here?"

"Of course not, they might spare you, or another train might pass before they get here. But these are distant possibilities, and your life is at stake. To keep on waiting is an unforgivable imprudence!"

"Can't I convert later on just as well?" "Of course, but perhaps it will be more difficult than it is now; repeated sins become habits and chains which are more difficult to break. Now, right away, please!"

You know this, Péguy. Our "awaiting" is based on the goodness of God, which shines especially in the actions of Christ, Who is called in the gospel "the friend of sinners." The greatness of this friendship is known: when one sheep is lost, the Lord seeks until He finds it; when He has found it, He puts it happily on His shoulders, and brings it back home; and Christ says to everyone, "There will be greater joy in heaven over one sinner who repents than over ninety-nine righteous people who have no need of repentance."

The Samaritan woman, the adulteress, Zaccheus, the thief crucified on the right, the paralytic, and we ourselves have been sought, found, and treated this way. And this is another reason for astonishment!

But there is still another one, *the certain expectation of future glory*, as Dante again says. It is this certainty, placed alongside the *future*, lost in the misty distance, that creates the astonishment. And yet, Péguy, this is the situation of we who hope.

We find ourselves in the situation of Abraham, who, once he had received from God the promise of a most fertile land, obeyed and "set out," the *Bible* says, "without knowing where he was going," but certain all the same and trusting in God. We find ourselves in the state described by John the Evangelist, "Now we are children of God, but what we will be has not yet been made manifest." We find ourselves, like Manzoni's Napoleon, "set out on the flowering paths of hope," even if we do not know exactly the region to which the paths lead.

Do we have at least a vague knowledge of it? Or did Dante not know what he was saying when he tried to describe it as light, love, and joy? "Intellectual light" because up there our minds will see with perfect clarity what down here we have only glimpsed, God. "Love of the true good" because the goods that we love are only little drops, crumbs, fragments of good, while God is *the* good. "Joy transcending every sorrow" because there is no comparison between it and the sweetness of this world.

Augustine is in agreement when he calls God "beauty ancient and ever new." Manzoni is in agreement, down here "the glory that passed is silence and darkness." Isaiah is in agreement in his famous dialogue, "Cry out!" "What shall I cry?" "Cry thus, every man is like grass and all his glory is like the flower of the field. The grass dries up and the flower fades."

We too are in agreement with these great men, dear Péguy. Do some people call us alienated, poetical, and impractical? We will answer, "We are the children of hope, the astonishment of God!"

26

Confession Six Hundred Years Ago

Letter to Francesco Petrarch, 1974

Illustrious Poet,

In Italy and outside it, the sixth centenary of your death (1374-1974) is being celebrated this year.

Congresses, studies, and publications stress this or that aspect of your character, this or that aspect of your personality, or your immense literary work.

Dead for so long a time, you turn out to be more alive than ever, evading the curiosity and attracting the attention of the people of today to the man of letters, on the very subtle psychologist, the politician, the impassioned tourist, the sincere Christian and at the same time critic that you were, and a hundred other aspects.

Will someone also talk about you as a sinner, remorseful but relapsing, a Christian who often longed for holiness, but was incapable of making a truly clean break from sin and of renouncing the passions, great and small that were dear to you? I don't know. If they do, they will also have to speak about your attitude toward confession.

Because, illustrious Petrarch, you went to confession!

Writing from Rome to your friend Giovanni Boccaccio, you recounted the misfortune that had befallen you, an enormous kick that a horse had dealt to your precious knee, with fifteen days of atrocious pain. "But I accept everything on account of my sins," you wrote, "as a substitute for that penance that my confessor, who was too kind, did not impose on me."

The zeal you put into examining even the deepest reaches of your conscience is apparent in your books.

When you write of taking too much delight in your genius, your eloquence, the culture you have acquired and even with your physical appearance; when you reproached yourself with being avid for honors, ease, and riches, and with having too often given way to lust. You groan about the bonds of passion, which you do not succeed in breaking, of the power of the "perverse habit," and on the "most bitter taste" of your lapses.

Writing to your brother, a monk, you deplore your "desire for the most elegant clothes," your "fear that a hair will be out of place and that a slight breeze will disarrange the laborious styling of my hair." The iron used to curl your hair causes interrupted sleep and pain more atrocious than that inflicted by a "cruel pirate," but you don't feel you can stop. And you put to St. Augustine, your imaginary interlocutor, some disturbing problems: "The fall was mine, but the lying there, the not getting up, does not depend on me." "It does depend on you," Augustine responds. You reply, "But you can see that I weep over my miseries!" And Augustine, "It is not a matter of weeping, but of willing!"

Luckily, the correct principle never failed you: "God can save me," in spite of my weakness. The mercy of God puts fears to flight and resolves many problems.

————

At six hundred years distance, are we, the penitents of today, better or worse than you? Here is a question that makes me curious.

We have less of a disposition, it seems to me, to recognize the sins we have committed. We often say, "Holy Mary . . . pray for us sinners." "Father . . . forgive us our trespasses," "Lamb of God . . . have mercy on us," but very superficially. In practice, we justify ourselves under the strangest pretexts; we are free, autonomous, mature. We appeal to the "demands of nature, instinct, culture, and fashion."

The Bible, in the Book of Proverbs, presents the case of an adulterous woman this way: "She eats and wipes her mouth and says, 'I have done nothing wrong!'" That woman, dear Petrarch, is an emblematic figure, she depicts exactly a good part of our permissive Christian civilization.

As already with you, we do not lack tears; it is the will that is defective. Or rather, we often go so far as to unwill what we once willed with sin, to disapprove what we approved, but we do not succeed in doing what is more practical, to flee the occasions of sin. You who, even during your ascent of Monte Ventoux, brought with you the *Confessions* of St. Augustine, remember the case of Alipius. A strong man, capable of standing up to very powerful senators, he had come to Rome from Africa, and had conceived a "disgust and hatred" for the combats where gladiators killed each other to provide a show for the people. Some friends suggested that he attend the combat at least once. Alipius answered no, then he said, "I will be there, but as if I weren't there, and I will achieve victory over you and over the spectacle."

He went, then, as a challenge; in fact, after he had sat down in the amphitheater, he closed his eyes so that he would not even see. Unfortunately, he did not stop his ears. At one point an immense roar from the crowd made him start. He opened his eyes out of mere curiosity, but "to see that blood and to be steeped in cruelty were one and the same thing; not only did he not take his eyes from the spectacle, but he stared at it; he breathed in violence without being aware of it; he took pleasure in that struggle: he became drunk with the bloody pleasure. He was no longer the same man who had come: he looked, he shouted, he grew enthusiastic"; he came away bearing with him a fever, which impelled him to return, dragging along others. He corrected his error, but only a long time afterwards (*Confessions*, ch. 8).

Unfortunately, we all find ourselves a little in the line of the extraordinary weakness of Alipius (later a bishop and a saint). For this reason, in every confession we are exhorted to pray "I firmly resolve . . . to avoid the near occasions of sin," but....

I'm afraid that we are more incomplete than you in regard to trust in God. Agreed, God is the father of the prodigal son; Jesus is the Good Shepherd, Who brings the lost sheep back to the fold. He forgave the adulteress, Zaccheus, the good thief. All of us, or almost all, can get this far.

Some, however, conclude, "I will arrange it with Him directly" and do not follow you as far as talking about a confessor, who mediates between God and the sinner, thanks to the words of Jesus to the apostles, "Those whose sins you forgive shall be forgiven."

They do not understand that it is not up to the confessor to declare a remission of the sins that have already taken place, but to bring about the remission by a judgment.

And this kind of judgment cannot be left to a mere whim ("I like you, so I will absolve you"), but it must be based on certain and properly weighed elements, which only the penitent can furnish, by his own confession.

————

You found your confessor "too kind." In our time, those who go to confession indeed look for confessors who are kind, but not "too kind."

Augusto Conti, an illustrious philosopher, dedicated an entire chapter filled with affectionate gratitude in his book *The Awakeners of the Soul* to his confessors.

St. Jeanne de Chantal and other penitents declared themselves perfectly content with St. Francis de Sales, who in confession was a father and a skillful physician above all in infusing courage. "Sanctity," he said, "consists in combating our defects, but how can we combat them, unless there are some? How can we conquer them unless we meet them? Being wounded at times in this battle does not mean being defeated. The only ones who are defeated are those who lose their lives or their courage. A victor is anyone who decides to continue to fight."

He is the type of confessor that people expect today, firm but sensitive, a lover of God, but one who knows the problems of human beings.

It is true, however, that today, according to the desire of the Church, the accent is placed not on the accusation of sin, but rather on conversion, presented biblically as a distancing of ourselves from sin, but still more as a coming close to God and a loving embrace of Him. "Let yourselves be reconciled with God," said St. Paul. Today we repeat it and we wish the reconciliation to be preceded by reading and meditation on the word of God itself. In fact, we go to God, if He first calls us and speaks to us. We also desire that this word, when possible, come to us not one by one, but gathered in community.

You in the Middle Ages, dear Petrarch, made your confession a very personal and secret thing. Today, we think with nostalgia of the ancient times, when, after Lent was over, the bishop gave his hand to the first of the penitents and this one to the long chain of all the others, who were thus introduced into the Church for the solemn reconciliation.

—————

I don't know how often you went to confession.

In your Middle Ages people confessed often and seldom went to Communion. Today it seems that the opposite is happening; even devout people seem a little bit allergic to frequent and devotional confessions.

They make me think of the servant of Jonathan Swift. After they spent the night in an inn, Swift asked for his boots and saw that they had been brought to him still covered with mud. "Why on earth didn't you clean them?" he asked. "I thought it was useless," the servant replied. "After all, after a few miles of traveling they will only get dusty again!" "You're right, but now go and prepare the horses for our departure." Shortly afterwards the horses came stamping out of the stable and Swift too was in full travel dress. "But we can't leave without breakfast!" the servant observed. "It's useless," Swift answered. "After a few miles of traveling, you'll only be hungry again!"

—————

Dear Petrarch, neither you nor I, I think, follow the logic of Swift's servant. Will the soul become soiled again after confession? It is very probable. But to keep it clean now can do nothing but good. Especially because confession does not only take away the dust of sins, it infuses a special strength to avoid them and strengthens our friendship with God.

27

In What Kind of World . . .

Letter to Gilbert Keith Chesterton

Dear Chesterton,

During the last few months, Father Brown, your unexpected priest-detective, a creature typically yours, has appeared on Italian television screens. It's a shame that Professor Lucifer and the monk Michael didn't appear too. I would have liked to see them, as you described them in *The Ball and the Cross*, traveling in an airplane, seated opposite each other, Lent facing Carnival.

When the airplane was above London Cathedral, the professor hurled a curse in the direction of the cross.

"I am wondering whether this blasphemy will do you any good," the monk said to him. "Listen to this story. I once knew a man like you. He too hated the cross. He banished it from his house, from his wife's neck, even from the pictures. He said that it was ugly, the symbol of barbarism, contrary to joy and life. He became still more furious. One day he climbed up on the bell-tower of a church, tore off the cross, and hurled it from the top.

"This hatred ended up being transformed first into delirium and then into raging madness. One summer evening, he stopped, smoking his pipe in front of a very long picket fence; not one light was shining, not one leaf was moving, but he believed that he saw the long fence transformed into a host of crosses, joined to each other going up the hill and down the valley. Then, whirling his walking stick, he moved against the fence, as though against a host of enemies; however long the road was, he tore up all the pales he came across. He hated the cross, and to him every pale was a cross. When he got home, he continued to see crosses everywhere, he crushed the furniture, and set fire to his house; and the next day his body was found in the river."

At this point, Professor Lucifer looked at the old monk biting his lips and said, "You made that story up!" "Yes," answered Michael, "I made it up just now; but it expresses well what you and your unbelieving friends are doing. You begin with breaking up the cross and you end up by destroying the inhabitable world."

The monk's conclusion, which is also yours, dear Chesterton, is correct. Take away God, and what remains, what will become of the human race? What kind of world will we be reduced to living in? "Why, it is the world of progress," I hear people say, "the world of well-being!" Yes, but this famous progress is not all that it was hoped to be. It carries with it missiles, bacterial and atomic weapons, the current process of pollution, all these that, unless we take steps in time, threaten to bring all of humanity to a catastrophe.

In other words, progress with human beings who love each other, and consider themselves brothers and sisters and children of the one Father God, can be a magnificent thing. Progress with human beings who do not recognize their one Father in God, becomes a constant danger. Without a parallel personal, interior moral process, this progress develops, in fact, the most savage dregs of mankind, makes a human being into a machine possessed by machines, a number managing numbers, "a barbarian in delirium," Papini would say, "who instead of a club can make use of the immense powers of nature and mechanics to satisfy his predatory, destructive, and orgiastic instincts."

I know, many people think the opposite of you and me. They think that religion is a consolatory dream. It is supposed to have been invented by the oppressed, by imagining another, nonexistent world, where they will find later what today the oppressors are robbing from them. The oppressors organized it for their exclusive benefit, to keep the oppressed still under their feet and to lull to sleep in them that class instinct, which, without religion, would incite them to class struggle.

It is useless to recall that it was the Christian religion itself that favored the awakening of the proletarian consciousness, exalting the poor and announcing future justice. "Yes," they answer, "Christianity awakens the consciousness of the poor but then it paralyzes it, by preaching patience and replacing the class struggle with trust in God and gradual reform of society!"

Many people also think that God and religion, by channeling hopes and efforts towards a future and far-off heaven, alienate human beings, and distract them from committing themselves to a heaven that is close at hand, to be realized here on earth.

It is useless to recall to them that, according to the recent council, a Christian, precisely because he is a Christian, must feel more committed than ever to favoring a progress that is good for everyone, a social promotion which is for everyone. "It is still true," they say, "that you think of progress for a transitory world, in expectation of a definitive heaven, which will not come. As for us, we see heaven here, the end of all our struggles. We already glimpse its rise, while your God is called 'dead' by the theologians of secularization. We are with Heine, who wrote, 'Do you hear the bell? On your knees! They are carrying the last sacraments to a dying God!'"

Dear Chesterton, you and I indeed fall on our knees, but before a God Who is more relevant than ever. He alone, in fact, can give a satisfying answer to these three problems, which are the most important for everyone: "Who am I? Where did I come from? Where am I going?"

As for heaven, that we will enjoy on earth and on the earth only, and in a near future as the conclusion of the famous struggles, I would like people to listen to someone who is more talented than me and, without obscuring your merits, even than you: Dostoyevsky.

You recall Dostoyevsky's Ivan Karamazov. He is an atheist, and a friend of the devil. Well, he protested, with all his atheist's vehemence, against a heaven obtained thanks to the efforts, the labors, the sufferings, the martyrdom of innumerable generations. Our posterity happy thanks to the unhappiness of their predecessors! These predecessors who "struggle" without receiving their portion of joy, often without even the comfort of glimpsing the heaven issuing from the hell that they are going through! Multitudes of the suffering exterminated, human sacrifices who are simply the soil which serves to cause the growth of the future trees of life! "It is impossible!" says Ivan. "It would be a pitiless and monstrous injustice."

And he is right.

The sense of justice that is in every human being, of any faith, demands that the good done, the evil suffered be rewarded, that the hunger for life innate in everyone be satisfied. Where and how, unless in another life? And by who if not by God? And by what God, if not by the one of whom Francis de Sales wrote, "Have no fear of God, Who does not want to do evil to you, but love Him very much, because He wants to do you great good!"

The God Who many combat is not the real God, but the false idea that they have formed of God, a God Who protects the rich, Who only demands and claims, Who is envious of our advancement in well-being, Who constantly spies from on high on our sins to have the pleasure of punishing them!

Dear Chesterton, you know that God is not like that, but both just and good; Father even of the prodigal sons, whom He wants to be not wretched and miserable, but great and free, creators of their own destiny. Our God is so little a rival of human beings that He wanted them to be His friends, calling them to participate in His own divine nature and in His own eternal happiness. And it is not true that He demands too much from us; rather He is content with little because He knows very well that we do not have much.

Dear Chesterton, I am convinced along with you, this God will become known and loved more and more, by everyone, including those who today reject Him, not because they are wicked (perhaps they are better than both of us!), but because they are looking from a mistaken point of view! Do they continue to not believe in Him? Then He answers, "But I believe in you!"

28

—✺—

Restless People

Homily for the Feast of All Saints, 1973

1. In the first reading, the apostle John testifies that he has seen "an immense multitude, that no one could count, from every nation, race, people, and tongue!" (Rv 7-9). It was the throng of saints, which the Church wishes to honor together today. Composed of all the just who have died from Adam onward, this throng includes not only the saints whose names are known, but entire groups like the martyrs of Uganda, the Carmelites of Compiegne, and the Franciscan Sisters of Mary, who died in China singing the *Te Deum*. In that throng there are not only souls consecrated to God by the priesthood or religious vows, but countless fathers and mothers of families, and all those humble people who became saints in their own state in life.

"Of every race, nation, people, and tongue," says John, because in heaven every barrier is truly overturned, political, racial, cultural, or generational. Even suffering, of any kind, is banished. It is true, of course, that we do not know exactly what good things we will find in heaven; we know, however, from what evils heaven will free us. We do know that only there will the great dream of fraternity and happiness that is vital to the heart of every human being be fulfilled. The roads that lead there are many, but that happiness that is found there is identical. People come there from university positions, from parliamentary seats, from lawyers' studies, from doctors' offices, from sports stadiums, but also from the cells of sisters, from the kitchens where the servants wash dishes, from sickbeds, from miners' tunnels, from the factories of Marghera. When they arrive, they might discover that the mother of a family is higher than some of the nuns, that a worker is ahead of a priest, that a humble sister has precedence over some bishop. All, however, says St. John, in today's second reading, will be like God "because we will see him as he is" (I Jn 3:3).

2. But we are still on the road. In order to better arrive at the goal, it helps us greatly to single out in the great crowd of the saints some who were closer to the difficulties that we are experiencing today, living the gospel in situations similar to ours.

We are living, in fact, in a world of marvels. We have gone to the moon; Asia, Africa, and America are a few feet from us every evening on television. But all this makes us more isolated and lonelier than before, because the more the world broadens before us, the more we feel alone inside ourselves. We cannot engage in dialogue with the moon, or with Asia, but we can with the saints. A Chinese man, Jean C. H. Wu, on reading Thérèse of Lisieux's *Story of a Soul,* began to engage in a dialogue with the author — "Dear Thérèse, an angelic personality like yours cannot be a merely human work. The things you write contain the best of the doctrines of Buddha, Confucius, and Lao-Tse; they are not yours, they come from above. In order to arrive up above, I am joining you in following Christ" — and he converted.

3. We are very powerful, but what fragility in this power! Atomic bombs and missiles can blow up the world in a few hours. Drugs turn a strong and intelligent young man into an unconscious rag. Psychiatry and psychoanalysis reveal countless wars in which human beings can become unbalanced. The saints, on the other hand, rise before us as balanced, serene people who have understood the meaning of life. They have found the right road, they have traveled it courageously, and they seem to say to us, follow us!

4. The reality is that we gladly follow those who have met their responsibilities squarely. We give ourselves easily to those who have committed themselves to the end, risking everything, their whole lives. Words are something that we hear so many of today, from every side, a hill of promises, alluring. Behind them, however, there is at times emptiness. We often find ourselves facing a pure facade, a compromise. The saints, on the other hand, are authenticity, truth, and loyalty. They are more than teachers; they are witnesses. If they are teachers, it is because they are persuasive because

they are teachers who bear witness. The theologian St. Thomas, for example, spoke of God, but after having spoken at length with God. People followed Don Orione, Don Bosco, Joseph Cottolengo and gave them a great deal of money — why? Because they saw that they were poor in spirit and knew that the money they gave them went immediately into the hands of the poor, into the play centers for children, into the orphanages.

5. But we must not believe that the saints were nice, slumbering, or tranquil people. That is the way they appear on the windows or the statues in churches. In reality, they were "restless and disquieting" people, restless in the sense that they had to be doing something; inclined to evil like us, attracted by seductions like us, they were always at war or battling against their own passions.

A saint is a very strong-willed person, who continually acts against his own nature to think and act in the way Christ did. He is also a soul that the grace of the Lord constantly stimulates: "One more effort! Another sacrifice! A step forward towards the poor and the suffering! If you want to be certain you are doing your duty, do more than your duty!" At the same time that it helps the saint to do great things, the grace of God keeps him humble. "Without me, you can do nothing!" St. Vincent de Paul, counselor to the queen of France, was against having an ecclesiastic, an aristocrat, but incompetent, named a bishop. The mother of the rejected man, a great lady, on meeting the saint in the heat of anger, slapped him in the face in public. St. Vincent limited himself to saying to those who accompanied him, "You see, brothers, how far a mother's love can go!" St. Pius X answered those who said to him, "You are a saint," with "You got one consonant wrong, Madam. I am Giuseppe Sarto, not Giuseppe Santo!"

6. If we read and study their lives, the saints disturb us. "They did this and that, and they succeeded. Why can't I?" St. Augustine experienced this disturbing stimulus. He confides it to us in the eighth book of *The Confessions*. In Milan, an old priest told him that in Rome Marius Victorinus, the famous professor, had left paganism and converted to Christianity. Augustine was silent on the outside, but inside his soul was in turmoil: "I was on fire to imitate him." Ponticianus, a countryman of his from Africa,

spoke to him at length about St. Anthony, an Egyptian monk. He added that two officials who were friends of his, having read the life of St. Anthony, immediately decided to consecrate themselves to God, while their fianceés did the same.

The story stirred up a tempest in Augustine's heart. "People without culture," he said to himself, "are stealing heaven. I, with all my learning, am not capable of breaking away from my passions." After a short time he freely gave vent to his tears, and took the firm decision to give himself to the Lord forever.

My brothers and sisters, some people today cry "triumphalism" if we propose the example of the saints. But we are not boasting in doing this, as much as helping ourselves by their example. If it is true that we must be their companions in heaven, it is right that we be their companions and imitators on the roads that lead to heaven.

29

Honoring the Human Person

Homily for the Feast of the Assumption, August 15, 1976

The mystery that we are celebrating today can be summed up in these words: The Mother of God, "when the course of her earthly life was finished, was assumed into the glories of heaven, body and soul . . . so that she might be more closely conformed to her Son . . . the conqueror of sin and death" (*Lumen Gentium*, 59).

It says, "when the course of her earthly life was finished." We don't know, in fact, if Mary died and then rose and was assumed into heaven, or whether she passed directly from this world to heaven without first dying and rising.

It says, "was assumed"; we are to understand "assumed by God."

The Bible is silent about this mystery, and Pius XII, who proclaimed it a dogma in 1950, appealed to the "voice of the centuries." A voice which comes from afar and forms a thundering chorus of assent and has been manifested in a thousand ways from the earliest centuries. Among them, the following way is of value. Catholics, who have always been impassioned collectors and devotees of the relics of the saints, do not have any relics of the body of Our Lady, and no one knows [for certain] of any burial place for her.

Now that we have said this about the Assumption, it is important for us to bring to light what it teaches us.

1. *The first teaching.* God honors the human person. A psalm addressed to the Lord says, "What is man that you are mindful of him . . . and yet you have made him a little less than the angels, you have crowned him with glory and honor; you have given him power over the works of your hands, putting all things under his

feet" (Ps 8:5-7). Mary is a sister to us. In the Church she is one of us, near us, redeemed like us, though in a privileged way. If God has treated her with such esteem in the Assumption, let us recall that He has a similar esteem for us, her brothers and sisters. After the example of God, let us also try to always respect the human person, wherever we meet it. Jesus has taught us, under the person of the hungry, the thirsty, the poor, the child, there He is. What you do for the least of these, even the gift of a single glass of water, you do it for Him (cf. Mt 25:40; Mk 9:40).

St. Irenaeus wrote, *Gloria Dei vivens homo*, "a living human being is the glory of God." Some people ask, even the human being not yet born? Even only one, two, or three months after conception? Even him, he too is a human person, and the more fragile he is, the more he needs respect and care, both from his family and society — something that some of the press during the past few days have refused to recognize, and have even mocked. At Seveso a "toxic cloud" has risen, loaded with terrible dioxin, a dramatic and calamitous event. In the newspapers, through the work of writers who are at least hasty, [and who because of fear of widespread birth defects in pregnant women affected by the gas, suggested mass abortions], a "morally toxic cloud" has arisen, filled with unverified, rash, and exaggeratedly alarmistic statements, not respectful of values and people; this too is a dramatic and calamitous event.

2. *The second teaching.* With the Assumption, God wants to teach us how eminent our body is because it is a temple of God. Mary bore Jesus for nine months in her womb; we too, in another way, are bearers of God. I am not talking only about Holy Communion, in which we receive in us the true Body of Christ. It is a truth of the Catholic faith that those who are friends of God receive, in a mysterious but real way, the visit of God. They receive it in their spirit, but it also resonates in the body. "Whoever loves me," Jesus said, "will keep my words, and my Father will love him, and we will come to him and make our dwelling with him" (Jn 14:23). It is a very beautiful reality, which ought to enchant us. Unfortunately, because it is a reality which is only believed, but not seen, many ignore it; involved, carried away, fascinated, I

would say, almost morally subjugated, by other realities, this time indeed bodily and palpable. We witness, especially in summer, not the cultivation, but the mistaken worship of the human body. Women have the gift of beauty from God, which God Himself has caused to be sung and celebrated in the Bible. The Song of Songs speaks of a beautiful woman's cheeks between pendant earrings, a beautiful neck ornamented with pearls, and women's eyes that are like doves (Sg 1:10, 15).

Young men in the Bible, great friends of God, cared about their wives' looks; so with Jacob, who preferred Rachel to Leah because she was beautiful. The same Bible, however, admonishes us that beauty is a relative thing and that we need to remain within just limits in regard to it. The Book of Proverbs, for example, raises a hymn to women; it extols their domestic virtues and even their business enterprise, but hints, "strength and seemliness are her garments . . . grace is deceptive and beauty is fleeting, the woman who fears God is to be praised" (Prv 25:30). We know that the Lord has provided us with different psyches; it happens, usually, that a man looks at a woman; a woman not only looks at a man, but looks to see if the man is looking at her. Nothing wrong with that. However, it is one thing to make yourself looked at, that is, to make yourself beautiful, for your own husband, for a fiancé already won, or that you want to win, to be equal to your own social condition, not to make a bad impression in front of your friends, and another thing to act in the contrary way. "Beware," says the Bible to a man, "of the wife of another, of the enticements of a strange woman. Do not desire her beauty, because if the prostitute seeks a bit of bread, the married woman aims for a life of luxury. Can you carry fire in your bosom without burning your clothes or walk on red-hot coals without scorching your feet?" (Prv 6:24-28). A sermon old and ever new, on the occasions of sin we must avoid, of our own weakness that we should recall. The patriarch will appear to you to be a moralist and spoilsport on this point. But the words I quoted are from the Bible, the words of God. And it is the least, in these times and this permissive atmosphere, that one can say.

3. *The third teaching.* Our Lady, after Christ, is the first of all of us. The journey that she made we must also make one day too.

"Our homeland," it has been written, "is in the heaven and from it we also await a Savior, the Lord Jesus Christ. He will change our lowly body to conform them with his glorified body" (Phil 3:20-21). Let us note here two words, "homeland" and "we await."

If it is true that heaven is our homeland, the earth will become merely a colony for us; let us not be dazzled by appearances. In a train it is we who are moving; but it seems to us that it is the trees and houses that are not standing still. So it is in this world, we have the impression that we are going to remain here forever. This is an illusion, only in the other life are we going to remain forever.

A pilgrim, says a medieval legend, arrived at a castle and asked for lodging for the night. The castellan, standing to his right on the drawbridge, answered, "My castle is not an inn."

The pilgrim wrapped himself up in his cloak. "Before I leave," he said, "allow me one question, who lived here before you?"

"My father!"

"And before that?"

"My grandfather!"

"And after you?"

"My son!"

"But then, this castle really is an inn; each one of its masters lives there for a little while, then he gives up his place to another; it is truly a place of passage."

That pilgrim translates the biblical words, "for here we have no lasting city, but we seek the one that is to come" (Heb 13:14).

And "we await," says St. Paul. In tune with him, in the Mass we often say, "We are a pilgrim Church," a Church which is "awaiting the coming" of the Lord.

A coming that should not put fear in us, if we at least try to be good Christians. "Blessed are those servants," says Jesus, "whom the master finds vigilant on his arrival; Amen, I say to you, he will gird himself, have them recline at table and proceed to wait on them" (Lk 12:37). The Lord will be our servant! This is enough to move us to tenderness, even if exactly what the happiness of our heaven will consist of is now obscure to us.

The Lord a servant? But Our Lady is a good and wise servant, who for centuries has been invoked as a "protectress," "helper," and "rescuer." Today, people insist on wanting to situate her above all as a poor woman and on the side of the poor, and that is very fitting; let's keep in mind, however, that even those who are rich in money are sometimes very poor on account of the sins they have committed or because of hidden sorrows. Nor is it accurate to speak of Mary's poverty being "rediscovered" or "discovered."

Already St. Luke noted that in the temple Mary was able to bring only the offering of the poor. That Mary looked with particular fondness on the poor of every kind was known even to the thirteenth-century author of the little fable, *Le jongleur de Notre-Dame*, which was later adapted many times in French literature.

When the exhausted juggler of the country fairs became a monk, he had the impression that he was the most wretched of all in the convent. "The Father Prior," he said to himself, "writes learned discourses on Our Lady. Among the other brothers, some transcribe the discourses on beautiful parchment. Some paint miniatures in gold and blue. Some compose verses in honor of Mary. Some sculpt statues, and what do I do? I am nothing; I don't know how to do anything."

But when, to offer something to Our Lady in her chapel, the poor man, the despised man, set himself to perform his humble leaps and conjuring tricks, to whom did Our Lady appear? Not to the prior, not to the artistic brothers, but to him. It is to him, the poor tired, sweaty juggler, who had fallen heavily on the ground, that she descended from her throne, him that she graciously comforted, and with the hem of her blue mantle, dried the sweat from his brow.

A fairy tale, but a symbol of living reality, precisely because we are poor. May Our Lady help us now and at the hour of our death. Amen.

30

Love Can Do Everything

Angelus Address, September 24, 1978

*Y*esterday evening, I went to St. John Lateran. Thanks to the Romans, and the kindness of the mayor, and some of the authorities of the Italian government, it was a joyful moment for me. It was not joyful on the other hand, but painful, to learn several days ago from the newspapers that a Roman student was killed in cold blood for a trifling reason. It is one of so many cases of violence that constantly torment this poor restless society of ours. The case of Luca Locci, a seven-year-old boy who was kidnapped three months ago, has also come up again in the past few days.

People sometimes say, "We are living in a completely corrupt, completely dishonest society." This is not true. There are still so many good people, so many honest people. Rather, what should we do to improve society? I would say, each one of us must try himself to be good and to infect others with a goodness that is permeated through and through by the gentleness and love taught by Christ. Christ's Golden Rule was, "Do not do to others what you do not want done to you. Do to others what you want done to you" (Mt 7: 12, Lk 6:31). "Learn from me, for I am gentle and humble of heart" (Mt 11:29). And He was always giving. When He was placed on the cross, not only did He pardon those who crucified Him, but He made excuses for them. He said, "Father, forgive them, for they do not know what they are doing" (Lk 23:34). This is Christianity, these are the sentiments that, if put into practice, would so greatly help society.

This year marks the 30th anniversary of the death of Georges Bernanos, a great Catholic writer. One of his best-known works is *Dialogues of the Carmelites*. It was published a year after his death. He had prepared it working from a story by the German

245

writer, Gertrude von Le Fort. He had planned to have it performed in the theater.

To the theater it went. It was put to music and later projected on movie screens throughout the world. A very famous work. The event, however, was a historical one. Pius X, in 1906, right here in Rome, had beatified the sixteen Carmelites of Compiegne, martyrs during the French Revolution. During their trial, they were sentenced "to be put to death for fanaticism." And one of them, in her simplicity, asked, "Mr. Judge, please, what does fanaticism mean?" and the judge, "it is your foolish adherence to your religion." "Oh, Sisters," the Sister then said, "did you hear? They are condemning us for our attachment to our faith! What happiness to die for Jesus Christ!" They were taken out of the prison . . . and made to get on the fateful cart. Along the way they sang religious hymns. When they arrived at the scaffold of the guillotine, one after the other they knelt before their prioress and renewed their vow of obedience. Then they chanted the "*Veni Creator.*" The song, however, gradually became fainter, as the heads of the poor Sisters fell one by one, under the guillotine. There remained at last only the prioress, Sister Thérèse de Saint-Augustine, and her last words were these, "Love will always be victorious, love can do everything." Here is the right word, not "violence can do everything," but "love can do everything!"

Let us ask the Lord for the grace that a new wave of love towards our neighbor may pervade this poor world.

Chronology

Albino Luciani
Pope John Paul I

1912   October 17, Albino Luciani was born in Canale d'Agordo and baptized on the day of his birth at home.

Family:

Father, Giovanni Luciani 1872?-1952
Mother, Bortola Tancon 1879?-1948
Brothers, Federico, born 1915 (deceased) and Edoardo, born 1917
Sister, Antonia born 1920
Also two half-sisters from father's first marriage, Pia and Amalia

1912   October 19, the ceremonies of baptism were completed at the parish church of San Giovanni Battista in Canale d'Agordo by the assistant pastor, Don Achille Ronzon. There is an entry in the parish register for this and a commemorative plaque at the baptismal font in the church.

1918   October, began elementary school in Canale d'Agordo.

1919   September 26, confirmed by the bishop of Belluno, Giosue Cattarossi.

1920?   Received First Holy Communion.

1923   October 1, entered the minor seminary in Feltre.

1935   February 2, ordained deacon.

1935   July 7, ordained a priest by the bishop of Belluno, Giosue Cattarossi.

1935   July-December, served as assistant pastor in the parish of San Giovanni Battista in Canale d'Agordo under Don Augusto Bramezza.

1935   December, served as assistant pastor under Monsignor Luigi.

1937   July, appointed vice-rector and professor of theology in the Gregorian seminary in Belluno, under the rector, Monsignor Angelo Santin. He would continue to teach there until his appointment as a bishop in 1958, in addition to other duties in the diocese. In addition to theology, he taught at various times: canon law, patristics, catechetics, eloquence (preaching), history, scholastic philosophy, liturgy, sacred art, art history, pastoral theology, and administration.

1941   November, enrolled at the Gregorian University in Rome as a fourth-year student in theology.

1942   October 16, received lizenziato (undergraduate degree) in theology *magna cum laude.*

1947   February, defended his doctoral thesis in theology, "The Origin of the Human Soul According to Antonio Rosmini" at the Gregorian University in Rome.

1947   Spent two periods, March 8-June and August 26-September 12, in the sanatorium and later the hospital in Belluno, suffering from what was first suspected to be tuberculosis, but later turned out to be severe viral pneumonia. He spent the time in between recovering at his family's home in Canale d'Agordo.

1947   October, named secretary of the diocesan synod.

1947   November, appointed pro-chancellor of the Diocese of Belluno.

1947   December 16, named monsignor by Pope Pius XII.

1947   Appointed director of the Diocesan Catechetical Office by Girolamo Bortignon, bishop of Belluno.

1948   February 2, appointed provicar general of the diocese of Belluno.

1949   Appointed assistant to young women's section of Catholic Action in Belluno.

1949   August 9, reconfirmed as provicar general by Bortignon's successor, Bishop Gioacchino Muccin.

1949   December, published *Catechetica In Briciole.*

1950   March, published his thesis and received his doctorate in theology from the Gregorian University in Rome.

1954   February 6, appointed vicar general of the Diocese of Belluno by Bishop Gioacchino Muccin.

1956   June, named canon of the cathedral in Belluno.

1958   December 15, named bishop of Vittorio Veneto by Pope John XXIII.

1958   December 27, consecrated bishop in St. Peter's Basilica in Rome by Pope John XXIII.

1959 January 11, entered Vittorio Veneto and said his first Mass in the cathedral.

1962 October 11-December 8, attended first session of Second Vatican Council in Rome.

1963 September 28-December 4, attended Second Session of council in Rome.

1964 July 23, visited Lourdes with a pilgrimage of sick priests from Italy.

1964 September 13-November 21, attended Third Session of council in Rome.

1965 September 13-December 9, attended Fourth Session of council in Rome.

1966 August 16-September 2, traveled to Burundi in Africa to visit the diocesan mission and the priests from Vittorio Veneto serving there.

1969 December 15, appointed patriarch of Venice by Pope Paul VI.

1970 January 14, became president of the Episcopal Conference of the Triveneto.

1970 February 9, entered Venice for his first Mass in San Marco.

1971 January 27, visited Paris with a Venetian delegation to attend a benefit for the preservation of the city of Venice. Visited Cardinal Marty, the archbishop of Paris.

1971 June 12-14, traveled to Basil and Muttenz, Switzerland, for a pastoral visit to some Italian immigrants. Returned by way of Annecy (Savoy) and visited the tomb of St. Francis de Sales.

1971 June 29, visited Lourdes with a Venetian pilgrimage.

1971 October, served as one of Pope Paul's specially named delegates to the 1971 Synod of Bishops in Rome.

1972 June, elected one of the vice presidents of the Italian Episcopal Conference, and remained in this office until June 1975.

1972 September 16, Pope Paul VI visited Venice, and in front of a large crowd in the Piazza San Marco put his stole on Luciani's shoulders.

1973 March 5, Luciani was named a cardinal in consistory by Pope Paul VI.

1974 September-October, attended the Synod of Bishops on Evangelization in Rome as an elected delegate of the Italian Episcopal Conference.

1975 May 18, began trip to Germany, where he visited a number of Italian immigrant communities.

1975 November 6-21, visited the Diocese of Santa Maria a Rio Grande do Sul, Brazil, for the centennial celebrations of Italian immigration in Brazil. Visited a number of Italian immigrant communities, met with the Brazilian Episcopal Conference, and received an honorary doctorate from the Federal University of Santa Maria.

1976 January, published *Illustrissimi with Edizioni Messaggero* in Padua.

1977 July 9, visited the shrine of Fátima in Portugal, and spoke with Sister Lucia, the last surviving visionary of Fátima, in the Carmelite convent in Coimbra.

1977 September 10-13, served as official representative of the Italian Episcopal Conference at the 1000th anniversary of the first Marian Sanctuary in Croatia, in Split, Yugoslavia.

1977 October, attended the Synod of Bishops on Catechesis in Rome as an elected delegate of the Italian Episcopal Conference.

1978 August 6, the death of Pope Paul VI.

1978 August 9, Luciani celebrated commemorative Mass for Paul VI in the Basilica of San Marco in Venice.

1978 August 10, left Venice for the conclave.

1978 August 26, elected Pope after only one day of balloting.

1978 August 27, first radio message *Urbi et Orbi* with program for his pontificate.

1978 August 30, met with cardinals.

1978 September 1, meets with members of the press from around the world.

1978 September 3, installed as Pope, doing away with the coronation.

1978 September 6, first general audience talk "God, Neighbor and Ourselves."

1978 September 13, second audience talk on faith.

1978 September 20, third audience talk on hope.

1978 September 23, took possession of the Cathedral of St. John Lateran as bishop of Rome.

1978 September 27, fourth and final audience talk on love.

1978 September 28, died alone in his room about 11:00 p.m.

1978 October 4, funeral mass and burial in the crypt of St. Peter's Basilica.

1978 October 4, founding of the Missionary Servants of Pope John Paul I by the Seabeck family.

2002 August 26, Bishop Vicenzo Savio of Belluno-Feltre announced that research to promote the Pope's beatification had begun on the local level.

2003 June 10, the Vatican's Congregation for Sainthood Causes gave its consent to begin the canonical process on the holiness of the Servant of God, Pope John Paul I.

Mother Teresa of Calcutta

October 8, 1978

*H*e was the most beautiful gift of God. A ray of the sun of God's love that shone on the darkness of this world. And he was like a hope of eternal happiness. An ardent flame of the love of God. A proof that God always loves the world, and that through the Church, Christ is still with us, and that Christ always lives in the Church.

For the poor and the immigrants, he represented hope. Even our people in India felt him to be a father. Also when they knew that figure of John Paul I they said, "There is a Pope who is close to the heart of Mother Teresa because he is full of love for the poor."

His death is a mystery, we must accept; it cannot be explained in human terms. His passage has shown the vitality of the Church.